The Making of the Citizen-Worker

Over the course of the 19th century, European societies started thinking of themselves as "civilisations of work." In the wake of the political and industrial revolutions, labour as a human activity and condition gradually came to embody a general principle of order, progress, and governance. How did work become so central to our systems of citizenship and social recognition?

The book addresses this question by considering the French context in the long transition between the 1789 and 1848 revolutions and focusing on a specific "fragment" of history in the early 1830s marked by a pandemic crisis and the first consequences of industrialisation. It combines the analysis of both political institutions and social movements to retrace the rise of a labour-based social contract revolving around the "citizen-worker" as the quintessential subject of rights.

The first part of the book highlights the role played by the genesis of the modern social sciences and analyses it as a political process that established work as an "object" of governance and scientific investigation, thus fostering pioneering measures of welfare centred on work conditions. The second part focuses on the emergence of the concept of "working class" and the modern labour movement, which structured the world of work as a collective political "subject."

Federico Tomasello is Assistant Professor at the University of Messina. His research path has developed at the intersection between social and political theory and intellectual history. His latest publications include *From Industrial to Digital Citizenship: Rethinking Social Rights in Cyberspace* (2022).

Routledge Studies in the Modern History of France
Series Editor
Rachel Utley
University of Leeds, UK

Titles in the series:

French Soldiers' Morale in the Phoney War, 1939–1940
Maude Williams and Bernard Wilkin

Edmond Fleg and Jewish Minority Culture in Twentieth-Century France
Sally Debra Charnow

The Man Who Murdered Admiral Darlan
Vichy, the Allies and the Resistance in French North Africa
Bénédicte Vergez-Chaignon
Translated by Richard Carswell

The Making of the Citizen-Worker
Labour and the Borders of Politics in Post-revolutionary France
Federico Tomasello

For more information about this series, please visit: www.routledge.com/Routledge-Studies-in-the-Modern-History-of-France/book-series/FRENCHHISTORY

The Making of the Citizen-Worker

Labour and the Borders of Politics in Post-revolutionary France

Federico Tomasello

Routledge
Taylor & Francis Group
LONDON AND NEW YORK

First published 2024
by Routledge
4 Park Square, Milton Park, Abingdon, Oxon OX14 4RN

and by Routledge
605 Third Avenue, New York, NY 10158

Routledge is an imprint of the Taylor & Francis Group, an informa business

British Library Cataloguing-in-Publication Data
A catalogue record for this book is available from the British Library

Library of Congress Cataloging-in-Publication Data
Names: Tomasello, Federico, author.
Title: The making of the citizen-worker : labour and the borders of politics in post-revolutionary France / Federico Tomasello.
Description: New York : Routledge, 2023. | Series: Routledge studies in the modern history of France | Includes bibliographical references and index.
Identifiers: LCCN 2023004940 (print) | LCCN 2023004941 (ebook) | ISBN 9781032301143 (hardback) | ISBN 9781032301150 (paperback) | ISBN 9781003303497 (ebook)
Subjects: LCSH: Labor—Political aspects—France—History. | Labor movement—Political aspects—France—History. | Social movements—Political aspects—France—History.
Classification: LCC HD8428 .T66 2023 (print) | LCC HD8428 (ebook) | DDC 331.0944—dc23/eng/20230501
LC record available at https://lccn.loc.gov/2023004940
LC ebook record available at https://lccn.loc.gov/2023004941

ISBN: 978-1-032-30114-3 (hbk)
ISBN: 978-1-032-30115-0 (pbk)
ISBN: 978-1-003-30349-7 (ebk)

DOI: 10.4324/9781003303497

Typeset in Times New Roman
by Apex CoVantage, LLC

The Open Access version of the Chapter 2 is funded by Università degli Studi di Messina.

Contents

Acknowledgements

I am deeply grateful to the following institutions for giving me the opportunity to pursue my research path while I was writing this book: the Department of Philosophy and Cultural Heritage at the University of Venice, the Robert Schuman Centre for Advanced Studies at the European University Institute, the National Center of Competence in Research "On the Move" at the Université de Neuchâtel, the Department of Political and Legal Sciences at the University of Messina, and the Democracy Institute at Central European University. The "SPIN-Supporting Principal Investigators" grant programme created by Ca' Foscari University of Venice has provided the essential conditions enabling me to complete and deliver this volume. I wish to warmly thank the following individuals for their support and/or the exchanges we had regarding the contents of my work: Sergio Knipe, Costanza Margiotta, Dieter Gosewinkel, Dimitri D'Andrea, Émilien Fargues, Eugenia Delaney, Filippo Bignami, Fiorella Giacometti, Franco Maria Di Sciullo, Gianni D'Amato, Giorgio Cesarale, Giovanni Mari, Jean-Thomas Arrighi de Casanova, Jelena Džankić, Liav Orgad, Lorenzo Coccoli, Maarten Vink, Michele Spanò, Pablo Scotto, Pietro Costa, Salvatore Cingari, Wessel Reijers, and my editor at Routledge, Robert Langham. I am also grateful to my colleagues Dario Caroniti, Giuseppe Bottaro, and Italia Cannataro for their warm welcome at the University of Messina. Special thanks go to my mother Gianna and to my old friends in Florence: Dani, Eleonora, Fiamma, Mattia, Nichi, Valerio.

Introduction

Over the course of the 19th century, European societies started thinking of themselves as "civilisations of work." In the wake of the political and industrial revolutions, labour as a human activity and condition gradually came to embody a general principle of order, progress, and governance. It became a cornerstone for further advancements in terms of citizenship rights and social welfare, whereas growing movements and parties came to envisage work as the main pivot for political subjectivation and social transformation. The democratic constitutions sprung from the ashes of the Second World War (WWII) crystallised such developments by acknowledging labour as a crucial right and duty for all members of the national community. "Today all workers are citizens, and we have come to expect that all citizens should be workers," wrote one of the most influential theorists of citizenship, Thomas H. Marshall (1964, p. 233). His words bear witness to the fact that labour and citizenship became intertwined institutional areas because the former came to represent the main avenue for the substantial inclusion of citizens in the political community. Furthermore, modern systems of "social recognition" identify work and employment as the most prominent domain in which individuals can search for and measure their self-realisation and public appreciation. By investigating the political meanings of these trends, Hannah Arendt (1958, p. 4) argued that "the modern age has carried with it a theoretical glorification of labor and has resulted in a factual transformation of the whole of society into a laboring society."

The present volume aims to reconstruct some of the processes which have determined this political and social centrality of labour. It deploys a genealogical approach to explore the intellectual and political *genesis* of those principles that have made labour a central dimension for thinking of the modern subject. The idea of undertaking a study of this kind first arose from the debates sparked by the thesis on *The End of Work* and a coming era of jobless societies in the Western world (Rifkin, 1995). Such debates have contributed to the growing perception that a series of major phenomena characterising our century – such as technological change, globalisation, and neoliberal economic governance – have eroded the nexus between labour and citizenship marking mature industrial societies and their architecture of rights. This points to "the prospect of a society of laborers without labor" (Arendt, 1958, p. 4), or to the coming aporia inherent in a social order that becomes incapable of ensuring the kind of support which it had established as a

DOI: 10.4324/9781003303497-1

privileged avenue for social and political inclusion. This scenario does not simply concern the quantitative decline of work as full-time and long-term paid employment in Western societies, but also the transformation of the experience and meaning of labour in the public sphere. The present book aims to contribute to a deeper understanding of this contemporary crisis by retracing the way in which labour acquired its modern social and political meaning in the 19th century.

Especially in Mediterranean Europe, two generations by now would appear to have experienced the effects of the crisis or decline of labour compared the previous scenario of the "century of work" (Accornero, 2000). It is this generational experience that has inspired me to conduct political-historical research on the *beginning of work*, that is, on why the latter has become a linchpin of our systems of citizenship rights and social recognition. The objective is not to outline a possible return to the past, but to help envisage a kind of society in which labour as paid employment has a different role and diminished relevance.

This volume will explore the origins of our concept of labour and how it became the basis to claim citizenship rights by focusing on post-revolutionary France in the first half of the 19th century. This introduction justifies the choice of such a historical context (§ 1), outlines the volume's theoretical aims and points of reference (§ 2), and describes its structure (§ 3).

1 1848 and the meaning of labour

Calls to recognise the ethical value and political meaning of work, with the aim of affirming its social centrality, emerged slowly and relatively late in the European consciousness. Ancient thought assigned primacy to the contemplative life over the active, thereby stressing the intellectual significance of "idleness" over the industriousness of work, which was regarded as a marker of the condition of slavery or servitude. In Roman civilisation, the term *labor* meant "toil" and in medieval Christendom work preserved this character as a mere immanent necessity. It was mostly perceived as forced activity marked by the sufferings consequent upon man's expulsion from the Garden of Eden, devoid of any significance beyond the concepts of expiation and sacrifice, and lacking the kind of recognition that was instead granted to warrior or religious virtues. It was only in the early modern era that these representations gradually started changing and work began to be charged with an ethical significance for the first time, particularly in the wake of the Reformation and among Calvinist communities (Weber, 1930, 1978). In 1690, Locke's *Treatises on Government* identified work as the only legitimate source of property, and in 1759 Voltaire's *Candide* described it as "the only way to make life endurable" and to escape "the convulsions of restlessness" or "the lethargy of boredom," thereby anticipating the consecration of the citizen-worker by the French Revolution.[1] In 1789, Sieyès' pamphlet *What is the Third Estate?* fostered the revolutionary process by stating that private works (*travail particuliers*) and public services (*fonctions publiques*) are all that a nation needs to exist and prosper (Sieyès, 1997). Thus, it denounced the inactive condition of privileged orders as a burden for the social body and announced that in the coming society of civil equality, there was no longer any room for – or even political acknowledgement of – those who did not work.

It is necessary, however, to pay attention to the concept of work celebrated by the Revolution, which also includes the idea of "entrepreneurship" or "economic activity," encompassing both the employees' manual labour and the use of capital and title deeds for productive purposes. This notion did not yet distinguish between those selling their own labour force and business owners, who were often directly involved in the manufacturing process. Both figures made up the Third Estate, whose redemption was sealed in the summer of 1789 by celebrating the virtue of work, even though this did not involve the awarding of any political meaning to the condition of the supplier of manual labour designated by the term "worker." On the contrary, by abolishing craft guilds, the Revolution radically undermined the political significance which had been directly attached to one's professional condition within the corporative system.[2]

It was not until the political revolution had fully merged with the industrial one that a clear-cut semantic distinction came to be drawn between entrepreneurs and workers, employers and employees. It was only through the division of labour promoted by capital investments in mechanised production that the notion of workers – or of "working classes" – acquired a meaning close to the contemporary one, ultimately coming to designate a specific condition, primarily defined by a relationship of employment and subordination. This semantic change also reflected the development of an increasing social rift between the bourgeoisie and the workers. This growing opposition – that contrasted with the French Revolution's aims and principles – shaped the whole course of the 19th century in Europe, permeating it with an undercurrent of social conflict. It contributed to fostering the new revolutionary break of 1848, which split the century in half and marked the moment when the opposition in question exploded, establishing – especially in France – the condition of wage labour as a matter of political contention (cf. De Boni, 2002; Scotto, 2021, and the Conclusion to the present volume). This development led to the gradual emergence of the "citizen-worker" as a central subject of rights and to a transformation of the very idea of labour, which came to be identified with that of paid employment (Tomasello, 2022).

The genesis of the process that this book aims to retrace can thus be identified in the decades between the watershed moment of 1789 and the new revolutionary turning point of 1848, when the question of wage labour acquired full political significance for the first time. Within this long period of transition, the present book focuses in particular on the phase which followed the July 1830 revolution and the Orléanist regime's establishment, when the first attempt was made to convert the principles of liberalism into actual policies and governance practices. It was in those years that the "social question" emerged in France and came to be referred to as such for the first time (Castel, 2003); and it was at this moment that the first real workers' mobilisations occurred.

Compared to the better-established readings that identify 1848 as the symbolic point of emergence of the constituent power and political meaning of wage labour, exploring this emergence through a focus on the 1830s makes it possible to encompass a more profound set of problems and a broader range of actors. It enables us to retrace those processes by which, from the wider field of issues brought together under the label "social question," wage labour emerged in its specificity and gradually became established at the centre both of liberal strategies to deal with pauperism and of those emancipation projects by which a socialist discourse took shape. Within the vast literature on these topics, little attention has been paid so far to the mutual interactions between these two sides. The present book aims to offer a contribution in this direction by considering both political institutions and social subjectivities; both the emergence of institutional measures designed to make wage labourers the focus of public policies and the development of emancipation projects focusing on the condition of the working class and thus influencing the nascent socialist movement. By intertwining these dimensions, the present volume combines different topics that have been largely studied in their specificity but not significantly analysed in their mutual relationship. Although most of the literature on early-19th-century France has stressed the growing opposition between liberal and socialist discourses, this book points to their convergence in promoting the social and political significance of work. To do so, it explores the parallel geneses of the labour movement and of new institutional practices aimed at governing urban pauperism through the discipline of wage labour.

Exploring both of these dimensions makes it possible to grasp the genesis of the modern political significance and social role of labour in its historically defined character, which stems from the contingent intertwining of a series of events, discourses, and phenomena. In other words, it enables us to appreciate the transient and diverse nature of the determining factors by which the relationship between work, politics, and subjectivity acquired a particular shape, which the events of 1848 crystallised for the first time in a way destined to mark the following 150 years of European history. Focusing the analysis on the two decades preceding the 1848 break means observing the complex field of debates, actors, perspectives, and conflicts that were at stake before such crystallisation. In this sense, the present work is intended to follow in the footsteps of those studies that, over the last few decades, have attempted to free the history of France in the years 1815–48 from that teleological perspective which has long viewed it as merely a phase of "transition" towards the "mature" one of democracy, capitalism, and the labour and socialist movement (Rosanvallon, 1985, 1994).

2 Work and the production of subjectivity

In exploring how labour became a central dimension for thinking of the modern subject and the production of social and political subjectivity, I will be referring to both semantic sides of the term "subject." On the one hand, we have the side of etymology, *sub-jectum*, which corresponds to the investigation of the way in which the figure of the wage worker was placed at the centre of a strategy to integrate the subaltern classes into the State through the founding of a labour-based system of social protections, duties, and rights. On the other hand, we have the side of *agency*, which points to the process of subjectivation that enabled the world of work to acknowledge itself as a collective subjectivity, to represent itself in a unitary way as a "class," and to develop the kind of initiatives and discourses that were to bring together under the label "labour movement."

Both these sides contributed to making work that experience by which individual subjects could represent themselves as citizens and achieve social recognition. Both led to the progressive emergence of systems of social rights and protections revolving around the figure of the citizen-worker, to the point of establishing the defence of "work" – of the interests and needs of the labour world – as a sort of political imperative for modern democracies (Honneth, 2003). This gradual extension of the sphere of rights and policies to that of work coincides with a redefinition of the very boundaries of the field of politics. What this book aims to retrace is precisely the "invention" of the political significance of labour relationships, the affirmation of the political status of wage labour as a new "regime of truth" that reshaped the borders of politics.[3]

The genesis of this "regime of truth" will be investigated here by emphasising the diverse field of factors that shaped it. Such a field appears irreducible to the mere dynamics of power and knowledge aimed at including subalterns in the sphere of the governed by turning wage labour into a means of governing inequalities. The emergence of the political meaning of labour can only be understood by intertwining the analysis of such dynamics with that of the development of a social movement aimed at representing wage workers as political actors and labour as a condition for claiming new rights. Far from fulfilling a sort of necessity immanent in history, in the development of industrial societies, or in the nature of the modern subject, the new social role and political significance of work stemmed from the changing interplay of these and other factors – among which the present study focuses in particular on pandemic crises and the rise of the social sciences. We must therefore measure the variable impact of such factors in specific contexts and in relation to contingent developments without imposing the determinism of a one-sided interpretation of what is actually a complex process. To grasp this complexity, the present book will pay particular attention to the production of "social representations," which will be investigated by drawing upon the press, publications by social and political movements, parliamentary debates, and all those sources which enable us to study the way in which an unprecedented connection between work and politics came to be established on the level of public debate, political discourse, and public opinion. This process, however, only becomes fully intelligible if we also include the dimension of social history and those materials that reflect the rapid emergence of the social question and of the first struggles of the labour world.

Within the varied field of the factors that determined the process under investigation, a key role will be assigned here to the nascent social sciences, owing to their capacity to establish new social representations bearing powerful truth effects because of their allegedly scientific nature. Hence, this book also concerns the genesis of modern social sciences. Yet, the latter will not be explored as an independent intellectual development based on the definition of new concepts, models, and theories, but rather as a "political" process responding to a twofold contingent necessity that emerged over the course of the 19th century: on the one hand, the need to define strategies and tools to deal with the social consequences of the Industrial Revolution and the issue of pauperism; on the other hand, the need to complete the political revolution by overcoming the limits revealed by the previous century's theories (Spaemann, 1959; Karsenti, 2013; Procacci & Szakolczai, 2003). Chapter 1 delves into this double necessity by addressing the field of problems that shaped French political thought in the post-revolutionary climate and the way in which different authors came to focus on the concept of *society* to overcome the previous doctrines of the social contract and of popular sovereignty. As we shall see, the epistemological framework of the modern social sciences emerged from this philosophical shift from the problem of the foundation of sovereignty and the State to that of social relations and the norms governing *society*. The latter concept gained increasing attention and circulation in those years as a means to describe the new kind of social relations that sprung from the demise of the "organic constitution" of the Ancien Régime based on hierarchical orders and intermediate bodies. The rise of sociology then contributed to establishing the idea of society as a sort of "natural" constant feature of the coexistence between human beings (Castoriadis, 1975; Donzelot, 1984; Moscovici, 1996; Foucault, 2004; Latour, 2006; Luhmann, 1997).

The processes by which society came to be conceptualised, produced, and shaped in order to establish within it the means to govern modern liberties in 19th-century France provides the fundamental background to frame the creation of that connection between work, politics, and citizenship which this book aims to explore. Hence, the latter also intends to engage with those studies – mostly inspired by Foucault's genealogical method – which have analysed the 19th-century production of "the social" as an intermediate dimension between the civil and the political and between the State and individuals; a dimension designed to reduce the pressures of political struggles, and paving the way for the rise of both sociology and the ideas of social rights and "welfare State" (Donzelot, 1977, 1984, 1988, 1991; Smart, 1982, 1990; Ewald, 1986; Procacci, 1989, 1993; Rabinow, 1995; Osborn & Rose, 1997; Rose, 1999). However, so far these "genealogical" investigations have never specifically addressed the issue of wage labour.[4] This gap may be explained by the fact that the production of subjectivity in the labour world is a multifaceted process that cannot be reduced to the dimension of governance dispositifs and knowledge-power practices – which is what this kind of literature generally focuses on. Instead, it requires us to combine such a dimension with that of the active political initiative of those actors who fostered the rise of the modern labour movement. The present volume aims to address both these dimensions by combining a "genealogical" approach with recent trends in the historiography of the labour movement.

3 The social sciences and the working classes

The subject of this book is a multifaceted one and its interpretation entails the development of a dynamic intersection of elements pertaining to intellectual, social, and legal history, political and social theory, and the history of the social sciences. The sources used will therefore include major theoretical-political texts, treaties and investigations on urban pauperism and work conditions, daily newspapers and influential journals, movement booklets and brochures, administrative and government documents, legal texts and the parliamentary debates behind them, literary works, and memoirs by leading figures from that period. Intertwining these sources means broadening the range of texts that pertains to the history of ideas and questioning their usual hierarchical divisions, so as to include all elements enabling us to describe the spirit of an epoch and the political cultures that reflect it.

This is the aim of Chapter 1, which introduces the historical climate under investigation by evoking some of the events that punctuated the emergence of the social question. It then sets these events within the framework of the problems that in those years inspired leading authors and doctrines, finally introducing the two currents of political thought that most contributed to shaping the debates on which the following chapters focus: "doctrinaire" liberalism and Saint-Simonian socialism. This arrangement of the chapter reflects a consolidated tendency within the history of political thought, a tendency to rethink the "textual analysis" of works within a broader interpretation designed to set them within the context in which they operated – that is, within the "political life" of their day – for the purpose of bringing out the connections between political theory and practice (Skinner, 1969, 1974; Rosanvallon, 2003).

After this introductory chapter, the volume is divided into two parts, which display two different perspectives on the book's topic. We might label these viewpoints as the *objectivation* and the *subjectivation* of work, that is the shaping of the labour world as an "object" of governance and scientific investigation, and as a collective political "subject." On the basis of this distinction, the *first part* of the volume considers institutional practices aimed at integrating the subaltern classes into the State by establishing wage labour as a means of governing poverty and social inequality. This analytical dimension includes the development of liberal theory into a doctrine of governance, the birth of labour law, and the genesis of the modern social sciences as an attempt to systematically understand pauperism to better govern it. The *second part* then retraces the rise of social movements that assumed labour conditions as the main platform for claiming new rights. This analytical dimension deals with the emergence of the modern workers' movement and the development of socialism as a political discourse based on labour emancipation

In the first part of the volume, Chapter 2 addresses the interpretations of the emerging social question in the field of post-revolutionary French liberalism. It focuses on the cholera outbreak of 1832 to describe how it fostered unprecedented and dramatic representations of urban pauperism chiefly marked by feelings of panic and distress with respect to the new "dangerous classes" brought into being by the Industrial Revolution. By analysing the pandemic crisis, the chapter shows that these subjects were initially perceived not merely as a different social class, but also – and especially – as a different "race," according to a conception exemplified by the metaphor of "new barbarians" invading the manufacturing cities. Yet, we shall also see how the pandemic crisis stimulated the rise of social research on the subaltern classes aimed at elaborating pioneering welfare policies as risk reduction strategies.

Chapter 3 focuses on the genesis of the modern social sciences, which took industrial urban pauperism as their first object of investigation. It considers the first social enquires on the subaltern classes undertaken in the aftermath of the pandemic crisis and the representations of post-revolutionary industrial society produced by these treatises. The latter are analysed to single out the transformation of the initial image of the "dangerous classes" and "new barbarians" into that of the poor yet decent and virtuous working class. In such a way, the chapter describes how the "social question" gradually evolved into a "labour question" and a mighty project of social integration centred on wage labour.

Chapter 4 addresses the effects of these social enquiries on French policy and legislation by focusing on two subjects in particular: the employment record book as a crucial tool for the governance of manpower in the 19th century and the 1841 law on child labour as the first legislative intervention in the field of employment relations. These matters are analysed to describe the genesis of modern labour law as a process of juridical codification of wage work conditions and the rise of social security measures centred on the worker as an emerging subject of rights. Then, the chapter considers how initiatives of social inquiry were also adopted in the field of socialist and workers' movements, so as to introduce a shift from the sphere of governance to that of social subjectivities, which is the focus of the following chapters.

The second part of the volume focuses on the process of political subjectivation that took the name of "labour movement" and on the formation of the "collective singular" *working class* as the pivotal condition for the rise of such a movement (Koselleck, 1975, 1979). In other words, it retraces the way in which the *working class* became a single consistent category able to encompass and include the various representations hitherto associated with the complex universe of the subaltern classes. Chapter 5 sets out from the Lyonnais weavers' insurrection of November 1831, which historians have generally envisaged as marking the "birth" – or the symbolic point of origin – of the modern labour movement in Europe. It retraces different historical readings of this event to show how they have nurtured different conceptions of the idea of workers' movement and of the very notion of working class. To single out these concepts, the chapter delves into the traditional Marxist interpretation of the Lyon insurrection and analyses how this was debated and reframed by the "new social history" school and subsequently by the impact of the so-called "linguistic turn" on labour history research.

On the basis of these readings, Chapter 6 aims to provide an original interpretation of the rise of the French labour movement and of its historical-political significance by focusing on the way in which the 1831 insurrection was understood and represented by its contemporaries and the actors involved. It draws upon working-class, republican, and socialist sources to retrace the reception of the concept of "class" in these discursive fields and investigate how the latter assigned a new, social meaning to this notion by setting it in relation to other terms such as "people," "proletariat," and "workers." In such a way, the chapter describes the emergence of the "collective singular" *working class* as a unitary representation within which the still heterogeneous universe of the subaltern classes was able to identify and envisage itself as a collective subjectivity. Hence, the rise of the labour movement is framed as a subjectivation process developed first of all on the level of political discourse (Sewell, 1980; Rancière, 1981; Stedman Jones, 1983; Scott, 1988; Berlanstein, 1993). The main argument is that the genesis of this subjectivity can be understood as a "discursive formation and practice" aimed at redefining the boundaries of the political field and the very meaning of politics. Based on this argument, the conclusion frames the new revolutionary break of 1848 as an initial moment of crystallisation for the processes under consideration. Then, it considers how an architecture of rights revolving around the citizen-worker – that is, a model of citizenship and a system of social recognition based on labour – emerged through the interaction between the processes of "objectivation" and "subjectivation" of labour described in the two parts of the book.

Notes

1 "For when man was put into the Garden of Eden, he was put there *ut operaretur eum*, to work; which proves that man was not born for rest," Voltaire (1963, pp. 295–299).

2 Even the idea of the "right to work" that emerged during the revolutionary process was merely understood as the individual civic right to freely choose one's own occupation under conditions of equal competition with other citizens, without the kind of regulations and hierarchies enforced by guilds. Then, census suffrage systems in the 19th century generally regarded the condition of the manual labourer as the threshold below which people could not enjoy political rights (cf. § 1.4). On the history of the idea of work, see Tilgher (1929), Negri (1981, 2002), Weiss (2009), Theocarakis (2010), Damerow (1996), Lytle (2020), Garver (2020) Montenach and Simonton (2020), Walkowitz (2020), Thompson (2020), Perrotta (2020), Lucassen (2021), Faitini (2023).

3 I am here introducing the concept of "invention," which I will sometimes be resorting to designate the performative effects that certain languages and political discourses produced in the climate under consideration: this is the case, for example, with the syntagm "working class" and with the way in which this "collective singular" (Koselleck, 1975, 1979) would appear to have foreshadowed the composition of a world of labour that was still varied and fragmentary, and closer to the widespread expression "working classes." As for the notion of "regime of truth," I am using it in the sense defined by Michel Foucault (1977a, p. 23, 1977b, p. 13, 2012, pp. 13–14) to indicate the way in which truth is produced, promoted, and regulated through a series of political mechanisms, techniques, and procedures based on the entanglement between social relations of power and the field of knowledge and "scientific" discourse. Furthermore, I will sometimes be resorting to the originally Weberian notion of "world image" (*Weltbild*), understood as a systematic understanding of our position in the world that defines the horizon of our expectations, and the tools needed to achieve them (Weber, 1974, 1978; Kalberg, 2004; D'Andrea, 2011).

4 More specifically, these genealogical investigations on the 19th century have focused on topics such as the family (Donzelot, 1977), the welfare State (Ewald, 1986, 1996), statistical knowledge (Hacking, 1990), poverty (Dean, 1991; Procacci, 1993, 1998), public security and policing (Neocleous, 2000; Napoli, 2003; Campesi, 2016), the free market (Harcourt, 2012), social sciences (Karsenti, 2013), and pandemics (Delaporte, 1986; Aisenberg, 1999). Given the relevance of wage work in the 19th-century social context, it is remarkable that these important studies have not specifically focused on this topic. Two important but partial exceptions are: Castel (2003), which focuses on the *long durée* to retrace the transformations of the social question from the Middle Ages, and Foucault (2015), which is the latest of his Collège de France lecture series to have been published as a volume and devotes several pages to the rise of wage labour.

References

Accornero A. (2000), *Era il secolo del lavoro*, Il Mulino, Bologna.

Aisenberg A.R. (1999), *Contagion: Disease, Government and the " Social Question " in Nineteenth-Century France*, Stanford University Press, Stanford.

Arendt H. (1958), *The Human Condition*, University of Chicago Press, Chicago.

Berlanstein L.R. (ed.) (1993), *Rethinking Labor History: Essays on Discourse and Class Analysis*, University of Illinois Press, Champaign.

Campesi G. (2016), *A Genealogy of Public Security. The Theory and History of Modern Police Powers*, Routledge, London and New York (or. ed. *Genealogia della pubblica sicurezza. Teoria e storia del moderno dispositivo poliziesco*, Ombre Corte, Verona 2009).

Castel r. (2003), *From Manual Workers to Wage Laborers: Transformation of the Social Question*, Transaction, New Brunswick (or. ed. *Les Métamorphoses de la question sociale, une chronique du salariat*, Gallimard, Paris 1995).

Castoriadis C. (1975), *L'institution imaginaire de la société*, Seuil, Paris.

Damerow P. (1996), The Concept of Labor in Historical Materialism and the Theory of Socio-Historical Development, in *Abstraction and Representation. Boston Studies in the Philosophy of Science*, vol. 175, Springer, Dordrecht. https://doi.org/10.1007/978-94-015-8624-5_11

D'Andrea D. (2011), The World in Images. Subjectivity and Politics in Max Weber. *Humana.Mente* (18), September: 87–104.

De Boni C. (2002), *Il diritto al lavoro nel 1848. Antologia di scritti e discorsi*, Mimesis, Milano.

Dean M. (1991), *The Constitution of Poverty. Toward a Genealogy of Liberal Governance*, Routledge, London.

Delaporte F. (1986), *Disease and Civilization: The Cholera in Paris, 1832*, MIT Press, Cambridge and London.

Donzelot J. (1977), *La police de familles*, Minuit, Paris (Eng. trans. *The Policing of Families*, Pantheon Books, New York 1979).

Donzelot J. (1984), *L'invention du social. Essai sur le déclin des passions politiques*, Fayard, Paris.

Donzelot J. (1988), The Promotion of the Social. *Economy and Society*, 17(3): 394–427.

Donzelot J. (1991), *The Mobilization of Society*, in Graham Burchell, Colin Gordon, Peter Miller (eds.), *The Foucault Effect: Studies in Governmentality*, University of Chicago Press, Chicago, pp. 169–179.

Ewald F. (1986), *L'État providence*, Grasset, Paris.

Ewald F. (1996), *Histoire de l'Etat providence: les origines de la solidarité*, Grasset, Paris.

Faitini T. (2023), *Shaping the Profession. Towards a Genealogy of Professional Ethics*, Brill, Boston.

Foucault M. (1977a), *Discipline and Punish. The Birth of the Prison*, Vintage Books, New York (or. ed. *Surveiller et punir. Naissance de la prison*, Gallimard, Paris 1975).

Foucault M. (1977b), The Political Function of the Intellectual. *Radical Philosophy*, 17, Summer, pp. 12–14 (or. ed. La fonction politique de l'intellectuel, 1976, in: Dits et écrits, vol. II: 1976–1988, Gallimard, Paris 2001, pp. 109–114).

Foucault M. (2004), *Sécurité, territoire, population. Cours au Collège de France 1977–1978*, Seuil-Gallimard, Paris.

Foucault M. (2012), *Du gouvernement des vivants. Cours au Collège de France 1979–1980*, Seuil/Gallimard, Paris, pp. 13–14.

FOUCAULT M. (2015), *The Punitive Society. Lectures at the Collège de France 1972–1973*, Palgrave Macmillan UK (or. ed. *La Société punitive. Cours au Collège de France 1972–1973*, Gallimard-Seuil, Paris 2013).

GARVER V.L. (ed.) (2020), *A Cultural History of Work in the Medieval Age*, Bloomsbury Academic, London.

HACKING I. (1990), *The Taming of Chance*, CUP, New York.

HARCOURT B.E. (2012), *The Illusion of Free Markets: Punishment and the Myth of Natural Order*, Harvard University Press, Cambridge.

HONNETH A. (2003), Redistribution as Recognition, in Nancy Fraser, Axel Honneth (eds.), *Redistribution or Recognition? A Political-Philosophical Exchange*, Verso, London and New York, pp. 110–196 (or. ed. *Umverteilung oder Anerkennung?: eine politisch-philosophische Kontroverse*, Suhrkamp, Frankfurt am Main 2003).

KALBERG, S. (2004), The Past and Present Influence of World Views. Max Weber on a Neglected Sociological Concept. *Journal of Classical Sociology*, 4(2): 139–163.

KARSENTI B. (2013), *D'une philosophie à l'autre: les sciences sociales et la politique des modernes*, Gallimard, Paris.

KOSELLECK R. (1975), Geschichte, Historie, in Otto Brunner, Werner Conze, Reinhart Koselleck (eds.), *Geschichtliche Grundbegriffe: lexikon zur politisch-sozialen Sprache in Deutschland*, vol. 2, Klett-Cotta, Stuttgart, pp. 647–717 (Basic Concepts in History: A Historical Dictionary of Political and Social Language in Germany).

KOSELLECK R. (1979), *Vergangene Zukunft: Zur Semantik geschichtlicher Zeiten*, Suhrkamp Verlag, Franfurt am Main (Eng. trans. *Futures Past: On the Semantics of Historical Time*, Columbia University Press, New York 2004).

LATOUR B. (2006), *Changer de société – Refaire la sociologie*, La Decouverte, Paris.

LOCKE J. (1690), *Two Treatises of Government*, Awnsham Churchill, London.

LUCASSEN J. (2021), *The Story of Work. A New History of Humankind*, Yale University Press, New Haven.

LUHMANN N. (1997), *Die Gesellschaft der Gesellschaft*, Suhrkamp, Frankfurt am Main.

LYTLE E. (ed.) (2020), *A Cultural History of Work in Antiquity*, Bloomsbury Academic, London.

MARSHALL T.H. (1964), *Class, Citizenship and Social Development: Essays*, Doubleday, New York.

MONTENACH A., SIMONTON D. (2020), *A Cultural History of Work in the Age of Enlightenment*, Bloomsbury Academic, London.

MOSCOVICI S. (1996), *The Invention of Society: Psychological Explanations for Social Phenomena*, Polity, Cambridge.

NAPOLI P. (2003), *Naissance de la Police Moderne. Pouvoir, normes, société*, Editions La Découverte, Paris.

NEGRI A. (1981), *Filosofia del lavoro: storia antologica*, Marzorati, Milano.

NEGRI A. (2002), *Per una storia del concetto di lavoro nella cultura filosofica ed economica occidentale*, in S. Zaninelli e M. Taccolini (a cura di), *Il lavoro come fattore produttivo e come risorsa nella storia economica italiana*, Milano, Vita e pensiero, pp. XVII–XXXIX.

NEOCLEOUS M. (2000), *The Fabrication of Social Order. A Critical Theory of Police Power*, Pluto Press, London.

OSBORNE T., ROSE N. (1997), In the Name of Society, or Three Theses on the History of Social Thought. *History of the Human Sciences*, 10: 87–104.

PERROTTA C. (2020), *Unproductive Labour in Political Economy. The History of an Idea*, Routledge, London.

Procacci G. (1993), *Gouverner la misère: la question sociale en France, 1789–1848*, Seuil, Paris.

Procacci G. (1989), Sociology and Its Poor. *Politics and Society*, 17(2): 163–187.

Procacci G. (1998), *Governare la povertà. La società liberale e la nascita della questione sociale*, il Mulino, Bologna.

Procacci G., Szakolczai A. (2003), *La scoperta della società. Alle origini della sociologia*, Carocci, Roma.

Rabinow P. (1995), *French Modern: Norms and Forms of the Social Environment*, University of Chicago Press, Chicago.

Rancière J. (1981), *La nuit des prolétaires. Archives du rêve ouvrier*, Fayard, Paris.

Rifkin J. (1995), *The End of Work*, Putnam, New York.

Rosanvallon P. (1985), *Le moment Guizot*, Gallimard, Paris.

Rosanvallon P. (1994), *La monarchie impossible. Les Chartes de 1814 et 1830*, Fayard, Paris.

Rosanvallon P. (2003), *Pour une histoire conceptuelle du politique*, Seuil, Paris.

Rose N. (1999), *Powers of Freedom*, CUP, Cambridge.

Scott J.W. (1988), *Gender and the Politics of History*, Columbia University Press, New York.

Scotto P.B. (2021), *Los orígenes del derecho al trabajo en Francia (1789–1848)*, Centro de Estudios Politicos y Constitucionales, Madrid.

Sewell W.H. (1980), *Work and Revolution in France: The Language of Labor from the Old Regime to 1848*, CUP, Cambridge.

Sieyès E.J. (1997), *What Is the Third Estate*, in Marc A. Goldstein (ed.), *Social and Political Thought of the French Revolution 1788–1797. An Anthology of Original Texts*, Peter Lang, pp. 105–129 (or. ed. *Qu'est-ce que le Tiers état?* Paris, January 1789).

Skinner Q. (1969), *Meaning and Understanding in the History of Ideas. History and Theory*, 8(1): 3–53.

Skinner Q. (1974), Some Problems in the Analysis of Political Thought and Action. *Political Theory*, 2(3): 277–303.

Smart B. (1982), Foucault, Sociology and the Problem of Human Agency. *Theory and Society*, 11(2), 120–141.

Smart B. (1990), On the Disorder of Things: Sociology and the End of the Social. *Sociology*, 24: 3.

Spaemann R. (1959), *Der Ursprung der Soziologie aus dem Geist der Restauration*, Kösel, München.

Stedman Jones G. (1983), *Languages of Class: Studies in English Working Class History, 1832–1982*, CUP, Cambridge.

Theocarakis N.J. (2010), Metamorphoses: The Concept of Labour in the History of Political Economy, *The Economic and Labour Relations Review*, 20(2): 7–37. https://doi.org/10.1177/103530461002000202

Thompson V.E. (ed.) (2020), *A Cultural History of Work in the Age of Empire*, Bloomsbury Academic, London.

Tilgher A. (1929), *Homo faber. Storia del concetto di lavoro nella civiltà occidentale*, Libreria di Scienza e Lettere, Roma.

Tomasello F. (2022), From Industrial to Digital Citizenship: Rethinking Social Rights in Cyberspace. *Theory and Society*. https://doi.org/10.1007/s11186-022-09480-6

Voltaire F-M. (1963), *Candide: Or, Optimism*, St. Martin's Press, New York (or. ed. *Candide ou l'Optimisme*, Genéve 1759).

WALKOWITZ D.J. (ed.) (2020), *A Cultural History of Work in the Modern Age*, Bloomsbury Academic, London.

WEBER M. (1930), *The Protestant Ethic and the Spirit of Capitalism*, Allen & Unwin, London (or. ed. *Die protestantische Ethik und der Geist des Kapitalismus*, Archiv für Sozialwissenschaften und Sozialpolitik, Bd. XX und XXI, 1905).

WEBER M. (1974), The Social Psychology of the World Religions. In H.H. Gerth, C. Wright (eds.), *From Max Weber*, Routledge, London, pp. 267–301 (or. ed. 1920).

WEBER M. (1978), *Economy and Society (1922)*, UCP, Berkeley, CA.

WEISS Y. (2009), Work and Leisure: A History of Ideas. *Journal of Labor Economics*, 27(1), January. https://doi.org/10.1086/596993

1 The post-revolutionary context

This chapter introduces the social, intellectual, and political climate in which the issues at the centre of the present book must be framed. It sets out from the fragment of history between November 1831 and June 1832 by presenting a series of events that shook the French public debate which had developed over the course of the long post-revolutionary period of transition (§ 1.1). Starting from these momentous events, the chapter develops an intersection between different subjects with the aim of framing the concepts and processes under investigation in the context in which they occurred. To do so, it first illustrates the common field of problems that embodied the "spirit" of this time and with which French society had to deal in those years. We thus explore a range of issues, concerns, and contradictions that made the climate in France in the first half of the 19th century so rich in original ideas and groundbreaking visions (§ 1.2). Then, we look at the impact that the rise of industrialisation and its social consequences had on this climate to introduce the central issue of the present book, that is, the emerging connection between labour and citizenship rights (§ 1.3). Finally, we turn to consider the two currents of political thought that most shaped the processes that are the focus of the following chapters: "doctrinaire" liberalism (§ 1.4) and Saint-Simonian socialism (§ 1.5). These two currents provide the fundamental theoretical-political coordinates to understand both the structuring of a liberal governance strategy with respect to the labour world – which is the focus of the first part of this book – and the emergence of a process of political subjectivation centred on workers' conditions – which we examine in the second part.

1.1 The 1831–32 fragment

"1848 did not invent anything. On the contrary, 1830 – and the three following years – marked a real crisis, the invention of ideas, the inception of movements," writes Daniel Halévy (1913, p. 57). "1831 and 1832 . . . contain the most peculiar and striking moments of history; and these two years, amid those that precede and follow them, stand out like mountains," writes Victor Hugo in *Les Misérables*,

DOI: 10.4324/9781003303497-2

enshrining in Europe's memory the fragment of history that constitutes the starting point of the present investigation:

> a political and a social disease declaring themselves simultaneously in the two capitals of the kingdom . . .; in Paris a civil war, in Lyons a servile war; . . . plots, conspiracies, insurrections, and cholera adding to the gloomy rumor of ideas the gloomy tumult of events.
>
> (Hugo, 1893, pp. 1 and 34)

"Servile war" broke out on a livid November morning, when the *canuts* – the silk-weavers of Lyon – drove the National Guard out of the working-class suburb of Croix-Rousse.[1] Historians were to identify this insurrection as the symbolic starting point of the labour movement in Europe. For the *canuts*, however, this was only the dramatic outcome of their open dispute with silk merchants over the price of their products. The merchants' refusal to negotiate led the weavers to drive all workshops in the suburb to a halt and to announce a general mobilisation (cf. § 6.1). To face the latter, Lieutenant Rouget summoned the National Guard, but only a few hundred men heeded the call. These were immediately attacked by the workers and driven out of Croix-Rousse. The silk-weavers' resistance then turned into a general offensive involving the whole of Lyon: a battle that lasted for two days, costing the lives of 177 people and forcing the authorities to barricade themselves in the Hôtel-de-Ville and eventually abandon the city together with the army. At dawn on 23 November 1831, "there was no other government in Lyon except that of the revolt" (Monfalcon, 1834, p. 74), and this continued to be the case for the next ten days, during which the silk-weavers thwarted all attempts to create some form of self-government by the "social-republicans" of the newspaper *La Glaneuse* and by the Carbonari exiles of the *Volontari del Rodano*.[2] The workers instead affirmed their loyalty to the Orléanist regime established during the revolutionary days of July 1830 and restored the power of the only remaining authority in the city: the Prefect. So on 3 December, without encountering any resistance, a garrison of 26,000 soldiers led by the Prince and welcomed by the local inhabitants regained control of Lyon. "The people were shocked when they saw themselves without masters. They feared for their own sovereignty," writes Louis Blanc (1844, p. 354) – evoking the paradox of a victorious insurrection which refused to tackle the question of political power, as it had been triggered by a subordination issue that responded to a different logic of domination.

> The July revolution [of 1830] had raised only political, governance issues; society was in no way threatened by such issues. What happened next? Social issues were raised. A struggle between classes took place. This is what the upheavals in Lyon have revealed. . . . Social issues, domestic upheavals, and disagreements in society have been added to the political issues, and we are

> now faced with this twofold difficulty: a government to be established and a society to be defended.
>
> (Guizot, 1863, p. 359)

This is how François Guizot commented on the events in Lyon, stressing the unprecedented nature of the problems they raised and the urgent "need to defend society" that spells out the political rationale of Orléanist liberals with regard to the emergent "social question" (cf. § 1.3). The debate sprung from the Lyonnais insurrection was destined to affect the development of all political discourses over the following years, as it marked "an essential turning point in the way in which French society perceived itself and its inner divisions" (Rosanvallon, 1992, p. 261). In the eyes of its contemporaries, the *révolte des canuts* was a break that led them to question the shared representations and views of the world which they had developed over the course of the long post-revolutionary transition (cf. Chapters 5 and 6 on the historical-political significance of this event).

"What a chasm the Lyon events have opened up! The whole country has been moved to pity at the sight of this army of ghosts consumed by hunger," stated Auguste Blanqui (1971, p. 68) in his famous self-defence of 1832, in which historians have identified the first instance of the use of the term "proletarians" in its modern, political sense (cf. § 6.2). Blanqui's republican vanguard and other similar clubs and associations were blamed by the pro-government press and Orléanist pundits for all the minor riots that erupted in the wake of the Lyon insurrection. This was a way to dispel the liberal elites' growing fears about what Prosper de Barante called the increasing "general tendency among the lower classes to resort to the strength of numbers" (1894, p. 393): a tendency that had the effect of evoking and newly disputing the very meaning of the revolutionary uprisings of 1830 that had given rise to the "July regime" (cf. § 6.1). "The Lyon movement was a local and spontaneous one; nonetheless, it was one of the symptoms or warning signals of a more general state of sickness," writes Charles de Rémusat (1959, p. 38). Such words bear witness to an emerging perception of social unrest as something "pathological": a disquiet which an event of an altogether different sort, namely the *cholera epidemic*, contributed to turning into genuine feelings of dread.

First announced in Paris on 29 March 1832, the disease claimed almost 13,000 victims in the following month alone. This death toll immediately brought profound forms of social inequality to light, triggering the psychosis of "the poisoning of the people" among the lower classes: the obsessive thought that the disease was a way for the elites to do away with the surplus population – in a context marked by debates on Malthus' theories about demographic equilibrium. The sick refused admission into hospital, lynchings of alleged plague-spreaders occurred, and the uprising went hand-in-hand with the epidemic. The 1,800 ragmen of Paris raised barricades against public health measures that deprived them of their sole means of livelihood, while the political prisoners at Sainte-Pélagie reacted to the first death in their gaol by staging a revolt with the support of the republicans, who sought to break them out. The fear of social unrest and political conflicts thus became intertwined with the fear of contagion, leading the wealthy classes to abandon the city in the belief that "popular miasmas" from the decadent and unsanitary poor neighbourhoods were a crucial vector for the spread of the disease (cf. §§ 2.3–2.4).[3]

On 16 May, even the head of government, Périer, fell victim to cholera after being infected during a visit to the sick poor at the Hôtel-de-Dieu. A few days later, General Lamarque, a leader of the opposition, met the same fate. In Paris during June, the republicans took advantage of his funeral to stage the greatest insurrection in the twenty-year history of the "July Monarchy." "The movement of 1832 had in its rapid explosion and mournful extinction so much grandeur that . . . [it] is assuredly a characteristic hour among the stormy hours of this age," writes Hugo when introducing his account of the battle waged by the thousands of armed militants who broke up the funeral cortège to occupy key junctions in the capital (Hugo, 1893, pp. 353–354). The insurgents raised hundreds of barricades, and to tear them down 40,000 soldiers and national guardsmen opened fire for the first time on the people of Paris. Over 300 people were killed in two days, leading the authorities to proclaim a state of siege.

> I believe that more courageous fighting was not seen even at Thermopylae. . . . The few who did not succumb did not beg to have their lives spared . . . with chests bared, they ran into the enemy and had themselves shot down.

Thus writes Henri Heine (1872, p. 217) to describe the last moments of a battle which could easily be seen as an extension of conflicts that had already been exacerbated by the cholera outbreak.[4] "The June uprising, which occurred just after the epidemic, is in all respects only the political continuation of the same crisis," writes Louis Chevalier in his matchless depiction of Paris during those years (1973, pp. 18–21), highlighting a continuity in terms of the actors, processes, and problems involved that lends the events just described "profound chronological unity."

In France, it was the fast pace and tragic quality of these events that marked the emergence of the "social question," of the labour movement, and of socialist discourse, as well as of the first attempt to translate liberalism into a mode of governance. To grasp the development of such processes, it is now necessary to frame the events constituting this fragment of history in the political and intellectual context of the time, in which they contributed to shaping new interpretations of politics and new representations of society.

1.2 Completing the French revolution

"The effect produced by the Lyon workers' uprising has been great . . . Will time heal this inevitable sickness of a popular revolution?" asked Prosper de Barante (1894, pp. 393–394), once again offering a "pathological" understanding of the social dynamics underlying the events that had unfolded since July 1830. François Guizot (1988, pp. 38 and 41) writes:

> Revolutionary France is neither stable nor constituted yet; uncertainty and confusion still reign within it; good and evil, truth and falsehood, the elements

> of order and the seeds of anarchy are brewing amid confusion and hazard; . . . like the Israelites, we have therefore both to settle and defend ourselves.

French authors and thinkers from this period regarded the time that had elapsed since the great Revolution of 1789 as a field of ruins overwhelmed by the powerful course of events that history seemed incapable of bringing into order (Chignola, 2011). In forty years, France had experienced all the regimes known to modernity, along with the traumas associated with each: the First Republic and the revolutionary Terror; the Empire and the Napoleonic Wars; the One Hundred Days of Napoleon's return and the subsequent invasion by Holy Alliance troops, which had brought the Cossacks to Paris; and the Monarchical Restoration with its White Terror, that is, the ultra-royalist reaction to the heir to the throne's assassination. Then, in 1830, another revolution occurred. The "Three Glorious Days of July" expelled the Bourbons once more and imposed a change of dynasty and the centrality of the Constitutional Chart together with a representative government based on extended census suffrage. Hence, they marked the beginning of the Orléanist liberal regime and of the peculiar institutional experiment known as the "July Monarchy."

As a result of this lengthy transition, punctuated by traumatic breaks, the French people appeared to be a wounded and divided social body that was still shaken by the traumas of the Terror, but also by the realisation that only the establishment of despotic regimes had managed to ensure political order. "Anarchy reigns in terms of reason, morals, and intelligence," writes René Chateaubriand (1848, p. 232); "the present is so utterly precarious," we read in the first issue of *La Revue Européenne*, "that the most inconsistent hopes, the most contradictory callings, perish amid so many ruins" (Carné, 1831, pp. 4 and 12).[5] In this troubled political and intellectual climate, the most unsettling effect of the long, post-revolutionary transition was identified as the erosion of the *social bond* and a widespread perception of social dissolution. "Your society is not a society or even its shadow, but a hotchpotch of beings which one would not know what to call . . . a menagerie, a flock, a mass of human beasts," writes Félicité de Lamennais (1840, p. 29), while Guizot bemoans the spirit of an epoch devoid of any "general and strong conviction capable of bringing people's spirits together" (Guizot, 1863a, p. 303: address of 5 October 1831). Hence, an aim common to different currents, authors, and doctrines in this period was to radically examine the bonds that held society together and enabled its reproduction. Even more than the traditional issue of defining the best political-institutional regime, the re-establishment, or re-invention, of the social bond – in a different form from both the "natural" order of the Ancien Régime and the contract between willing parties – came to be seen as the key challenge to bring the post-revolutionary transition to a stable point of arrival, that is, to *complete the French Revolution*.

By erasing the traditional system of class divisions and inequalities by birth, 1789 marked an unprecedented historical break. This corresponded to the shift from a society based on orders and guilds to one made up of generic "individuals." The Revolution inaugurated the era of civil and political equality by abolishing the intermediate bodies that had hierarchically organised the social order and the forms of political representation of the various strata of society during the Ancien Régime, rendering its structure directly visible and politically meaningful. The new social ontology resulting from this shift appeared to be depoliticised, individualised, and impossible to understand according to traditional categories. As Tocqueville remarked in a particularly vivid way, post-revolutionary society appeared to be ungovernable insofar as it was constantly permeated by a drive towards equality – an irresistible tendency towards the levelling of all differences and hierarchies – and by a form of liberty that atomised subjects, engendering isolation and indifference. The entire spectrum of French political thought in the first decades of the 19th century would thus seem to have been pervaded by a common tendency to investigate the laws ruling and driving this new social ontology – the society of individuals – to find where the means of governance of modern liberties could be applied within it, and to rethink the social bond without drawing upon the constructivism of contractarian doctrines.

These issues became the centre focus of a "problematic community" that brought together all the leading political thinkers of the first half of the 19th century: Henri de Saint-Simon, Benjamin Constant, Auguste Comte, François Guizot, René de Chateaubriand, Alexis de Tocqueville, M.me de Staël, and Félicité de Lamennais.[6] Despite their different perspectives, these authors shared the assumption that 1789 had caused an irreversible break, marking the beginning of a different "social state of the world" (to quote Tocqueville) and that, therefore, it was necessary to develop a new "classification" of post-revolutionary society capable of justifying an order worthy of the era of civil equality. This intellectual climate found unity and coherence in the shared question of how to complete the French Revolution – that is, how to translate its liberal and egalitarian principles into a political system capable of ensuring political order without resorting to authoritarian means. What the present research aims to retrace in connection to this field of problems and intellectual-political climate is the role that labour and the interpretation of its social and political functions came to play in the search for a post-revolutionary order.

The feelings of uncertainty produced by the political disorder and breaks marking the first decades of the 19th century added to the widespread distrust towards the ideas of the past and the doctrines of the previous century. Enlightenment philosophies and social contract theories were blamed for the way in which politics had given itself over to constructivism, the mere law of numbers and force, and the rule of passions that could only be held in check by authoritarian systems. The principles of the general will and of popular sovereignty were deemed responsible for the Terror's excesses and for a political lack of restraint that had ultimately shattered common sense and shared truths.[7] Hence, the challenging need to envisage a new, post-revolutionary epoch by forgoing the very doctrines that had brought it about. The challenge gradually became to establish a rational government capable of "objectifying" politics in such a way as to release it from the dominion of passion and bring the Revolution to completion without repeating its mistakes. As we shall see, "doctrinaire" liberalism (§ 1.4) and Saint-Simonian socialism (§ 1.5) are quintessential expressions of this field of problems, as they explored it with the aim of translating its theoretical interpretation into political praxis.

The epistemological framework of the modern political and social sciences emerged precisely out of this need to react to the perceived failure of classical political philosophy and to rethink the social bond in terms other than those of the contract between willing individuals. This meant leading political ideas beyond the constructivism of theories that conceived of politics as separate from the social sphere, thereby exposing it to the disorder of passions (cf. § 1.4). Rather, it was a matter of applying political theory to society in such a way as to develop representations capable of identifying where the means of governing modern individual liberties in the era of civil equality could be applied. The need was felt for doctrines that no longer stemmed from mere philosophical speculation, but which were capable of becoming rooted in common sense and social relations and, at the same time, of developing a new scientific approach to politics.[8] It was around the notion of *society*, then, that initial attempts were made to "define the range of tensions, contradictions, and problems deriving from the modern ideas of liberty and equality" (Chignola, 2004, p. 11). This corresponded to a shift towards a "different philosophy," which was now to assign to the concept of society the central position that the speculation of the previous century ascribed to political power and its foundation (Karsenti, 2013). The present book aims to explore how this theoretical shift towards the dimension of society – which fostered the birth of the modern social sciences – also corresponded to the rise of a powerful new representation of the modern subject: the dyadic figure of the "citizen-worker" as the quintessential subject of rights.

1.3 The rise of the "social question"

The events recalled at the beginning of this chapter contributed to exacerbating the sense of disquiet pervading the French scenario of the early 1830s, as they revealed the emergence of the "social question" of pauperism. The rise of this new form of exclusion and deprivation in the post-revolutionary society of individuals added a problematic new depth to the political uncertainties marking this epoch of "civilisational crisis," filling it – as we shall see in the next chapter – with the "general expectation of a return of the Barbarians" (Michel, 1981, p. 195). The spread of industrial pauperism was to play a major role in the process that – throughout the 19th century – came to assign political and social meaning to labour, establishing it as a key dimension to think of the modern subject. The strategy that the present book will deploy to retrace such a process is to observe the rise and development of the social question through a perspective that connects labour to citizenship in order to describe how these two dimensions became intertwined institutional areas. To do so, it will essentially frame the idea of citizenship as a bundle of rights, that is, as a legal status that bestows specific rights on those who are legally recognised as member of the political community (Marshall, 1992). Based on this notion, the following chapters explore the way in which labour became a crucial carrier of citizenship rights while at the same time transforming the contents of these rights by incorporating a social depth. To frame such an exploration, we must now consider the institutions and rights of citizenship established by the revolutionary break of

1789 and how they were affected by industrialisation processes and the rise of the social question.

The 1789 *Déclaration des droits de l'homme et du citoyen* stated that "all the citizens have the right of contributing personally or through their representatives to [the] formation" of the law, which "must be the same for all" (art. 6). On these bases, the French Revolution established civil equality before the law and institutionalised political rights as citizen rights on a national level. This marked a significant turning point insofar as not even the 1815 Bourbon Restoration was able to repeal the principles of civil equality. Political rights, instead, remained a field of contention throughout the 19th century, but 1789 marked their first emergence on a national level (Tilly, 1995; Hammersley, 2015). Through the principles of equal political rights and civil equality, the modern citizen emerged as the quintessential subject of rights and embodiment of equal membership in the political community. These principles established the legally homogeneous national citizenry and brought about a consistent definition of modern citizenship (Brubaker, 1989, 1992). Although limited to free men, the main feature of this institution was egalitarianism: modern citizenship emerged as a powerful driving force of *equality* among the members of a nation by defining a region of general human equality in the legal-political sphere, despite all the material differences shaping the other spheres of human existence. "Like civil rights, political rights derive from a person's capacity as a citizen. These legal rights are identical for every person, whether his property happens to be great or small," Sieyès (2002, Ch. 3, 17) wrote in his famous pamphlet *What Is the Third Estate?*[9]

In parallel with the spread of these legal-political principles, industrialisation began to transform post-revolutionary society, leading to the rise of new inequalities in the social domain. Besides the principles of civil and political equality, Revolutionary Declarations affirmed private property to be a "natural," "imprescriptible," "inviolable and sacred right of man": industrialisation turned out to be a driving force for *inequality* in such a domain. The post-revolutionary society based on civil equality recognised private property as a legitimate source of inequalities in spheres other than the civil and political ones, according to principles – such as those of talent, work, fortune, and ability – not based on the old and immutable privileges by birth (cf. §§ 1.4–1.5). The advent of an industrial regime of production and commerce created the conditions for almost limitless inequalities of wealth and property, since the transition from hand production to machines fuelled by steam energy led to an unparalleled increase in the amount of goods that could be manufactured and exchanged.

Early-19th-century political and social theorists perceived and described industrialisation as a deeply ambivalent movement producing the simultaneous and antithetical growth of unprecedented prosperity and of new forms of deprivation and social exclusion. Steam energy, mechanisation, and the division of labour enhanced the productivity of low-skilled workers, whose condition as equal citizens was deeply affected by the inegalitarian dynamics brought about by the capitalistic use of industrial technologies. The latter fostered the rise of both industrial pauperism as a new form of exclusion resulting from the lack of any property and capitalism as a new form of class privilege. "As the conditions of men constituting the nation become more and more equal, . . . as the mass of the nation turns to democracy, that particular class which is engaged in manufactures becomes more aristocratic," Alexis de Tocqueville (1994, p. 556) wrote, arguing that "if ever a permanent inequality of conditions and aristocracy again penetrate into the world, it may be predicted that this [industrialisation] is the channel by which they will enter."[10] Hence, at the same time as the modern principle of citizenship based on civil equality was making it possible to overcome the old status-based structures (Marshall, 1992), industrialisation was paving the way for new forms of human hierarchy, dependency, and subordination originating within the industrial workplace and production process.

The establishment of civil equality among citizens – that is, the foundation of modern citizenship – went hand in hand with the abolition of all those intermediate bodies and orders that shaped feudal societies by defining their hierarchical and differential system of rights and duties based on natural and divine law. A system of legal equality among citizens instead required the creation of an "empty space" between individuals and the State by removing all the traditional structures of legal-political inequality. Such structures also included guilds, which organised employment on the local level, and were therefore considered to be in conflict with the civil right to freely chose one's work, but also provided a system of social security. In this context, industrialisation processes involved a workforce that was deprived of any property and social protection. As we shall see in the next chapter, it fostered a massive influx of migrant workers, propertyless citizens, working poor, paupers, and proletarians into manufacturing cities. These internal migrants found themselves alone as individuals before society and the State: a new condition of deprivation that in the 1830s was first named through neologisms such as "pauperism" and "proletariat" (cf. §§ 3.1.2 and 6.2).

The growth of this class of propertyless citizens and its unsettling state of social exclusion and deprivation embodied a stunning contradiction with respect to the egalitarian principles of citizenship affirmed by the Revolution. This tension soon became a major issue and defining element in 19th-century European societies and the full inclusion of these subjects into a substantial condition of equal citizenship progressively emerged as the main challenge for these societies. In a famous treatise on the social question (cf. § 6.3), Eugène Buret proclaimed that:

> The wretched condition of these populations is incompatible not only with the hopes of civilisation, but with its very existence. One must either find an effective remedy to the affliction of pauperism, or else prepare for the overthrow of the world.
>
> (Buret, 1840, p. 74).

Addressing such a threat implied identifying political strategies and legal "technologies" able to mitigate the contradiction between the equal membership affirmed by the political revolution in the legal sphere and the new social inequalities produced by the Industrial Revolution. As we shall see in the next chapter, in the

1830s this contradiction was named the "social question," since it revealed a new dimension – the *social* dimension – consisting of problems and subjects that appeared to be excluded from the regulations and systems of rights established by the modern institution of national citizenship (cf. § 2.1). As Karl Polany (2001, pp. 108, 267–268) has illustrated, the rise of the industrial age brought about the emergence of society as a new continent for political and legal theory: "pauperism and political economy . . . formed part of one indivisible whole: the discovery of society. . . . It came to us through living in an industrial society. . . . It is the constitutive element in modern man's consciousness." While previous political theories – especially the social contract and Enlightenment doctrines – focused on the foundations of sovereignty, political power, and legal rights, the post-revolutionary landscape of the 19th century, marked by industrialisation processes, brought the issue of *social relations* to the centre stage.

The new challenges posed by industrialisation revealed the emergence of the social dimension as a fluid and murky space which appeared to be impenetrable to politics, law, and administration. The development of civil and political rights in no way seemed to affect the substantial inequalities that shaped the social fabric and originated from the economic realm, to which the existing institutions of citizenship remained ultimately indifferent. The hypothesis that this book aims to develop is that the attaching of political significance to labour and its making as a crucial carrier of rights gradually emerged as a way to address the contradiction between legal-political equality among citizens and the new inequalities produced by industrialisation within the social order established by the Revolution. In the next chapters, we see how workplaces, the industrial sphere, and labour conditions were gradually identified as the key critical areas where such a contradiction had to be mitigated. Hence, we explore how the recognition of certain rights within the industrial domain of labour emerged and fostered the rise of pioneering principles of welfare and social rights. Before beginning this exploration, let us consider the two currents of thought and ideas that provide the political background against which these processes must be understood.

1.4 Doctrinaire liberalism

The political thought of the "doctrinaires" is rooted in the tradition of French liberalism sprung from the interpretation of the Revolution that was crystallised by Benjamin Constant in *Des effets de la Terreur* (1797), and which later consolidated into opposition to the Restoration regime centred on the defence of the Constitutional Charter.[11] Under Camille Jordan's philosophical guidance and Pierre-Paul Royer-Collard's political leadership, doctrinaire liberalism developed the ideological infrastructure and institutional framework of the July Monarchy, which it furnished with great statesmen – most notably, François Guizot, but also Prosper de Barante, Victor de Broglie, and Charles de Rémusat.[12] In such a way, doctrinaire liberalism inextricably bound its own theoretical-political experience to the institutional one of Orléanism. The doctrinaires who hailed from noble or *haut-bourgeois* families that had embraced the Revolution and then fallen victim to the

Terror – are an expression of the post-revolutionary climate in France, which they reinterpreted according to a *juste milieu* vision aimed at establishing a kind of politics and government opposed both to a return to absolutism and aristocratic privileges, and to the advent of democratic egalitarianism and popular sovereignty. Hence, the spread in the Orléanist field of the formula "society must be defended" (cf. § 2.2) alluded to the twofold aim to defend the society established by the Revolution against attempts to revert to the constitution of the Ancien Régime and, at the same time, to protect it against the risks that the very revolutionary process had engendered by fuelling political passions, excesses, and extremes.

Through this perspective, the political thought and institutional praxis of the doctrinaires deployed the first attempt to turn liberal theory into a form of governance. This aim also led them to radically call into question certain canonical assumptions of classical liberalism, especially regarding individualism and the concept of society and its relationship with power (cf. § 1.4.1). On the institutional level, these theoretical developments coincided with the identification of the principle of *capacity* and capacity-based representation as the overall logic by which a just compromise could be struck between aristocracy and democracy so as to bring an end to the prolonged, exceptional state of disorder caused by the "revolutionary" obsession in French politics (cf. § 1.4.2). The politics of governmental liberalism developed by the doctrinaires offer the background against which to frame the topic of the first part of the book, which is the establishment of labour as an object of administration, scientifical knowledge, and governance.

1.4.1 Social powers

Rémusat traces the birth of the doctrinaires' "party" back to the turn of the 1820s, arguing that "the political problem at the time was this: to create a *libéralisme gouvernemental*" (1959, p. 324). Indeed, doctrinaires' theory and politics express the first attempt to translate liberalism into a form of governance and institutional praxis in continental Europe. Such an aim also led them to mark significant discontinuities with respect to previous liberal theory, in particular with regard to the way it framed the relationship between political power and society. Doctrinaire liberalism combined a radical critique of Rousseau's theory of the social contract with an attempt to distance itself from the individualism that had shaped the 18th-century liberal tradition. The latter rested on the idea of an empty space between the State and individuals, and of an isolated subject that pre-existed society and whose rights liberalism sought to defend. By conceiving of society as an autonomous sphere capable of regulating itself, traditional liberalism aimed to act as its champion against the prerogatives of the government, thereby developing an ineffective policy of opposition.[13] The doctrinaires regarded this juxtaposition between power and society as a merely theoretical artifice. Against 18th-century individualism, they argued that society *de facto* owes its existence to bonds of mutual recognition based on a "rule" that our *reason* enables us to accept, along with the relationships which such bonds establish.[14] According to doctrinaire theory, political power – which is to say, the "government" – is merely an expression of this rule. It shapes and enables society's existence, coexisting with it in a relationship of constant symbiosis. The criticism of individualism thus became the starting point for an overall reassessment of traditional liberal doctrine and of the way in which it conceived of society and of its relationship with political power. Far from being two opposite and conflicting dimensions – Guizot writes – "society and government mutually imply each other; . . . The idea of society necessarily implies the idea of rule, of a common law, which is to say of government." This "necessary coexistence of society and government" makes the former an intrinsically political dimension that "shows the absurdity of the hypothesis of the social contract," which "presents us with the picture of men already united together into a society, but without rule, and exerting themselves to create one" (Guizot, 1880, Vol. I, p. 86).

This assumption of a natural mutual implication between power and society enabled doctrinaire thought to sidestep the problem of the "origin" or "foundation" of the political order, on which the distinction between State and civil society was based, to deny the modern logical correlation between sovereignty and representation, and hence to also deny the foundational political role of free will. The criticism of contractualist doctrines thus led to the overall questioning of major assumptions in modern political philosophy, starting from the very distinction between the State and civil society. Doctrinaires questioned such a distinction through a kind of pragmatics of power that undermined both the conception of a foundational relationship between political authority and society and that of the precedence of individuals over society (Manent, 1987). Hence, they developed a dynamic and essentially *social conception of power* insofar as they framed the latter as the "natural" consequence of those relations of "superiority" and "influence" that "turn a multitude into a society and make it capable of preserving itself against anarchy without resorting to absolute power" (Guizot, 1988, p. 105). In contrast to what social contract philosophies suggest, power is not a sort of "object" that is held and ceded; rather, it must be understood as something which flows through societies and gives them shape and order, without ever being fully absorbed into a stable centre.[15] Therefore, every lawful attribution of sovereignty – which by definition is one and indivisible – to an individual or collective figure inevitably contains the seeds of despotism.[16]

However, against the idea of sovereignty – and the Legitimists' notion of divine right – the doctrinaires did not endorse a reduction of political power to the bare minimum in the name of the self-regulatory autonomy of society, but rather the principle of *representative government*. The latter embodies a kind of political power that must constantly prove its legitimacy, insofar as it "does not recognize the sovereignty of right as an intrinsic attribute of any person or collective body; on the contrary, all powers are expected to strive to discover and faithfully apply the rule that ought to govern their actions" (Guizot, 1880, p. 87). Doctrinaire theory is characterised precisely by this principle of the governmentalisation of power based on the notion of "representative government." The latter is conceived of as one of the powers imbricated in society, whose strength and magnitude depend on its capacity to represent the multitude of social powers – the forms of authority and influences lending shape and order to society – and to co-opt them into existing institutions.[17] This political power has to be a faithful representation of society's material constitution and therefore must constantly verify that it adheres to the social powers. It was through this dynamic conception of government as a flexible dispositif applied to the social body that the doctrinaires sought to overcome a crucial problem for modern political philosophy. This was the institution of political power through a constructivist mechanism essentially external to and autonomous from society, and therefore requiring abstract and complex forms of mediation such as the idea of a social contract as the foundation of sovereignty.

> [The] true means of government . . . reside in society itself and cannot be separated from it. It is there that they must be sought, and it is there too that one must leave them in order to make use of them.
>
> Guizot (1988, pp. 106–107)

Society is the "general force" from which government draws its own "particular force." The latter depends on the government's ability to represent society faithfully by establishing a relationship of ontological and isomorphic continuity that precedes the fictional construction of the social contract and representation of wills.[18] Against the classic "external means" of government, "machines resting on the surface" of society "which do not have any roots in its bowels and do not draw upon the principle of its movement" (ibid.), the doctrinaires thus promoted the search for political technologies capable of penetrating the folds of society to find some foothold. Power must constantly communicate with society to understand its needs, and thus ensure that society will recognise it as legitimate and "be reflected" in and "encapsulated" by it. "It is needs that we must study" to "delve into this society which the Revolution has crafted for us; it is necessary to probe its depths, to explore it in all directions," writes Guizot (1820, p. 155). This will to know society marks the distance between the doctrinaire theory and the previous tradition in political philosophy, which focused on the origins of power, establishment of sovereignty, and foundation of rights. For the doctrinaires, it was no longer a matter of developing a general theory of power, but rather a pragmatics of power that was sociologically qualified insofar as it was designed to identify those areas where the means of governing post-revolutionary society could be applied. As early as 1816, Guizot wrote:

> The men entrusted with managing the social order have a pressing need to know both the *theory of the society* they must govern and the *theory of the institutions* that are their means of governance. By a theory of society, I mean the sum of facts that constitute the state of this society and of the laws by which such facts are combined and coexist.[19]

What emerges in doctrinaire theory, then, is this tension – common to all French political thought of the 1820s and 1830s – to associate the exercising of power with methods for the investigation of society. The very doctrine of capacity-based representation – that will be the focus of the next section – expresses the effort to translate this tension into actual political institutions. This idea that the foundations of politics must now be sought within social relations results from the doctrinaires' effort to rethink the relationship between political power and society without drawing upon the constructions implied by the notions of sovereignty, the people, contract, and general will. These they replaced with the concept of representative government as a flexible technology for the exercising of a form of power whose matrix nonetheless remains exclusively social. This principle of the governmentalisation of power was intended as a way to bring the French Revolution to an end by directly linking politics to society and disconnecting it from the disorder of political passions and frenzies. Thus, doctrinaire theory broke away from certain canonical assumptions on the basis of which modern political thought had conceived of the relationship between the State and civil society, and revealed a necessary connection to the kind of sociological knowledge whose basic concepts Auguste Comte was starting to define in those same years in his *Course of Positive Philosophy*.[20]

1.4.2 Capacity-based government

For doctrinaire liberalism, completing the Revolution meant, first of all, bringing into power a constitutional elite that might legitimately govern the *nouvelle France* according to the principles of civil equality enshrined by 1789, as well as keeping with the values of order implied in the conservation of the monarchical form of government. This objective implied a twofold effort. On the one hand, it was a matter of affirming a classification of post-revolutionary society based on a new and dynamic principle which was no longer derived from any privileges by birth, and which reflected subjective values and abilities rather than a class-based logic. At the same time, doctrinaires sought to reject the kind of democratic egalitarianism on which the "false and deceitful principle of universal suffrage" rested. The means to such a twofold goal was found in the principle of *capacity*, which the doctrinaires sought to assert as the general principle of governance for a society made up of individuals, and which was expressed in institutional terms through the doctrine of *capacity-based representation*.

"Power would never have been established among equals," wrote Guizot (1988, p. 125), illustrating his essentially historical and social conception of power, which in his view was rooted in the "natural" inequalities between the subjective capacities of human beings. Guizot identified representative government as the political technology that made it possible to co-opt these natural and legitimate "forms of superiority" into the institutions, to gather the "fragments of social power," and to "constitute" them as political power. "It is necessary to discover all the elements of legitimate power that are disseminated throughout society and to organise them into an actual power; that is to say to concentrate them, and to realise public reason and public morality, and to call them to the occupation of power", added Guizot (1880, Vol. II, pp. 49–50): "what we call representation is nothing other than a means to arrive at this result". Electoral suffrage constituted the key element in the dynamics of communication and self-reflection which political power needed to establish in society in order to "extract from the bosom of society itself" the new capacity-based aristocracy of the reason that had the right to govern France, and by whom the latter had the right to be governed.[21]

Hence, voting was primarily seen by doctrinaires not so much as a right, but as a "function," a "means of governance," and a "social power" that had to work harmoniously with all other powers: hence, to exercise it, it was necessary to show that one had the required capacity to do so according to one's own interests and those of society. In other words, doctrinaires' theory aimed to subordinate access to political rights to the prove of one's "faculty to act according to reason" and to "act freely and reasonably in society's interest" by discerning general affairs. Such a faculty was supposed to enable *political capacity* to contribute to the election of representatives. Capacities are understood as objective qualities which predate legislation and constitute "the natural principle, the necessary condition" for the right to vote: "in society there are natural, legitimate electors, ready-made electors, whose existence precedes the thought of the legislator and whom he must simply endeavour to discover" (Guizot, 1861, pp. 384–387). It is this objective need to know society that makes the capacity-based doctrine a sociologically-qualified science of government which primarily conceives of representation as a means to develop those maps and images of society that political power must produce to directly identify the best strategies to govern the social body.[22] This kind of sociological understanding of political power allowed doctrinaires to abandon the ideas and constructions implied by the modern theories of political representation and sovereignty.

According to doctrinaire thinking, democratic representation is a formal device that involves "all individuals, merely because they exist, without demanding of them anything more." It counts their wills and pretends to embody them via representatives. By contrast to this "arithmetical machine," capacity-based suffrage "considers what the kind of action is on which individuals are consulted; it examines what the degree of capacity required for this action is", Guizot (1880, Vol. I, p. 110) writes: "it then summons those individuals who are supposed to possess this capacity – all such, and such only. Finally, it seeks a majority among those who are capable." Hence, capacity-based representation requires a complex and dynamic electoral device that changes in relation to the object and scale of the election. And it is also supposed to change over time because it is necessary for individuals' capacities to be constantly evaluated to avoid the crystallisation of institutional positions that no longer reflect social reality. Guizot stresses the changing character of political capacity, which varies in extension depending on the "material and moral development of society" and the progress of civilisation. Insofar as everyone is equipped with reason, this extension is potentially general, and any census must be understood merely as one proof of the people's capacity, not as the only proof, and certainly not as one valid for all time (Tomasello, 2018).[23]

The theory of capacities is thus far more complex than the census system that represents its only historical expression. It may be identified as a relevant point of origin for contemporary discourses on "merit" and "meritocracy" as a general principle for the governance of multiple institutions. It also offers a pioneering assessment of the theoretical and political limits of democratic representation, but it is precisely at this level that the doctrinaires show their greatest limit: a striking short-sightedness with respect to the historical movement towards equality that marked their age. Tocqueville (1852) was to emphasise this by accusing the doctrinaires of having "always been one revolution too late." The implicit equation between the multitude and the tyranny of numbers, the masses and disorder, popular sovereignty and despotic terror, which is implicit in doctrinaire theory as a whole, makes their principle of capacity structurally deaf to the problem of the subaltern classes' integration into the State, which the emergence of the social question in those very years had actually established at the centre of the debate.

This aspect is evident in Guizot's attempt to identify the criteria for political capacity. He does so by distinguishing three "social classes." On the one hand, we have the class of people whose condition enables them "to devote themselves almost exclusively to the cultivation of their own intelligence" – as in the case of those with a life income – and the class of those whose activity makes them acquainted with facts enabling them to grasp general relations and interests – as in the case of those who invest their capital. On the other hand, we have the mass of individuals whose state of need prevents them from "moving beyond the tight circle of their individual interests," as they are forced to provide for themselves and others by selling their work (Guizot, 1863, pp. 389–390). Hence, the limit beyond which it is legitimate to assume that political capacity no longer applies – that is, the threshold of political incapacity – is set at the condition of wage labour, which according to Guizot's theory of capacities "entails a drastic reduction of the sphere of citizenship" (Pasquino, 1991, p. 119). This theory, therefore, proved radically inadequate for grasping the constituent power of the link between labour and citizenship that was emerging, to the point of becoming a major focus of the break marked by 1848. In commenting on the revolutionary events of that year, Guizot (1849, pp. 86–89) was to bemoan "the meaning which the word labour carries in the language of this anti-social war," designed to develop "in the spirit of workers devoted to material labour a feeling that theirs is the only kind of labour worthy of this name and possessing the rights associated with it" (cf. § 6.6).[24]

The following chapters investigate precisely the gradual reversal of this assumption concerning the mutual exclusion between the condition of wage labour and the sphere of citizenship, which led wage labour to become a major source of citizens' rights and protections. The hypothesis I will be presenting is that, far from suddenly finding concrete expression in the events of 1848, this political emphasis on the value of wage labour gradually developed from the early 1830s onwards, and that through their political praxis, the doctrinaires unwittingly contributed to its emergence insofar as they faced the need to develop strategies to address the social question. While it is correct to state that the doctrinaires' political thought proved strikingly indifferent to the 19th-century problem of the subaltern classes' exclusion and deprivation, the same cannot be said about the political activity they engaged in during the July Monarchy. The theory of doctrinaire liberalism only becomes fully intelligible in the light of the efforts to put this theory into practice through the policies and institutional practices deployed by the Orléanist government (Rosanvallon, 1985). The first part of this book therefore delves into what

Robert Castel (1995, p. 379) calls "the social side of a capacity-based governmentality," which developed through the need to deal with issues related to pauperism. The momentous reform of primary schools which Guizot carried out as Minister of Education can be considered an example of this, since it envisaged the "teaching staff" as a fundamental intermediary between the government and society. Yet, the main institutional initiative that we will consider is Guizot's reopening of the Academy of Moral and Political Sciences, which became an essential workshop for the development of modern social sciences by making pauperism the object of an increasingly in-depth and organised analysis that brought the centrality of workers' conditions into focus (cf. § 2.6 and §§ 3.2 and 3.3). We will see how, even in the liberal sphere, the need to develop strategies to address the social question brought attention to wage labour conditions as a field of knowledge, administration, and social security policies that anticipated – if only in an extremely ambivalent way – the modern connection between labour and citizenship.

1.5 Saint-Simonianism: between sociology and socialism

Claude-Henri de Saint-Simon's thought and that of Guizot and the doctrinaires emerge from a shared field of problems and aims, even though the former interprets it through an authoritative anticipation of socialist discourse, while the latter approach it in an attempt to establish a liberal mode of governance. This shared core clearly emerges from the centrality that Saint-Simon too assigns to the idea of *capacities* (or abilities) as the general principle by which to overcome the logic of aristocratic privilege and to establish a new classification of society capable of fulfilling – and at the same time closing – the French Revolution.[25] Pierre Macherey (1992) has investigated the proximity between these two perspectives by identifying a shared notion of "social relationships" on the basis of which both Saint-Simon and Guizot developed their theories, in an effort to re-establish the social bond in a form other than the contract between wills.[26] Both thinkers turned to history and historical knowledge to distance themselves from the philosophical theories of the previous century and to identify the French Revolution as the outcome of a centuries-old process. Saint-Simon viewed this as the last of the "critical epochs," which now needed to be stabilised by developing a new balance between "organic" relationships. Hence, he credited Guizot with having spread the very understanding of national history which he himself favoured, namely as the outcome of a long struggle between two different people or races (cf. §§ 2.1 and 2.2).[27] Saint-Simon also developed this view by collaborating with another leading liberal historian of the French bourgeoisie, Augustin Thierry, who acted as his first secretary from 1814 to 1817.[28]

Thierry's successor was Auguste Comte, whose development of Saint-Simonian "positive philosophy" is usually credited with having laid the epistemological foundations of modern sociology. Yet, "it is to Saint-Simon that one must, in full justice, award this honour," wrote Émile Durkheim (1959, p. 104), who credited him with this "new enterprise" intended to find a place "between the formal generalities of metaphysical philosophy and the narrow specialisation of the particular sciences." Like the doctrinaires, Saint-Simon contributed to the rise of modern social sciences by pursuing the entirely political aim of establishing a rational government capable of ordering the social dynamics created by the Revolution. In this case too, interest in developing pioneering forms of the social investigation was fuelled by the political will to develop a classification of post-revolutionary society apt to identify a new hierarchical order suited to the age of civil equality – which is to say, one founded on capacities as opposed to attributes inherited at birth. Compared to doctrinaire liberalism, Saint-Simon's thought is marked by greater social depth and by more explicit sociological ambitions. These are expressed by the aim of developing a "social physiology," understood as a "science of observation" designed to address "political problems . . . by the same method and in the same way that today one treats sciences relating to other phenomena."[29] Hence the pioneering effort to develop a scientific representation of society, which – according to Durkheim (1959) – makes Saint-Simon the real source of the first assumptions at the basis of both *sociology* and *socialism* (cf. also Picon, 2003; Maddaloni, 2011, pp. 28 ff.). Indeed, his thought and the Saint-Simonian movement are also commonly regarded as a crucial milestone in the emergence of French socialism and as an important point of reference in early workers' struggles (cf. Marx & Engels, 1848, Ch. 3). As we shall see in Chapter 6, one crucial element for the development of the latter was the reception in the labour world of the notion of "association," based on which the Saint-Simonians interpreted the issue of the re-establishment of the social bond in post-revolutionary society (cf. §§ 6.3–6.4).

It is precisely this shared sociological and socialist matrix that makes Saint-Simonianism a remarkable point of juncture between the two parts of the present study, that is, between the objectivation of labour as a field of knowledge promoted by the nascent social sciences, and the political subjectivation of labour promoted by socialist discourses and the workers' movement. In other words, the Saint-Simonian perspective allows us to appreciate the connections between, on the one hand, the emergence of a scientific form of knowledge about society that found in industrial pauperism and labour conditions its first object of enquiry (the focus of the first part of this book) and, on the other hand, the development of a socialist discourse that conceived of labour as a powerful tool for political subjectivation, namely for the development of that historical-political subjectivity that came to be known as the labour movement (the focus of the second part of the book). To grasp this interplay and frame Saint-Simon's doctrine within its context, we must now consider the way in which it was interpreted by his followers through the establishment of a movement that found a central place in French political debate in the early 1830s.

1.5.1 The sociology of association

After Saint-Simon's death in 1825, it was most notably Olindo Rodriguez, Amand Bazard, and Prosper Enfantin who strove to keep the Saint-Simonian newspaper *Le Producteur* in print and to draft an *Exposition de la Doctrine saint-simonienne*, which provided a crucial impulse for the spread of an otherwise unsystematic and fragmentary philosophy (Enfantin et al., 1854). "At the time, the stage was entirely occupied by the Saint-Simonian school," writes Louis Blanc, stressing "the great influence" of the movement in those years.[30] This culminated in the acquisition of one of the leading French newspapers, *Le Globe*, which already brought together the Restoration's liberal opposition. It featured contributions by Rémusat and Guizot, among others, and was a prominent mouthpiece during the 1830 Revolution. In the wake of the latter, the paper's founder, Pierre Leroux, joined the Saint-Simonians' ranks, paving the way for the next step: the conversion of the newspaper into the *Journal de la doctrine de Saint-Simon* (later *De la religion saint-simonienne*) and the choice to distribute it freely in the capital's streets.[31]

This was a striking gesture in a context in which the press still had a very limited circulation, and it reflected a basic aim of the Saint-Simonian programme: "reforming the physical, moral, and intellectual condition of the poorest and most numerous class." The centrality of this catchphrase, combined with the rejection of bourgeois individualism, makes it possible to frame this movement within the nascent socialist discourse.[32] However, it is no less true that the other cornerstone of the doctrine was largely liberal, that is, the formula "to each according to his capacity, to each capacity according to its works," which for the democrat Louis Blanc implicitly supported the social inequalities entailed by the capitalist system.[33] Hence, Saint-Simonians expressed only a relative principle of equality: on the one hand, it opposed all inequalities by birth and by law but, on the other, it assigned legitimacy to those which were useful for production and its social organisation. The latter forms of inequality were seen as resulting from differences between individuals in terms of their capacities and the fruits of their labour. They were regarded to be justified after the establishment of the universal right to education.

> True equality – Saint-Simon writes in *Du système industriel* – means that each person derives benefits from society in exact proportion to his social investment, that is to say, to his positive capacity: this equality is the natural foundation of industrial society
>
> (Saint-Simon, Enfantin, 1865–78, Vol. VI, p. 17).

In this case, the principle of capacity underlies the plan for rational management of industry (rather than of the government, as in the doctrinaires' case), designed to abolish the pathologies associated with the regime of industrial competition and bourgeois individualism so as to pave the way for a "universal association" based on the natural brotherhood of mankind and on the peaceful coexistence of people. "Emancipation of the poor classes, which are the most numerous; universal association; holy equality between man and woman – such is the future towards which we stride," wrote a militant, who summed up the key ideas of political Saint-Simonianism as follows: "privileges of birth are the cause of poverty and war; it is by replacing it with retribution according to one's works that happiness and peace will reign" (Bazard, 1831, p. 4).

The sociological drive of Saint-Simonianism is primarily linked to the aim of investigating the way in which the advent of industrial technologies could impact and transform social relationships in the post-revolutionary scenario. Like other "utopian" movements inspired by the dawning of the industrial age, Saint-Simonians assumed that industrial technologies made it possible to create new forms of political membership and social organisation capable of overcoming the inequalities produced by capital-driven industrialisation and outdated political institutions and principles of governance. Positivistic faith in technological change as a powerful force of social progress led these movements to plan forms of governance based on techno-scientific principles and aimed at overcoming the organisation of the political community based on State sovereignty. These "apostles of industrialism" sought to bring social technology up to the same level as industrial technology by establishing an organic integration of society based on industrial cooperation and human fraternity. The objective was to turn politics into a positive science of production and political power into the rational administration of society according to scientific knowledge (Saint-Simon, 1952, 1975; Manuel, 1956). These social engineering principles expressed an attempt to build a new form of political membership aimed at reabsorbing the State within the fabric of industrial society and at reorganising it as an association of producers.

This perspective made Saint-Simonian doctrine focus on the assessment of what conditions are responsible for the association between men (rather than those governing and defending society as in the doctrinaires' case). Such an approach aimed to replace the problem of the governing of society with that of the realisation of *association*, understood as the establishment of a social relation that makes it possible to overcome bourgeois individualism without having to draw upon the political constructs of sovereignty or the social contract. Instead, the Saint-Simonian idea of the association was based on the political emphasising of the immanence of the brotherhood which naturally binds human beings together and leads them to cooperate. The association is that form of the social bond capable of turning the government of men founded on the centuries-old relationship of command and obedience into a straightforward "administration of things" founded on the cooperative bond stemming from the relationship of interdependence and mutual attraction between human beings. Hence, the dissolution of the State into "a workers' association" was envisaged as the "ultimate goal" of the progressive historical succession of "critical" and "organic" epochs, in which "states of antagonism" – different social groups hampering one another through relations based on domination – slow down the ultimate emergence of the "state of association," which unites the "human family" through the "division of labour." "The only law" governing the development of the human species is this "uninterrupted progress of association," its constant expansion from the original core of the family to the "universal" form of the "association of all men . . . in all spheres of their relationships" (Enfantin et al., 1854, pp. 99–101).

In the second part of the present book, we will consider the crucial role that this idea of association played in a process of political subjectivation of labour that led to the emergence of the modern workers' movement. Specifically, we will observe how – in the aftermath of the *révolte des canuts* of 1831 – this idea was received and rethought in the labour world, where it acquired new meaning by interacting with other notions – such as those of "class," "people," and "proletariat" – used to describe the subjects which burst into public debate as a result of the events described at the beginning of this chapter. We shall see how the reception of the idea of association in the labour world came to play a key role in stimulating new forms of the coalition and struggle that moved beyond the legacy of guilds, cutting across the boundaries between different trades (Sewell, 1980; cf. §§ 5.4 and 6.3).[34] At the same time, we shall see how the emerging political significance of labour, in turn, had relevant repercussions for the Saint-Simonian movement, reorienting it towards increasing attention to workers' conditions (Rancière, 1981; cf. §§ 6.4 and 6.5).

Notes

1 The succinct reconstruction of the events in Lyon that I am presenting here – and to which I will be returning in § 6.1 – is chiefly based on the following sources: the account provided by Prefect Bouvier-Dumolard (1832); the report for the Chamber by President of the Council of Ministers Périer (1831); the accounts by the *Journal des débats* between 25 November and 5 December 1831, the pioneering historical reconstruction by Monfalcon (1834); and the documents collected by the publisher Baron (1832), and by Collombe (1832) and Mazon (1831). The point of view of the artisans involved in the insurrection can especially be found in the 27 November and 4 and 11 December 1831 issues of the weekly *L'Écho de la fabrique* (on which cf. §§ 5.4 and 6.3) and in the report produced for the government by silk-weavers Bernard and Charnier (n.d.). For a detailed analysis of the Lyonnais insurrection of 1831 and its historical-political meaning, cf. Chapters 5 and 6.

2 "The workers' occupation of the city has continued for eight days; but it exists in name only. . . . It seems as though the victors have abdicated. . . . The workers still wield power, yet do not know what to do with it," Monfalcon writes (1834, pp. 92 and 95). *All translations from the original French sources are my own.*

3 As we shall see in the next chapter, the theories about contagion, the isolation measures, and the harsh administrative measures taken in an attempt to save what could still be saved, just like the articles in the bourgeois press, bear witnessed to the fear – a primarily physical, biological fear – of that mass of humans that in a few decades had settled in the old heart of the city, transforming it beyond recognition (cf. §§ 2.3–2.4).

4 The author is describing the Cloître Saint-Merry barricade, to which Hugo devotes many pages of *Les Misérables*. It was here that Gavroche met his maker and that, for the first time since the trauma of the Terror, the red flag was used again as a symbol by the insurgents, together with black one bearing the old revolutionary slogan "The Republic or death" (see Hazan, 2002, pp. 314–399; Baehrel, 1952, pp. 62–93). Insurgents and soldiers fell together in the very same streets where, two months earlier, cholera had struck most violently. The memory of the epidemic was brought back by the bitter fighting, the disregard for death, the rancour shown by both the insurgents and the bourgeois divisions of the National Guard, and the feeling of dread that gripped the capital once more. The insurrection was followed by over 1,500 arrests, and the state of siege endured until 29 June, when it was *de facto* nullified by a ruling of the Court of Appeal which decreed the military tribunes unfit for trying the insurgents. On this event, see the court documents in Marrast (1832) and the research by Bouchet (2000a, 2000b).

5 This important magazine was founded in 1831 by Lamartine, Carné, and Cazalès in an effort to reconstruct "the system of common sense" on the basis of Félicité de Lamennais' "new Catholic philosophy."

6 I am borrowing the expression "problematic community" from Pierre Rosanvallon (1985, p. 75), who speaks of a "real golden age of political philosophy," of a "genuine workshop for contemporary political thought," fuelled by the need "to develop a political science and to establish a sociology, to rethink at once the political and the social sphere."

7 "Even after 1830 the problem endured, as the meaning of words had not yet become the expression of a common sense assigned to ideas," Riot-Sarcey (1998, p. 77), pointing to the creation of shared meanings as the challenge at the heart of a political arena whose "borders are still hazy."

8 "According to clearly different perspectives, Auguste Comte, Guizot, and Bonald became sociologists owing to a *nécessité problématique,*" i.e. a shared need to address certain problems, writes Rosanvallon (1985, p. 96), interpreting the "birth of sociology" as a "response" to the perceived failure of classical political doctrines and to the need to "lend shape and intelligibility to a society which no longer has any foothold [*prises*] from which it can be both understood and guided."

9 "Inequalities of property and ability are no different from inequalities of age, sex, height, and the like. They do not affect civic equality" (Sieyès 2002, Ch. 6, 76).

10 Chapter 20 of *Democracy in America* is entitled "How an aristocracy may be engendered by manufactures." As we shall see especially in Chapters 3 and 5, industrialisation in France emerged and developed at a much slower pace than in Britain. Yet, in the early 1830s its social consequences were significant enough to attract broad attention and spark heated debates (cf. § 3.1.2).

11 See Schmitt (1928) concerning the doctrinaires' constitutional theory and their affirmation of the "sovereignty of the Charter": "this curious personification of written laws was meant to raise the law, with its guarantee of bourgeois liberties, . . . above all political power. . . . this encompassed the genuinely political question of whether sovereignty lay with the prince or with the people; the answer was simply: neither with the prince, nor with the people, but with the 'constitution'" (p. 21). On the Charters of 1814 and 1830, see Morabito (2008) and especially Rosanvallon (1994), who seeks to define it as the "English moment" in French history and to release it from its subaltern condition with respect to the better-known "Jacobin moment."

12 Jordan died in 1822, yet remained an important theoretical point of reference for the doctrinaires, a group that was not narrowly defined: to the aforementioned names we can add Hercule de Serre, Pellegrino Rossi, Victor Cousin, Jean-Philibert Damiron, and Théodore Jouffroy.

13 "Like the government, the opposition too is required to have a system and a future. It does not govern, yet government is a necessary goal for it," wrote Guizot (1988, pp. 210–211). On the relationship between the doctrinaires and the liberal tradition, see Manent (1987), Stuurman (1994), Mélonio (1994), Craiutu (2003), and Jennings (2011).

14 The doctrinaires' notion of "reason" is not associated – as in Kant or the *philosophes* – with the autonomy of the will, but with the evident nature of the rule itself, which the course of civilisation makes intelligible to an increasing number of individuals. Against the constructivism of previous centuries' philosophies, the doctrinaires developed a conceptual framework that was fully shaped by their *historiographical studies* and political-philosophical use of *history* (cf. §§ 2.1–2.2). The relationship between power and society is inferred not through theoretical speculation, but through the analysis of centuries of civilisation as a slow process of adopting political institutions to the changes in power relationships underlying the constitution of society by alternating the dominance of various elites and principles of legitimacy. This is the fundamental conceptual core of the history courses that Guizot held at the Sorbonne in 1821–22 (*Histoire des origines du gouvernement représentatif*) and then – after a period in which he had been stripped of his teaching assignments by the ultra-royalists – in 1828–29 (*Histoire de la civilisation en France*) and 1829–30 (*Histoire de la civilisation en Europe*). Hence the historical

representation of the French Revolution of 1789 as the legitimate and natural outcome of a centuries-old struggle, which had finally "set political power" in the "region" where those interests lay whose legitimacy the course of history had gradually established, affirming the civil equality of all citizens before State law (Guizot, 1959, pp. 79–80).

15 Power "is spread throughout society as a whole; it circulates through it swiftly, only just visible in every place, yet present everywhere," Guizot (1984, p. 114). The legitimacy of this power is not established by law, but – as in the archetypal case of paternal authority – by the capacity for reason necessary to acknowledge the correct duty to safeguard it.

16 In 1822 Guizot made the criticism of the concept of sovereignty the topic of his only strictly philosophical-political work, which was published posthumously (Guizot, 1985). On this important text, see Lefort (1994).

17 "When I speak of government, I include in this word all kinds of power existing in society, from domestic powers that do not extend beyond the family to public powers that are at the head of the State," Guizot (1880, vol. II, p. 272). Government, in other words, is understood here as a sort of "dynamic social operator" that ensures a form of "non-separate mediation," since its mission is to directly constitute the social relations of power and authority as political power without the filter of sovereignty (Rosanvallon, 1985; Chignola, 2011).

18 This is an isomorphic continuity also because it rests on an organicist conception of society and of its relationship with government (cf. Omodeo, 1970, pp. 66–97). According to Guizot, society and the government are to be understood as "one and the same being," and the latter serves as the "head" of the former: for just as the head governs the body because it possesses a "general cognition" of its needs, so the government ought to possess a general cognition of society's needs, insofar as "in the social body, as in the human body, nothing is insensible and everything holds together" (Guizot, 1817, p. 278, 1988, pp. 112–118 and 130).

19 Thus writes Guizot in annotations to his translation of Friedrich Ancillon (1816, p. 14, note 3, my italics).

20 "It is on the level of sociology, and not of an indistinct political philosophy" that the doctrinaires "overcome the limits of utopian liberalism . . . political philosophy and sociology thus become inseparable," writes Rosanvallon (1985, p. 96). Chignola (2011, p. 77) speaks of a "sociological register that grafts the notion of power upon all the circuits of action in which man's social spirit is expressed."

21 The essential principles of Guizot's theory of capacity can be found in Guizot (1861, pp. 379–420) and in his parliamentary addresses of 8 February and 5 October 1831 (Guizot, 1863, vol. I, pp. 211–217 e pp. 303–322). On Guizot as a major forerunner of elitism, see Pareto (1978, pp. 53 ff.); on his interpretation of the French Revolution, see Pozzi (1989); on his polemic against the Legitimists, see Clerici (2012).

22 From this perspective, other classical liberal principles – such as freedom of the press and the publication of parliamentary debates and government deeds – are redefined as functions structuring the relationship of self-reflection between government and society.

23 After the 1830 Revolution, the doctrinaires fought to deconstitutionalise the electoral census and to launch a debate on *adjonctions de capacité* that would allow certain citizens to be exempted from census conditions by adding other criteria connected to their education, profession, or intellectual contributions (see Odilon Barrot, 1875, pp. 255 ff.). Suffrage rights were therefore to be understood according to this dynamic logic, which nonetheless was always included within that of *variable* rights – deriving "from the sole personal merits of each man" – which is to say, quite apart from the sphere of universal and inviolable rights belonging to mankind as a whole. According to Guizot (1959, pp. 79–81), the French Revolution had the "honour" to assert the latter rights, while at the same time ensuring that the principle of civil equality might allow individual capacities to govern society without becoming crystallised as privileges. The

doctrinaires' public law theory – as chiefly defined by Pellegrino Rossi – rested on this distinction between universal "equal" rights governing the civil sphere of individual existence and freedom, and "special," variable "unequal" rights pertaining to the political dimension of social existence and government.

24 A few months before the revolution, Guizot addressed the following words to the Chamber, which left an enduring mark in his biography: "The day of universal suffrage will never come. There will never be a day when all human creatures, whatever they may be, will be called upon to exercise political rights" (Guizot, 1864, vol. V, p. 380: address of 26 March 1847).

25 In English-language publications, the French term *capacités* is translated as either "capacities" or "abilities," depending on the author and context.

26 M. Riot-Sarcey (1998, p. 121) writes: "How do the capacities dear to Guizot fundamentally differ from those defined by Saint-Simon? The great establishment of industry that Saint-Simon dreamt of would have mobilised the same talents, the same minds as the doctrinaires' representative government. . . . The public of the Saint-Simonians was identical to that of the liberals." Besides, after the disbanding of the movement in late 1832, leading Saint-Simonians such as Michel Chevalier became Orléanst statesmen.

27 Durkheim (1959, p. 127) emphasises the consistency and proximity of Saint-Simon's theory of history with respect to Guizot's, especially when it comes to the interpretation of medieval communes and the role they played in the development of the modern bourgeoisie, attributing a more "impartial" and rigorous interpretation of the Revolution to the former thinker.

28 Saint-Simon developed the basic principles of his theory between 1814 and 1824, initially collaborating with Thierry in the drafting of *De la réorganisation de la société européenne* (1814), *Opinion sur les mésures à prendre contre la coalition* (1815), and the section of *Industrie* entitled *Des nations et de leurs rapports mutuels* (1817): these texts are now included in Saint-Simon (2012). For their English translation see Saint-Simon (1952, 1975). On Saint-Simon's claim to have anticipated Guizot's conception of national history, see Bazard *et al.* (1831, pp. 102 ff).

29 C-H. de Saint-Simon, *Mèmoire sur la science de l'homme et Travail sur la gravitation universelle* (1813), in Saint-Simon and Enfantin (1865–78, Vol. III, p. 189). As is widely known, this author's approach – which is centred on the issue of capacities – led to a classification of society based on the distinction between "artists," "scientists," and "industrialists," and to the idea that the last two should be the leaders of the new post-revolutionary order. The principle that science should exercise hegemony over mankind was first expressed by Saint-Simon in *Lettres d'un habitant de Geneve a ses contemporaines* (1803).

30 Blanc (1844, p. 360): "the Saint-Simonians displayed a perfect understanding of the laws which were to govern mankind in the future. . . . With a vigour supported by a considerable talent and extensive studies, this school exposed all the scourges of the century, shattering a thousand prejudices, driven by profound ideas. . . . The influence it exercised was great and it endures to this day."

31 Founded by Paul-François Dubois and Pierre Leroux in 1824, *Le Globe* became the official organ of Saint-Simonianism in January 1831. By 1832, it had become the fifth-most widely circulated French newspaper, with roughly 4,000 copies a day: see *Tableau de tous les journaux politiques, scientifiques, industriels qui se publient à Paris* (1832, BNF, impr., in-fol., Q2) and Aguet (1960). The Saint-Simonian movement paid close attention to the sphere of public opinion and the power of the press (cf. Chevalier, 1831a), but on 20 April 1832 *Le Globe* ceased publication on account of financial and political difficulties.

32 Saint-Simonianism is centred not on the individual, but only on the contribution which the individual can provide to the social usefulness of industry; and it is this

'anti-individualism' which led to its final break with liberal reformism, bringing it closer to socialism (Procacci, 1998, p. 134).

33 "An apparently just and wise formula, which is actually subversive and unjust," writes Blanc (1844, p. 360), accusing the Saint-Simonians of being blind to the inequalities implied by this formula, which at the time was indeed perceived as being close to the doctrinaires' proposal. Note that even Pierre Leroux eventually distanced himself from Saint-Simonianism because he was critical of the inequality underlying the logic of capacities (as well as of the fact that under Enfantin's leadership the movement had increasingly come to resemble a religious sect).

34 Significantly, as we shall see in Chapter 6 (§ 6.4), the liberal elites turned to Saint-Simonian doctrine to make sense of the Lyonnais insurrection of 1831 and to identify those responsible for it. In this regard, it is worth noting how Guizot described Saint-Simonian doctrine and its political impact: "outside the arena where these tumultuous scenes were taking place, and beyond the political parties that were vying for the government of France, other struggles were being waged; other reformers were aspiring to dominate the future. It was in 1831 that Saint-Simonianism and Fourierism, after much work, made their most resounding appearance. . . . shaken by some of the errors of our time, particularly in the field of political institutions, and with a better understanding of the importance of the principles of authority, discipline, and hierarchy than the radical school, Saint-Simon and Fourier felt they had been called to straighten out the French Revolution and, at the same time, to push it to its ultimate and final limits . . . but their doctrines and general tendencies merely aggravated the anarchic perturbation in the popular masses" (Guizot, 1959, p. 167).

References

AGUET J-P. (1960), Le tirage des quotidiens de Pans sous la Monarchie de Juillet. *Revue suisse d'Histoire*, 62: 216–286.

ANCILLON F. (1816), *De la souveraineté et des formes de gouvernement*, translation and notes by François Guizot, Lenormant, Paris.

BAEHREL R. (1952), La haine de classe en temps d'épidémie, *Annales. Economies, Sociétés, Civilizations*, 7: 562–593.

BARANTE P.B. DE. (1894), *Souvenirs du Baron de Barante de l'Académie française*, vol. IV, Calman-Levy, Paris.

BARON A. (1832), *Histoire de Lyon pendant les journées des 21, 22 et 23 novembre 1831*, Baron, Lyon.

BAZARD S.-A. (1831), *Aux femmes, sur leur mission religieuse dans la crise actuelle*, Brière, Rouen.

BAZARD S.-A., ENFANTIN B.-P., CARNOT Y., FOURNEL E., DUVEYRIER C. (eds.) (1831), *Doctrine de Saint-Simon. Exposition. Première année: 1828–1829*, L'Organisateur, Paris.

BERNARD C., CHARNIER P. (n.d.), *Rapport fait et présenté à M. le président du Conseil des ministres, sur les causes qui ont amené les événemens de Lyon, par deux chefs d'ateliers*, Impr. de Charvin, Lyon.

BLANC L. (1844), *Histoire de dix ans 1830–1840*, vol. 1, Société Tipographique Belge, Bruxelles.

BLANQUI L.-A. (1971), *Textes Choisis*, Éditions Sociales, Paris.

BOUCHET T. (2000a), Histoire d'un cheminement vers l'oubli (1832–1862), *Revue d'histoire moderne et contemporaine*, 47(1): 113–130.

BOUCHET T. (2000b), *Le roi et les barricades, une histoire des 5 et 6 juin 1832*, Selì Arslan, Paris.

Bouvier-Dumolard L. (1832), *Compte rendu des événemens qui ont eu lieu dans la ville de Lyon au mois de novembre 1831*, Tenon, Paris.

Brubaker R. (1989), The French Revolution and the Invention of Citizenship. *French Politics and Society*, 7(3), Summer: 30–49.

Brubaker R. (1992), *Citizenship and Nationhood in France and Germany*, Harvard University Press, Cambridge, MA.

Buret É. (1840), *De la Misère des classes laborieuses en Angleterre et en France: de la nature de la misère, de son existence, de ses effets, de ses causes, et de l'insuffisance des remèdes qu'on lui a opposés jusqu'ici, avec les moyens propres à en affranchir les sociétés*, 2 voll., Paulin, Paris.

Carne L. de (1831), Du problème social au Dix-neuvieme siècle. *Revue Européenne*, 1: 4–22.

Castel R. (1995), *Les Métamorphoses de la question sociale, une chronique du salariat*, Gallimard, Paris (Eng. trans. *From manual workers to wage laborers: transformation of the social question*, Transaction, New Brunswick, NJ 2003).

Chateaubriand F.R. de (1848), *Mémoires d'outre-tombe*, vol. V, Penaud, Paris.

Chevalier L. (1973), *Laboring Classes and Dangerous Classes in Paris During the First Half of the Nineteenth Century*, Howard Fertig, New York (or. ed. *Classes laborieuses et classes dangereuses*, Plon, Paris 1958).

Chevalier Michel (dir.) (1831a), *La presse*, L'Organisateur, Paris.

Chignola S. (2004), *Fragile cristallo. Per una storia del concetto di società*, Editoriale Scientifica, Napoli.

Chignola S. (2011), *Il tempo rovesciato. La Restaurazione e il governo della democrazia*, il Mulino, Bologna.

Clerici A. (2012), Contro l'uguaglianza, contro il privilegio. Il giovane Guizot e i suoi critici (1820–1821), in L. Scuccimarra, G. Ruocco (a cura di), *Il governo del popolo, vol. 2: Dalla Restaurazione alla guerra franco-prussiana*, Viella, Roma, pp. 47–70.

Collombe B. (1832), *Détails historiques sur les journées de Lyon et les causes qui les ont précédées*, Charvin, Lyon.

Constant B. (1797), *Des réactions politiques. Seconde édition, augmentée de l'examen des effets de la Terreur*, s.d, s.l., BNF ark:/12148/cb30265428n

Craiutu A. (2003), *Liberalism Under Siege. The Political Thought of the French Doctrinaires*, Lexington, Oxford.

Durkheim É. (1959), *Socialism and Saint-Simon*, Routledge, London (or. ed. *Le socialisme. Sa définition, ses débuts, la doctrine saint-simonienne*, Alcan, Paris 1928).

Enfantin B-P., Bazard S-A., Carnot H., Fournel H., Duveyrier C. (1854), *Doctrine saint-simonienne: exposition, première année, 1828–1829*, Au bureau de l'organizateur, Paris (or. ed. 1831).

Guizot F. (1817), Du conseil d'état. *Archives philosophiques, politiques et littéraires*, 1(3), September.

Guizot F. (1820), *Du gouvernement de la France depuis la Restauration et du ministère actuel*, Ladvocat, Paris.

Guizot F. (1849), *De la démocratie en France*, Plon-Masson, Paris.

Guizot F. (1861), Elections, ou de la formation et des opérations des collèges électoraux (1826), in F. Guizot (ed.), *Discours académiques suivis de trois essais de philosophie littéraire et politique*, Didier, Paris, pp. 379–420.

Guizot F. (1863), *Histoire parlamentaire de France. Recueil complet des discours prononcès dans les Chambres de 1819 à 1848 par M. Guizot, Vol. 1: 1819–33*, Lévy, Paris.

Guizot F. (1864), *Histoire parlamentaire de France. Recueil complet des discours prononcés dans les Chambres de 1819 à 1848 par M. Guizot, Vol. V: 1844–8*, Lévy, Paris.
Guizot F. (1880), *Histoire des origines du gouvernement représentatif et des institutions politiques de l'Europe depuis la chute de l'Empire roman jusqu'au XIVe siècle*, 2 vol., Dider, Paris (course of 1820, first published in 1851).
Guizot F. (1959), *Mémoires pour servir à l'histoire de mon temps (1859)*, Laffont, Paris.
Guizot F. (1984), *De la peine de mort en matière politique (1822)*, Fayard, Paris.
Guizot F. (1985), *Philosophie politique: de la souveraineté (1822)*, in F. Guizot (ed.), *Histoire de la civilisation en Europe*, Hachette, Paris.
Guizot F. (1988), *Des moyens de gouvernement et d'opposition dans l'état actuel de la France*, Belin, Paris (or. ed. 1821).
Halévy D. (1913), *La jeunesse de Proudhon*, Les Chaiers du Centre, Paris.
Hammersley R. (2015), Concepts of Citizenship in France During the Long Eighteenth Century. *European Review of History*, 22(3): 468–485.
Hazan E. (2002), *L'invention de Paris. Il n'y a pas de pas perdus*, Seuil, Paris.
Heine H. (1872), *De la France*, Lévy, Paris (or. ed. *Französische Zustände*, Campe, Hamburg 1832).
Hugo V. (1893), *Les Miserables*, IV, trans. M. Edouard Jolivet, vol. I, George Barrie & Son, Philadelphia (or. ed. 1862).
Jennings J. (2011), *Revolution and the Republic. A History of Political Thought in France Since the Eighteenth Century*, OUP, Oxford.
Karsenti B. (2013), *D'une philosophie à l'autre: les sciences sociales et la politique des modernes*, Gallimard, Paris.
Lamennais F.R. de. (1840), *Le pays et le gouvernement*, Pagnerre, Paris.
Lefort C. (1994), *Libéralisme et démocratie*, in S. Stuurman (dir.), *Les libéralismes, la theorie politique et l'histoire*, AUP, Amsterdam, pp. 5–25.
Macherey P. (1992), Aux sources des "rapports sociaux". Bonald, Saint-Simon, Guizot. *Genèses*, 9: 25–43.
Maddaloni D. (2011), *Visioni in movimento. Teorie dell'evoluzione e scienze sociali dall'Illuminismo a oggi*, Franco Angeli, Milano.
Manent P. (1987), *Histoire intellectuelle du libéralisme. Dix leçons*, Calman-Levy, Paris.
Manuel F.E. (1956), *The New World of Henri Saint-Simon*, Harvard University Press, Cambridge, MA.
Marrast A. (ed.) (1832), *Procès des vingt-deux accusés du cloître Saint-Méry; événements des 5 et 6 juin 1832: suivi de pièces justificatives*, Rouanet, Paris.
Marshall T.H. (1992), *Citizenship and Social Class*, Pluto, London (or. ed. 1950).
Marx K., Engels F. (1848), *Manifest der Kommunistischen Partei*, London.
Mazon J-F.R. (1831), *Événements de Lyon, ou les trois journées de novembre 1831*, Guyot, Lyon.
Mélonio F. (1994), *Les libéraux français et leur histoire*, in S. Stuurman (dir.), *Les libéralismes, la theorie politique et l'histoire*, AUP, Amsterdam.
Michel P. (1981), *Les barbares 1789–1848. Un mythe romantique*, PUL, Lyon.
Monfalcon J-B. (1834), *Histoire des insurrections de Lyon en 1831 et en 1834*, Perrin, Lyon.
Morabito M. (2008), *Histoire constitutionelle de la France (1789–1958)*, Montchrestien, Paris.
Odilon Barrot M.C. (1875), *Mémoires posthumes*, vol. I, Charpentier, Paris.
Omodeo A. (1970), *Studi sull'età della Restaurazione*, Einaudi, Torino.
Pareto V. (1978), *Les systèmes socialistes*, Droz, Généve.

Pasquino P. (1991), Sur la théorie constitutionnelle de la monarchie de Juillet, in M. Valensise (dir.), *F. Guizot et la culture politique de son temps*, Seuil, Paris, pp. 111–128.

Périer C. (1831), *Communication faite au nom du gouvernement à la chambre des députés sur les troubles de Lyon par M. le président du conseil*, Imp. Royale, Paris.

Picon A. (2003), Utopian Socialism and Social Science, in T.M. Porter, D. Ross (eds.), *Cambridge History of Science, Vol. 7. The Modern Social Sciences*, CUP, Cambridge, pp. 71–82.

Polany K. (2001), *The Great Transformation. The Political and Economic Origins of Our Time*, Beacon Press, Boston (or. ed. 1944).

Pozzi R. (1989), *François Guizot*, in B. Bongiovanni e L. Guerci (a cura di), *L'albero della rivoluzione. Le interpretazioni della Rivoluzione francese*, Einaudi, Torino, pp. 150–171.

Procacci G. (1998), *Governare la povertà. La società liberale e la nascita della questione sociale*, il Mulino, Bologna.

Rancière J. (1981), *La nuit des prolétaires. Archives du rêve ouvrier*, Fayard, Paris.

Rémusat Ch. de. (1959), *Mémoires de ma vie, t. II: La Restauration ultra-royaliste. La Révolution de Juillet (1820–1832)*, Plon, Paris.

Riot-Sarcey M. (1998), *Le réel de l'utopie. Essai sur le politique au XIXe siècle*, Alvin Michel, Paris.

Rosanvallon P. (1985), *Le moment Guizot*, Gallimard, Paris.

Rosanvallon P. (1992), *Le sacre du citoyen. Histoire du suffrage universel en France*, Gallimard, Paris.

Rosanvallon P. (1994), *La monarchie impossible. Les Chartes de 1814 et 1830*, Fayard, Paris.

Saint-Simon C.H. de (1952), *Selected Writings of Henri Comte de Saint-Simon*, ed. F.M.H. Markham, Basil Blackwell, Oxford.

Saint-Simon C.H. de (1975), *Selected Writings on Science, Industry and Social Organization*, ed. Keith Taylor, Holmes & Meier, Teaneck, NJ.

Saint-Simon C.H. de (2012), *Œuvres complètes*, édition critique éditée par J. Grange, P. Musso, P. Régnier, F. Yonnet, 4 vols., 3504 pp., Presses Universitaires de France, Paris.

Saint-Simon C.H. de, Enfantin P. (1865–78), *Oeuvres de Saint-Simon & d'Enfantin*, Dentu, Paris.

Schmitt C. (1928), *Verfassungslehre*, Duncker & Humblot, Berlin.

Sewell W.H. (1980), *Work and Revolution in France: The Language of Labor from the Old Regime to 1848*, CUP, Cambridge.

Sieyès E.J. (2002), *Qu'est-ce que le Tiers état?* Boucher, Paris (or. ed. 1789).

Stuurman S. (dir.) (1994), *Les libéralismes, la theorie politique et l'histoire*, AUP, Amsterdam.

Tilly C. (1995), The Emergence of Citizenship in France and Elsewhere. *International Review of Social History*, 40(S3): 223–236.

Tocqueville A. de (1852), *Discours prononcé en 1852 à la Séance annuelle de l'Académie des Sciences morales et politiques*. Retrieved from: www.asmp.fr/travaux/solennelles/president/1852_tocqueville.pdf

Tocqueville A. de (1994), *Democracy in America*, Fontana Press, London (or. ed. 1835).

Tomasello F. (2018), Il governo della storia. La dottrina delle capacità politiche nel pensiero di François Guizot, in Rossella Bufano (a cura di), *Libertà uguaglianza democrazia nel pensiero europeo (XVI-XXI secolo)*, Milella, Lecce, pp. 130–148.

Part I

Objects: Work and the social sciences

2 Epidemics and subaltern classes

"It must ultimately be understood that, beyond the parliamentary conditions of an authority's existence, there is a social question that needs to be addressed," the daily newspaper *La Quotidienne* stated on 18 November 1831, commenting on the Lyonnais weavers' insurrection (cf. § 1.1). This editorial is usually credited with having introduced the expression *question sociale* into the French debate (Castel, 2003, p. 25). From that moment onwards, such a neologism was destined to designate one of the major challenges faced by 19th-century European societies: the condition of deprivation and exclusion of the emerging industrial poverty and the plebeian subjectivities which the events considered in the previous chapter had catapulted to the centre of the political stage. In the first instance, the representations of such a condition appeared to be chiefly marked by fear and outrage with respect to the new subaltern classes brought into being by the Industrial Revolution.

This first part of the book focuses on the interpretations and representations of the social question which emerged in the liberal field to retrace their transformation, whereby those initial feelings of fear gradually gave way to a mighty project of social integration centred on wage labour conditions. The cholera epidemic of 1832 will be identified as a crucial moment in such a process, a moment which fostered unprecedented and dramatic perceptions of urban pauperism epitomised by the two images of "dangerous classes" and "new barbarians." We will explore the way in which such images gradually turned into that of the poor yet decent and virtuous working class. To this end, the present chapter analyses how the pandemic crisis stimulated the rise of social research on the subaltern classes with the aim of developing new security policies and risk reduction strategies. The next chapter then considers the first major enquiries into urban pauperism, to retrace how they brought the question of wage labour into focus as an object of scientific study and public governance. Chapter 4 will eventually explore the impact of those social investigations on French policy and legislation, so as to interpret the genesis of modern labour law. As such, these three chapters aim to retrace a single development that may be described as the process of "objectification" of the realm of wage labour as a field of knowledge and administration. This aim implies establishing a dynamic intersection between social history (the critical junctures giving rise to the social issues which theory was intended to address), intellectual history (the

DOI: 10.4324/9781003303497-4

interpretations and representations of such issues), and legal history (the measures adopted to translate those interpretations into practice).

2.1 The new barbarians: genealogy of a metaphor

On 8 December 1831, the academic and journalist Saint Marc-Girardin commented on the Lyonnais workers' insurrection (cf. § 1.1) in a *Journal Des Débats* editorial that sparked a heated controversy:

> The sedition in Lyon has revealed a serious secret, that of the strife that is taking place within society. . . . Our commercial and industrial society has its bane like all other societies. This bane is its workers. . . . Commercial competition today has the same effect as folk migrations had in the past. Ancient society is dead, because peoples set in motion the wastelands of the north, and clashed with one another, until they gradually fell upon the Roman Empire. Today, the *barbarians* threatening society are to be found not in the Caucasus or in the Tatar steppes; they are in the suburbs of our own manufacturing cities. . . . It is there that the threat to modern society lies, it is from there that the barbarians may come who will destroy it. . . . It is not a matter of choosing between republic and monarchy, but of the very *health of society*.
>
> (*Journal Des Débats*, 8 December 1831, p. 1, emphasis added)[1]

It is precisely from this figure of the subaltern classes as *nouveaux barbares*, or a "bane" threatening the "health of society," that we must set out to understand the elites' initial perceptions and representations of the nascent social question. And it is through this kind of image that a working-class subjectivity emerged in the European imaginary at the outset of industrialisation. Herein lies the controversial origin of the process which was to lead to the image of the honest, working-class father figure whose laboriousness stands as the foundation of constitutions, political parties, and citizenship rights. From this perspective, the shocking comparison with the barbarian invasions seems prophetic today in the way it describes the momentous impact of what the Lyon insurrection was bringing to light for the first time: the political meaning of labour. Girardin himself was to stress this point, thirty years later, when recalling the controversies sparked by his editorial:

> I compared the workers seeking to make their way into our society to the barbarians who in another age invaded the Roman Empire and became the origin of modern peoples. But there was no disgrace or insult in this. . . . The barbarians of the 4th and 5th centuries are no longer considered monsters. . . . The barbarian invasions amounted to a renewal of the world and, along with the establishment of Christianity, contributed to founding a new civilisation, of which we are the heirs and custodians. The Goths, Heruli, and Franks have long been historically rehabilitated.
>
> (Girardin, 1859, pp. 143 and 156)

The strength of the editorial lay in the fact that it described contemporary reality by appropriating a central figure in the historiographical debate on the French nation's origins (cf. § 2.2), assigning it a new meaning. To grasp this aspect we must first note that Girardin had just recently been appointed Chair of History at the Sorbonne as the successor of François Guizot, who had made historiography a weapon of the liberal opposition to the Bourbon Restoration and supporters of the Old Regime (cf. § 1.3). He had done so by focusing precisely on the interpretation of the barbarians and their invasions of France in the Middle Ages.

Guizot, like the Thierry brothers and other early-19th-century bourgeois historians, described the barbarian age as a disorderly one in which there was "no society," but only a general freedom that was exercised through violence, and yet constituted the matrix for those *modern liberties* that had been unknown to ancient civilisations, to the Roman world, and to medieval Christendom. "Despite this combination of brutality, materialism, and foolish selfishness," Guizot wrote, "the taste for individual independence is a noble, moral sentiment" which "was introduced into European civilisation precisely through the barbarians of Germany."[2] In the barbarians' modes of life, this post-revolutionary liberal historiography saw the matrix of a kind of freedom which the course of civilisation had reshaped by making property rather than brute force the primary means of exercising it. The evolution of European civilisation made property the new means to satisfy the ancient, independent barbarian spirit, which was thus translated into the codified liberty of the bourgeois citizen and property-owner. Foucault (2005, p. 197) has described this interpretation as a model for "the filtering of the barbarian" which, in post-revolutionary France, liberal authors set in contrast to other historiographical models to turn it into a weapon in the fight against the supporters of the Old Regime through the distinction between the "bad" barbarism of the invading Franks from Germany and the "good" barbarism of the native Gauls – which had inhabited France since the 5th century BC.[3] Thirteen centuries of national history were thus portrayed by bourgeois historians as a long struggle between two barbarian "races," to present the 1789 Great Revolution as the outcome of this centuries-old clash, as an ultimate rebalancing of history that did justice to centuries of oppression.

The evocative power of the *Journal des débats'* editorial thus lay in how it interpreted contemporary reality through a reference that was extremely relevant to the debate on the significance of national history and the French Revolution. By this gesture, however, Girardin also gave the notion of barbarism a semantic twist, by replacing its historical meaning with a metaphorical one. He juxtaposed the image of the historical barbarians, who had come from afar to invade and conquer, to that of the "new barbarians" – metaphorical yet no less dangerous ones – who from the backward agricultural heartland of the nation had migrated into the urban spaces transfigured by the Industrial Revolution, bringing their savage attitudes and primitive behaviours with them. Through this metaphorical image of barbarism, his editorial crystallises the first and most compelling representation of the industrial subaltern classes, whose relevance social and intellectual historians have not failed to emphasise. The first to do so was Louis Chevalier (1973), who stressed the spread of this representation and its impact on public opinion in the

19th century, turning it into an emblem of those "dangerous classes" which lie at the centre of his evocative portrayal of Paris in the first half of the 19th century. Such was the relevance of Girardin's image that Pierre Michel (1981) spoke of the emergence of a genuine "romantic myth" of the barbarian. Thus, the latter figure became a "metaphor translating . . . the marginality of the proletariat with respect to bourgeois civilisation" (Chignola, 2004, p. 448). The historical fascination with the barbarians who, by destroying the old world, had sown the seeds of modern liberties thus became fear of their return: a metaphorical yet equally destructive return, as it was connected to the unleashing of primal urges and instincts that civilisation had reshaped, yet not removed.

The metaphor of barbarians is one of the great representations of the 19th-century lower classes; and it too, in a way, "filters" the historical image of the barbarian so as to highlight certain specific elements. The first is an ambivalent attitude towards a society which is at the same time destructive (posing the constant threat of disorder, violence, and turmoil) and marked by the desire for appropriation – appropriation of the goods that civilisation produces. Then there is the tendency towards nomadism and the incurable aversion to work, "the restless obsession with movement and idleness," as Eugène Buret put it:

> The poverty-stricken are reminiscent of these Saxon bands who, in order to flee the yoke of the Norman conquest, hid under forest trees, in their nomadic independence. . . . An uncertain existence is the first resemblance between the poor and the savage. . . . Beggary [and] vagrancy [are] a premeditated return to barbarism.
>
> (Buret, 1840, Vol. II, pp. 1–8)[4]

The historical barbarians were nomads who moved through bloody conquests, and whose independent spirit was embodied by a rejection of work and the exercising of violence: the new barbarians are those who migrate from the countryside, establishing their primitive and idle attitudes in manufacturing cities, thereby exposing them to the threat of social collapse. In their anti-social traits, these people are "hyper-natural" and evoke a kind of freedom that has never been socialised. Only the discipline of work might bring these subjects into modern bourgeois civilisation by removing them from that condition of foreignness/outwardness with respect to society that brings it close to the historical barbarians.

"It is not an insult to any part of the human species to compare it to the barbarians, but simply a way of saying that this part is *outside* current society," Girardin (1859, p. 157, emphasis added) writes again, presenting the issue of "how to let them in" as the crucial challenge.[5] "*The barbarian is always* trampling at the frontiers of states, crashing against the walls of the city," writes Foucault, highlighting this very condition of outsiderness.[6] Yet in the case of the 19th-century barbarians, this outwardness becomes merely figurative and paradoxical: for whereas the historical barbarians came from faraway lands, the metaphorical ones are *internal* barbarians who are a genuine product of industrial society, which never ceases to create them. And it is precisely this ambivalent outwardness – a radical yet only metaphorical one – that underpins the transition from the great historiographical figure of the barbarian to that of the new internal barbarians, the bringers of an invasion that is paradoxical because it is somehow "endogenous." The exodus of these *classes dangereuses* out of the agricultural heartland of the country thus marks the beginning of the metaphorical use of the barbarians' image, which extends down to the present day as one of the most evocative metaphors for social and urban disorder (Tomasello, 2015, pp. 208–215).

2.2 A different race: the dangerous classes

The figure of the barbarian became entrenched in the French imaginary through the debates between competing historiographical theories about "race war." Starting from the publication of Hotman's *Francogallia* (1573), authors such as Boulainvillier, Mably, Montlosier, and Thierry had – in different centuries – invoked an original racial difference – between the breed of the Germanic conquerors and that of the native Gauls – to explain conflicts within the French nation (Barzun, 1932; Dubois, 1972; Jouanna, 1976). They resorted to this idea of different "races" to address the question of the enemy and the "other," and to assert the legitimacy of a social order based on the primacy of the Crown, the aristocracy, or the Third Estate. Yet these notions of *race* had an exclusively historico-political nature: they were based on a historical event – an invasion and conquest – which had founded a relationship of political domination in the light of which this historiography sought to make sense of the French nation's entire history (cf. Rosanvallon, 1985, pp. 183–184). Therefore, using the figure of the barbarian to designate the new industrial pauperism also meant somehow bringing the concept of race into play – although at the time this did not yet possess the biological connotations it was later to be charged with.

In this respect, the shift from historical barbarians to metaphorical ones as a means to describe the rural masses' migration to manufacturing cities also reflects a tension within the concept of race, which has to do with a kind of otherness and idea of invasion of a completely different sort. The new barbarians are *internal* ones; they are the product of the very industrial civilisation that creates and ceaselessly reproduces them. Their behaviour falls outside the rules of civilisation which inform the social body and keep it alive, but their existence is the endogenous and inevitable outcome of the very dynamics which the social body engenders through the industrialisation processes. Their invasion, therefore, has a metaphorical and paradoxical character, and in the face of it is no longer a matter of guarding the frontiers, but rather of "defending society" – according to the expression which best encapsulates the attitudes of the liberal elites faced with the social question's emergence.

Michel Foucault drew upon this expression to describe how the historiographical discourse on the conflict between races was transformed in the first half of the 19th century. His thesis is that the liberal historiography of those years replaced the idea of war as the "web of history" with a philosophical dialectic describing the progressive universalisation of the bourgeois way of life and affirming "two transcriptions" of the traditional discourse on the "race war" (Foucault, 2005, pp. 59–60). On the one hand, we have that transcription which translates the historiographical discourse about the race war into the idea of class conflict according to a conception of history as the outcome of the struggle between different classes.[7] On the other, we have a "biological transcription" which draws its "vocabulary from a materialist anatomo-physiology" and "European policies of colonisation." Within this framework, "defending society" means acting against the biological threat of "the other race," which is "basically not the race that came from elsewhere or that was, for a time, triumphant and dominant, but that it is a race that is permanently, ceaselessly infiltrating the social body, or which is, rather, constantly being re-created in and by the social fabric" (Foucault, 2005, pp. 60–61). The metaphor of proletarians as the new barbarians reflect this kind of conception because it implies the notion of race and, at the same time, lends it a semantic nuance steeped in new references. We can indeed observe that a range of mentions of the native people of colonised lands come to integrate the comparison between industrial subalterns and barbarian invasions.

A significant contribution in this direction was provided by ethnology, which in these years acquired a specific epistemological status as the science of the classification of races, centred on the investigation of "primitive societies." As we shall see, its approach was also used to carry out some of the first enquiries on urban poverty (cf. § 3.1.1).[8] "The modernising of history and this comparative ethnology . . . imposed the racial stereotype of the barbarian," writes Pierre Michel, stressing the way in which the *détournement* of the figure of the barbarian became intertwined with the history of colonialism (1981, pp. 95, 196). Thus, René Chateaubriand compares the poverty of American Indian tribes to that of the French lower classes (cit. ibid., p. 259). Eugène Buret likens the tendency for alcoholism among the urban proletariat to that of the "native races of North America" and the "Negro of the African coast," who "sells his children and himself for a bottle of brandy" (1840, vol. II, p. 13). Jean-Baptiste Monfalcon describes the insurgent Lyonnais weavers as a "frenzied and barbarian throng" akin to the Native Americans, drunk "from the smell of blood" (1834, pp. 124–128). Louis-René Villermé notes the use of the "strange epithet white-Negroes" to describe the cotton workers of Lille (1989, p. 348). Such are the kinds of references informing the notion of race that underlie the metaphor of the new barbarians. Even the previously quoted editorial by Girardin, alongside its parallel with the ancient invasions, draws a comparison with the inhabitants of modern colonies:

> The sedition in Lyon is akin to the Santo Domingo insurrection: each factory-owner lives in his *fabrique* like a colonial planter among his slaves, one to a hundred.
>
> (*Journal des Débats*, 8 December 1831, p. 1)

In the early 1830s, Orléanist circles, liberal pundits, and the bourgeois elites represented the subaltern classes immigrating into manufacturing cities by comparing them simultaneously with the barbarians of Antiquity and the natives of the contemporary colonies. The use of the idea of barbarism as a metaphor to describe

19th-century subalterns thus also involved the concept of race resulting from public debates on colonised populations. The new "dangerous classes" were perceived as somehow foreign, as "external" to the social body of the nation, and were therefore compared to the "savages" of the colonies to indicate a sort of anthropological or even racial difference (Virdee, 2019).[9] This "racialisation" of the emerging European proletariat (Robinson, 1983) served to describe a condition of radical otherness and foreignness with respect to the bourgeois society established by modern political revolutions. In this sense, we can recognise the role that the very concept of race played in the genealogy of what was destined to become the notions of the proletariat and working class. The comparison between the insurgent workers in Lyon and barbarians is so significant precisely because it crystallises the perceptions of a social *difference* that is so profound as to appear somehow racialised. The new human breed which, with the impetus of an invasion, migrated into industrialised cities was perceived, first of all, in terms of a radical anthropological otherness: as a different race. The cholera outbreak of 1832 offers a striking illustration of this aspect and of the social representations described so far since the public authorities interpreted and faced the epidemic as a sort of new invasion by drawing upon the barbarism/civilisation dialectic and the image of a biological foundation for social differences.

2.3 The disease of civilisation

To grasp how the French authorities approached the cholera outbreak in 1832, we must, first of all, consider the way in which the political, scientific, and intellectual elites interpreted a threat that had clearly been looming on the horizon for a few years. The pandemic first broke out in India in 1817, but was stopped by the rigours of the Russian winter in 1824 (Pollitzer, 1960; Longmate, 1966; Hamlin, 2009). It resurfaced in 1826 when a new wave spread from the Ganges Valley to Persia. The existence of cholera had been known to Western medicine for centuries, but with this epidemic, the disease actually entered Europe for the first time. Hence, the authorities commissioned several studies about the "Asiatic journey" of cholera, and in 1831 inspectors were despatched to Russia, Hungary, and Poland, where the outcome of the anti-Russian battle for independence contributed to carrying the disease to Austria and Germany.[10] The westward march of cholera was indisputable, but in France – which had not experienced any epidemics since the plague of 1720 – the public debate on the disease drew upon the barbarism/civilisation dialectic to exorcise its threat. Charles de Rémusat recalled:

> We thought that these great plagues which historians spoke of only belonged to the Middle Ages; that they could no longer penetrate into such an advanced society: our climate, the wholesomeness of our country, our administrative measures, and scientific progress would protect us against it. How were we to imagine that a magnificent city such as Paris, just like the wretched cities of the Orient, would fall victim to an infection from Indochina?
>
> (Rémusat, 1959, Vol. II, p. 556)

This kind of attitude towards cholera was widely echoed by medical science, which regarded the maturity and quality of the *civilisation française* as a powerful antibody, stemming from the virtuous interplay of factors such as the country's geography, climatic conditions, scientific culture, and advanced customs. "The topographical situation in France is so advantageous that there is not much to fear from cholera in this country," we read in the *Mémoire* by military doctor Larrey (1831, pp. 27 and 33): "today, as in no other country of the world, have civilisation, industry, and commerce reached a higher level of perfection."

In the reports from the Royal Academy of Medicine, the geographical, climatic, and social features of the country from which cholera had spread, India, and the ways of life of the savage people of the Ganges Valley are set in contrast to the "superior" characteristics of French civilisation (Dubois, 1831). Considering the "progress" that France could boast of before the whole world, this Asiatic disease coming from sweltering, rainy regions governed by despotic, backward regimes and inhabited by barbarians seemed somewhat of an anachronism. The historical-political notion of civilisation was thus grafted upon the medical discourse, and through the concept of *milieu*, direct causal links were established between "health" and "civilisation." "Among which peoples" – asked the *Gazette médicale de Paris* – "has cholera wreaked havoc? Among *barbarian* or semi-barbarian peoples; but rest assured that in our advanced civilisation it will find a formidable obstacle."[11] This interpretation of the dynamics of the epidemic, based on the dialectic between civilisation and barbarism, adopted the latter notion in an ethno-anthropological sense, which was now added to and intertwined with the socio-historical meaning we have considered above.

In such a way, the appearance of the disease in Paris in the last days of March 1832 (cf. § 1.1) had the immediate effect of intensifying discourses that had already been associating proletarian ways of life with those of colonised people, thereby bringing the racial theme into play as well. "All men struck by this epidemic . . . belong to the popular class. . . . They inhabit the filthy alleyways of the Cité and of the Notre-Dame district," Eugène Roch (1832, p. 40) wrote, stressing the unequivocal fact that cholera had primarily spread in the working-class streets of the city centre. The living conditions of the rural populations who had recently settled there immediately suggested a comparison with the savage ways of life of the Indian tribes from which the scourge had spread. "The working classes stood before the privileged classes as India did to France. Within French society, the proletariat constituted a different race – a uniquely vulnerable one," François Delaporte writes in a fine study of the topic (1986, p. 2).

The parallel between new urban pauperism and barbarian or savage populations thus acquires new references, and the interpretation of the epidemic reveals several connections with that of the Lyon revolt. The two events are perceived and described as two expressions of the same social danger, of the same risk of "contamination" by barbarism – that of the internal migrants and that of the "savages" from the Ganges Valley.[12] Cholera and insurrection, poverty and illness, the epidemic and the uprising appear to be different symptoms of the same disease affecting society; a disease which is interpreted and described by intertwining medical and anthropological, scientific and social, moral and political language.

When, in the first half of the 19th century, the effects of the revolutionary abolition of intermediate bodies and craft guilds in France (cf. § 3.1) started becoming intertwined with the effects of the first industrialisation processes, the vagrant humanity that emerged from this conjuncture was at first literally perceived as another species. Portrayals of it do not stress any specific – social, economic, or cultural – difference, but rather its overall anthropological difference, which only the concept of race seemed capable of encompassing. The image of barbarians ultimately points to this high degree of human otherness, and the cholera outbreak realised the most dramatic historical crystallisation of this condition of separation and radical difference, exacerbating the perception of what was seen as an anthropological and racial, more than merely socio-economic, cleavage. When it comes to 19th-century France, any investigation of the genesis of what came to be known as the "working class" is bound to start from these images and perceptions of the social question as expressing a radical otherness and overall difference resting on an anthropological foundation.

More than anyone else, the social demographer Louis Chevalier (1973) has stressed these elements, that is, "the truly racial character of social antagonism in the Paris of this period" (ibid., p. 408).

> This was unquestionably a class struggle, but it was carried out by means of a struggle which its contemporaries themselves described as a struggle of race; a conflict between two population groups differing wholly from each other, but above all in body; a difference not merely social but biological.
>
> (ibid., p. 433)

Indeed, the very "term proletariat" was to emerge in the public debate still in close connection with "characteristics which were not yet economic. It had not yet been purged of the ethnic and physical antagonisms" (ibid., p. 364). In this context, the proletariat "is a race rather than a class and the word connotes a savage and barbarous way of living and dying rather than an occupational distribution or economic characteristic" (ibid.). Only in the light of this initial portrayal is it possible to grasp "the great reversal of the working-class position" which gradually took place through deeds and ideas, leading to the "new and triumphant concept of the worker . . . , the 'sublime' worker in which even bourgeois opinion was to acquiesce" (ibid. 394; cf. Gossez, 1956). It is precisely this gradual "reversal" of the figure of the new barbarians into that of the honest and industrious worker that I wish to retrace in the following pages by exploring a different set of references and problems – first of all, the interplay between the liberal interpretation of pauperism and the genesis of the modern social sciences.

To sum up the elements considered so far, we may say that the use of the metaphor of barbarism was rooted in a centuries-old debate through which French historiography had sought to make sense of the conflicts that the nation was experiencing by drawing upon the idea of an original division between different people, or races. In the first half of the 19th century, this interpretative grid was then applied again to the emergence of the new social cleavages and rifts that industrialisation processes and the resulting "social question" of urban pauperism were creating within the post-revolutionary bourgeois society based on civil equality. However, this racial approach was now charged with different meanings and with a new degree of otherness which we may describe as "biological" to stress its overall and fundamental character. Out of this image of the subaltern classes' general otherness, the wage labour condition gradually began to emerge as a *specific* difference capable of functioning as a means of governance and, at the same time, of social and political subjectivation. A difference among other differences, work conditions acquired their centrality through complex and multifaceted processes. The *contingent* nature of the latter must be stressed to carefully avoid any kind of historical determinism that understands labour as a kind of anthropological condition that is irreducible, essential, and basically coextensive with the modern subject.

We can thus assume the radical and general otherness embodied by the figure of the barbarian as the starting point of this intellectual-historical journey along the production of a labouring subject as one of the pillars of the post-revolutionary social order. It is now a matter of bringing into focus the trajectory which, from this figure of otherness, leads to other representations of the 19th-century subaltern classes, down to the "limpid" and unitary image that came to be known as the working class. My hypothesis is that, within this transition, a key role can be assigned to the genesis of the modern social sciences. I will look at such a genesis as a process shaped by the development of methods and practices for the empirical study of the social realm that made urban pauperism their first specific object of investigation, thereby gradually bringing into focus the figure of the wage labourer as a field of knowledge, governance, and emergent social policies.

2.4 Cholera and the genesis of the social sciences

The experience of the 1832 epidemic lent the image of the "dangerous classes" a meaning that extended far beyond that of a criminal threat, adding the perception of a sociobiological risk to the representations of urban pauperism that had emerged in the previous months. The cholera outbreak reinforced those discourses that the elite had developed in the wake of the Lyonnais weavers' insurrection of 1831 (cf. § 1.1 and 5.1), because the two events came to be regarded as symptoms of the same social malady: a disease which was breaking out in the insalubrious urban areas overcrowded with immigrant workers and then spreading as a result of their savage way of life. "The poverty in which the people are left to wallow draws, engenders, and nourishes the deadly disease," writes Antoine Métral (1833) in his *Natural, Moral, and Political Description of Cholera*.[13] The expression *miasmes populaires*, to which many attributed the disease's spread, bears witness to this understanding of the epidemic's dynamics, which seamlessly combined hygienic, political, and social considerations: "it is the morbidity of the popular city [districts] that makes the miasmas of cholera and those of insurrection spread at the same speed" (Rancière, 1981, p. 83). Indeed, as soon as the disease broke into Paris, rag-sellers rose against the public health measures, while the Republican inmates at Sainte-Pélagie reacted to the first death in their prison with an uprising. This foreshadowed the big insurrection that was to break out in June, sparked by the funeral for General Lamarque's death from cholera (cf. § 1.1). "People in their political zeal had never been more ready to fight," recounts Louis Blanc (1844, p. 406); "under the cholera, revolution was incubating," writes Lucas-Dubreton (1932, p. 55). Thus, when Dr Frayssinet states that "there is nothing more favourable to the spread and development of the epidemic than the state of exaltation dominant among populations subject to political excesses" (Delpech de Frayssinet, 1833, p. 167),[14] he echoes a well-established discourse that incorporated social, political, and moral categories into the medical-scientific description of cholera.

Such attitudes also reflect the difficulties faced by medical science in the attempt to establish a shared definition of cholera, capable of isolating it to grasp its causes and suggest a cure. Algid, blue, asphyxial, passive, Asiatic, spasmodic, typhoid-like, contagious, inflammatory, epidemic, asthenic: the wide range of adjectives used to define it bear witness to the many perspectives from which physicians sought to grasp the nature of cholera, which – not unlike the social question – emerged as a protean and hazy object that was difficult to understand and frame in a rigorous way.[15] The effort to develop a theory about cholera thus sparked a medical dispute that touched directly upon political discourse, as it juxtaposed two different medical-scientific perspectives that supported the implementation of different security measures and urban governance policies (cf. § 3.3.1). On the one hand, we find the perspective that understood cholera as a *contagious* disease and identified its cause as specific germs whose spread needed to be prevented. Hence, it promoted "sanitary measures," such as quarantine, designed to contain the spread of the disease by isolating the sick and dividing the urban population, as had been the case during major epidemics in the past. On the other, we find the "anti-contagionists," who in the wake of hygienist theories identified physiological causes connected to the contexts in which "miasmas" proliferated. Consequently, they advocated "salubrity measures" of public hygiene designed to improve unsanitary environments and the "living conditions" in urban spaces where the choleric infection was at risk of developing.[16] By juxtaposing a strategy based on the improvement of working-class living conditions with one designed to prevent contagion through the marginalisation of subjects at risk, this medical opposition between contagious disease and bacterial infection directly translated into the medical-scientific field different conceptions of the subaltern classes within the new social order forged by the political and industrial revolutions.

This debate opposing "contagion" and "infection," aimed at advancing different theories of cholera, thus implicitly reflecting different theories of society. At the same time, as we shall see, the effort to develop a theory – or rather a science – of society appears deeply influenced in these years by the event of the epidemic, which nourished organicist conceptions of society that incorporated a hygienist perspective into the budding one of the social sciences (cf. § 3.3.1). The pandemic enabled the penetration of medical metaphors into social and political debate based on a simple yet persuasive analogy: just as an inflammation limited to the intestine becomes a threat to the whole human body via cholera, so specific social pathologies such as riots or the unhealthy and immoral attitudes of the urban subaltern classes can put the health of the social body as a whole at risk.

"My mother has finally decided to leave Paris after five people have died on the corner of the street in which we live," Alexis de Tocqueville writes (1984, p. 115), bearing witness to the flight of the affluent classes at a moment when fear of contagion went hand-in-hand with fear of social and political conflicts. In the French capital, cholera caused 18,402 deaths in four months: this "scourge" – to use the journalists' favourite term – first broke out in the unsanitary poor neighbourhoods, but then from these "hotspots" the threat soon spread throughout the urban space, making it a risky and unpredictably hazardous environment. On 16 May 1832, even the head of government, Casimir Périer, succumbed to the illness. His death contributed to the feeling that the subaltern classes' living conditions might be a problem affecting French society as a whole, a problem that far exceeded the scope of philanthropy and charity and threatened the very social order. By this time, the social question clearly emerged in the terms in which Girardin's editorial envisaged it: as a "scourge" threatening "the health of society" as a whole (cf. § 2.1).

The effort to define cholera constantly shifted between medical and socio-political language and frameworks, as different explanations about the dynamic of the epidemic corresponded to different ways of understanding the social order. Cholera revealed the socio-biological roots of the problem of urban pauperism, fostering different perceptions and interpretations of the social question through an unprecedented intertwining of political and medical-scientific discourses that paved the way for new ways of governing poverty. Even among the liberal elites steeped in *laissez-faire* dogmas, the idea emerged that political power somehow had to deal with such problems to "defend society." That is to say that the government needed to act in a sort of "medical" way by developing a "scientific" knowledge of the subaltern classes' living conditions capable of suggesting policies for the prevention and immunisation of the social body – understood, in organicist terms, as a whole that can be threatened by the sickness of any one of its parts (cf. § 3.3.1). Thus, as a response to the social challenges raised by the events of this pandemic crisis, the need emerged to develop cognitive maps capable of grasping and describing the new depths of a complex social body to immunise it against ills potentially threatening the whole system.

This interaction between political discourse and medical language revolving around the concept of "social environment" (*milieu*) and an organicist conception of society played a relevant role in the genesis of the modern social sciences' epistemology. Exploring such a role offers a glimpse of a minor and less-known history of the birth of sociology, viewed not in terms of the development of great concepts, models, and theories but of social research *practices* that appear to be partially derived from the empirical method of medicine and driven by the political need to respond to the social challenges posed by the emerging industrial society. In the very years when Comte's *Course of Positive Philosophy* (1830–42) established the foundational theoretical assumptions of sociology, certain institutional and government circles started to promote initiatives for the empirical analysis of society to identify new security policies for the reduction of social, biological, and political risks. This drive to study and *classify* the new human species which was transforming manufacturing cities fostered the rise of unprecedented practices for empirical analysis of the subaltern classes' conditions.

2.5 The epidemic as a social question

As early as July 1831 a central health committee was established as a means of prevention in Paris, along with twelve district commissions and forty-eight neighbourhood ones, entrusted with "visiting" thousands of sites regarded as "insalubrious" (Boulay de la Meurthe, 1832). These commissions proceed to identify the unhealthiest buildings and areas, and to promote their sanitisation, the demolition of certain slums, the closing of alleys infested with "miasmas," and the disinfecting of streets with chlorinated water. These were exceptional measures inspired by an unprecedented effort to understand the urban and social roots of the pandemic threat, which nonetheless proved ineffective in preventing cholera, thus fostering the search for a more general level of understanding of those conditions that expose the urban fabric to threats such as an epidemic. This failure stimulated further research into measures aimed at managing the urban space as an environment posing constant hazards, to prevent new sociobiological risks. The trauma of cholera thus led to the first official social enquiry in French history: the *Rapport sur la marche et les effets du cholèra morbus dans Paris et les communes rurales du Département de la Seine*, commissioned by the prefecture to a committee headed by the demographer Louis-François Benoiston de Châteauneuf and including a group of ten doctors, scientists, public servants, and emergent social research experts such as Trébuchet, Villot, Chevallier, Devaux, Millot, Petit, Pontonnier, Parent-Duchâtelet, and, most notably, Louis-René Villermé (on whom, see § 3.3). This document offers an in-depth portrayal of Paris in the early 1830s, resulting from the attempt to systematically establish the "relationship of cholera mortality" with various demographic, climatic, geographical, urban, and social factors (Benoiston de Châteauneuf, 1832).

The *Rapport* examines the spatiality of the Department of the Seine in all its detail to single out conditions that might pose some kind of health risk or threat. The urban space is here envisaged as a "social environment" that can be described and investigated in a scientific way for the purpose of developing pioneering welfare measures inspired by systematic methods and practices for the empirical study of the social fabric (cf. § 3.3.1). The committee's diagnosis is clear: the central factor in the spread of the epidemic is *social conditions*, which is to say unhealthy ways of living in the poor neighbourhoods of the old city centre (Coleman, 1982; Delaporte, 1986). The report stresses that such neighbourhoods occupy one-fifth of the capital's territory yet house half of its population: "these streets, all of them without exception," and "these houses" have had "mortality rates that are double the average" (Benoiston de Châteauneuf, 1832, p. 30). Through the analysis of medical statistics on the epidemic, the committee affirms that the overcrowded areas inhabited by immigrant workers constitute the key centre onto which new security policies must be grafted to prevent new epidemic threats:

> These classes were pushed into the districts of Arçis, Grève, Cité, Saint-Denis, Saint-Martin, and Popincourt; into the *faubourgs* of Saint-Marceau and Saint-Victor, whose dirty, narrow, damp houses, without courtyards, without air, received in their dark recesses these new guests who came to pile up alongside the already too numerous inhabitants of these unhealthy neighbourhoods. . . . In these gloomy districts, the population vegetates sadly, the filth is disgusting, the air infected, the streets narrow, and death so active that it strikes more than anywhere else; the inhabitants are weak and puny, to the point that one in three called up for military service are exonerated.
>
> (Benoiston de Châteauneuf, 1832, pp. 30 and 202)

The *Rapport* on cholera first of all highlights the extremely high mortality rates in these poorer neighbourhoods, and hence a basic social inequality in the face of death. Clearly, this acknowledgement of inequalities is far from new and surprising, but what is striking is the fact that it is now "photographed" in an official document which derives further authoritativeness from the extensive use of statistics. The latter linked the epistemological and methodological framework of budding social research to that of the natural sciences, giving the former a scientific outlook that strengthened its normative character. This was further supported by the publication in 1832 of the first *Statistique géneral de la France*, which marked a turning point in the project – begun at the end of the previous century – of introducing the concept of measurement into the description of human and social phenomena.[17] This publication reflected a broader trend towards the professionalisation and regularisation of population statistics, which was defined as the "science of facts" and progressively replaced the term "political arithmetic" (Rabinow, 1995, pp. 59–61).

"In saturating the social space, the epidemic revealed its non-neutrality: the social selectiveness of the epidemic, which chiefly struck the poor, made people aware that conditions for order in the social space might, or might not, be produced," write Procacci and Szakolczai (2003, p. 68), stressing the importance of this event for the social sciences' genesis. "The cholera epidemic of 1832 was a watershed event," writes Paul Rabinow (1995, p. 30), because it "set the stage for a new understanding of social conditions" and "opened the way for new scientific discourses, new administrative practices, and new conceptions of social order." By revealing basic deep inequality in the face of death, this experience intensified and exacerbated the way in which French society perceived its internal rifts. But at the same time through this very trauma, a vivid need arose, even in the liberal field, for a political strategy to socially integrate the subaltern classes and include them into an actual condition of citizenship, a strategy that required the development of specific knowledge about their living situation. Let us now observe how such a need found practical development in the aftermath of the pandemic trauma and how the latter stimulated the rise of social research on poverty and pioneering measures of social security.

2.6 The moral and political sciences

The cholera outbreak fostered a change in the way in which French liberalism looked at urban pauperism and the management of problems associated with it. The dynamics of the epidemic nourished the idea – an idea no doubt conflicting with classical liberal principles – that to safeguard the social body as a whole, the political authorities somehow needed to take charge of the conditions of the subaltern classes, so as to "defend society" by immunising it against a risk that far exceeded the political sphere. The cholera crisis brought about representations and interpretations of the lifestyles, customs, and habits of the subaltern classes in terms of a "social pathology." The will to adopt safety measures to prevent the risk that the latter implied for the health of society as a whole thus stimulated the development of strategies and practices aimed at providing a scientific understanding of the social fabric, of subaltern urban subjects, and the major hazards associated with them (cf. § 1.3). "The fear of dangerous classes, the fear of a new irruption of barbarians into the depths of society, contribute to making social research one of the linchpins of the new kind of governance that is being developed," writes Rosanvallon (1985, p. 261), who uses the metaphor of the *État sociologue* to describe the original intertwining between political power and social enquiry which emerged in the early 1830s. Doctrinaire liberalism – committed to establishing an ideological infrastructure for the Orléanist regime and translating liberal theory into government policies for the first time in continental Europe (cf. § 1.4) – consistently interpreted this political-intellectual tension through several institutional measures. Particularly relevant is the decree of 27 October 1832 by which François Guizot, then Minister of Education, reopened the *Académie des Sciences Morales et Politiques* (ASMP).

This Academy was first established in 1795 by the Revolution and then suppressed by Napoleon owing to its Republican tendencies. Its new regulations of 1832 asserted the principle of election among peers, starting with the surviving original members (including Sieyès, Tayllerand, Destutt de Tracy, and Gérando) and defined its mission as the promotion of studies, social investigations, and research grants.[18] Among the thirty full members initially elected we find two leading figures in the cholera debate, Lous-René Villermé and François-Joseph-Victor Broussais – which shows how the ASMP project was driven by the same kind of issues that had emerged during the epidemic. Out of the Academy's five sections, it was especially the political economy and statistics that engaged with the issues considered so far: through the joint work of economists, mathematicians, doctors, civil servants, and jurists, it focused on the complex and hazy set of problems related to the social question, seeking to clarify it through the observation, "classification," and organisation of the social actors it involved. The Academy further encouraged the use of statistics to tackle the problems brought into play. The "physical and moral conditions" of the urban lower classes thus became the object of increasingly regular and systematic observations ranging from their biological constitution to their expression of political wills and passions – to prevent the unrest that might stem from them. In such a way, the ASMP became a crucial workshop for the genesis of the modern social sciences, which made pauperism the first specific object on which to develop a scientific method for the analysis of society.[19] Up until the 1848 revolution, the Academy played a leading role in the intertwining of political institutions with the emerging practices of social research that contributed to bringing workers' conditions into focus as the strategic area for the governance of urban pauperism.

The ASMP perfectly embodies "the connection between science and power which characterises the early July monarchy" (Leterrier, 1992, p. 656; cf. § 1.3). This Academy expresses the government's ambition to become both sociologist and the arbiter of sociological knowledge through the establishment of an instrument enabling it to act in the field of social research while delegating it, according to the liberal paradigm, to private initiative. In such a way, the Academy presented itself as a public yet independent body that was nonetheless closely connected to the political authorities, in relation to which it aspired to act not just as an adviser, but as an inspirer and in some cases – as we shall see in Chapter 4 – as the direct promoter of administrative and legislative measures. This hybrid, public-private configuration is precisely what enabled the ASMP to become an avenue for collaboration between different kinds of intellectuals and scientific approaches sharing an original interest in the subaltern classes and in new research practices aimed at scrutinising these classes' living conditions to orient government and administrative policies.

The social question immediately emerged as the central focus of the Academy's activities, giving rise – over the course of the 1830s – to major enquiries into poverty that marked a turning point in the processes we have been exploring so far. The image of otherness so radical as to acquire anthropological-racial connotations, and crystallised in the metaphor of barbarism, was now replaced by the tendency to take this very field as the object of a budding form of knowledge. The next chapter follows this development by considering the major social enquiries promoted by the ASMP over the course of the 1830s, to illustrate how they brought about new representations of the subaltern classes and a progressive redefinition of the "social question" as a "labour question." By retracing the evolution of the social investigation on poverty, we will see how the latter progressively began to distinguish specific problems and classify different figures within the dark and hazy universe of the subaltern classes – what had been initially represented as a single dangerous subject through the figure of the "new barbarians." Specifically, we will observe how the social enquiries promoted by the ASMP gradually brought into focus the condition of wage labour as a field of knowledge and a set of administrative practices that were designed to limit potential risks and brought about the first occupational medicine and labour law measures. Although these studies – consistently with the spirit of the Orléanist regime – were primarily driven by a conservative concern to stem the growing political pressure from the subaltern classes and by a moralising approach, they were to have powerful reformist outcomes in terms of policies and legislation, which will be the focus of Chapter 4.

Notes

1 Founded in 1789, the *Journal des débats* was the most authoritative mouthpiece and supporter of the Orléanist government.
2 Guizot (1828, pp. 150–151): "there is one element that must be clearly understood to get a true picture of what a barbarian was, and that is precisely the taste for individual independence, the pleasure of using one's strength and freedom amid the world's possibilities."
3 The same aspect is stressed by Rosanvallon (1985, p. 86 n. 2): "the history of civilisation is naturally that of a gradual cleansing of barbarism, through the separation of its positive principle (individual independence, equality) from its negative principle (confusion and anarchy)."
4 Cf. § 4.3 concerning this important treatise, which interprets poverty as a specifically modern phenomenon which, at the same time, is also a kind of return to the *état de barbarie* and "savage life" (Buret, 1840, Vol. 1, pp. 67–68).
5 "The workers' poverty is a social bane which must be cured through the broadest possible division of property," writes Girardin (1859, p. 154), bearing witness to the fact that the main strategy envisaged by the liberal elites in this period was "to make the proletarians property-owners." The aim of the present book is also to reconstruct the gradual transformation of this position into an integration strategy based instead on the broad extension of wage labour.
6 Foucault (2005, p. 195): unlike the "savage," the man of nature, who lacks history and leaves his condition behind by establishing the contract that founds society, the barbarian "does not emerge from some natural backdrop to which he belongs. He appears only when civilization already exists, and only when he is in conflict with it. He does not make his entrance into history by founding a society, but by penetrating a civilization, setting it ablaze and destroying it" (*ibid.*).
7 This perspective clearly finds its most authoritative development with Marx, who in any case attributes its conception to great historians of the French bourgeoisie such as Guizot and Thierry: "I do not claim – Marx writes to Joseph Weydemeyer in 1852 – to have discovered either the existence of classes in modern society or the struggle between them. Long before me, bourgeois historians had described the historical development of this struggle between the classes" (Marx, 1983, p. 62).
8 Particularly revealing in this respect is the case of the *Société des observateurs de l'homme* (1799–1804), among whose founders was Baron de Gérardo, who in the 1820s sought to apply the ethnographic principles developed for the study of "savage people" to the analysis of the urban poor (cf. § 3.1.1).
9 Even Louis Blanc describes the *canuts* of Lyon as "a long-subjected race" that is regarded as "inferior and degraded" (1844, pp. 354 and 345), whereas Alphonse de Lamartine writes: "these are what are, strictly speaking, called the proletarians, a race destined to populate the soil . . . a people sprung from the people, a nation within the nation, a displaced race" (1864, Vol. IV, p. 109). Note that François Guizot himself draws upon comparative ethnography to develop his interpretation of the historical barbarians: "I know but one means to represent . . . the social and moral condition of the Germanic *peuplades*: to compare them to the *peuplades* that, in modern times, in various areas of the globe, in North America, in the interior of Africa, and in northern Asia, are still at a roughly similar level of civilisation. . . . For us they become like a mirror that reveals . . . the image of the ancient Germanic peoples" (Guizot, 1853, Vol. I, p. 194).
10 This second pandemic of "Asiatic cholera" spread from the Ganges delta in 1826, reaching China in 1828, Persia in 1829, and then Poland, Hungary, Prussia, Germany, Austria, and Britain in 1831 (cf. Baehrel, 1952). Hegel died from it in Berlin on 14 November 1831.
11 Cit. in Leca (1982, p. 77, emphasis added): "civilisation, you see, is the best means to fight all epidemics." This kind of discourse was also adopted by the republican

opposition: "the admirable people of Paris . . . are not made to be served up to Asiatic Cholera and to die from the disease of slaves" (Société des Amis du Peuple, 1832, p. 4). On this topic, see also the Saintsimonian movement's pamphlets by Chevalier (1832) and Flachat (1832).

12 On 15 April 1832, in the republican newspaper *Le National*, Armand Carrel denounces "this way of understanding society . . . transposed from the events of Lyon to the circumstances of the terrible disease that is ravaging Paris," and represented by the reference to the "new barbarians."

13 Métral (1833, p. 160): the lower classes are here described as "a kind of hermaphrodite race: they belong neither to nature, since they are not like the savages, nor to society, since they are not civilised" (ibid., p. 24).

14 Among the possible causes of cholera, this surgeon lists "violent emotions," "passions of the soul," and hence too revolutionary drives and political unrest. Some journalists stress the role played by Polish political refugees in the westward spread of a disease that the clergy was portraying as a divine punishment for the impiety of a population that the previous year had gone so far as to plunder the archbishop's palace. "Labour movements are contagious," we read in the 26 November 1831 issue of *Le Temps*. On these matters, see Morris (1976), Bourdelais and Dodin (1987), and Bourdelais and Raulot (1987).

15 In March 1832, the public authorities circulated an *Instruction populaire sur les principaux moyens a employer pour se garantir du cholèra-morbus, et sur la conduite à tenir lorsque cette maladie se declare*. It reflects all the confusion surrounding this disease ("the less one is afraid, the smaller the risk one runs"), providing generic suggestions in terms of "cleanness," "sobriety," and moderation, and advising people to avoid the kind of situations which the popular classes were forced to deal with owing to their poverty (to avoid sleeping in crowded rooms, to wear woollen garments and not go barefoot, to wash one's clothes and take hot baths, to avoid wine of poor quality, etc.). Even the medical debates on possible "cures" for the disease reflect the same kind of confusion, suggesting treatments that range from leeches to coal, and from cold water to punch and even opium.

16 See esp. the addresses made by Louis Villermé, on whom see § 3.3, and by François Broussais, who supported the identity of the physiological and the pathological, and identified the origin of cholera as an inflammation of the intestine to be treated exclusively by external means, such as the use of ice and leeches (cf. *Gazette médicale de Paris*, April-June 1832 and Le Mée, 1998).

17 See also the *Rapport au roi sur les hopitaux, les hospices et les services de beinfaisance*, which was published by the Prefecture of Paris in 1837 and reflects the emerging "public health" approach (cf. § 3.3.1). "In the first half of the 19th century, statistical research in Paris responded to the population's concern, and actually witnessed a remarkable spread", exercising a considerable influence on public opinion (Chevalier, 1956, p. 624). As far as public statistics are concerned, demographic ones were first published in 1821 and those on murders and suicides in 1827, while the first meagre statistics on industry appeared in 1839. See Marietti (1949), Lazarsfeld (1961), Hacking (1982, 1990), and Porter (1986).

18 The first phase of the Academy lasted until 1803 and centred on the *Idéologues*' work. This group included intellectuals such as Condillac, Cabanis, and Destutt de Tracy, who already displayed a tendency to combine science and governance, social research and administration, in analysing the population's physical and moral conditions (see Simon, 1885). Victor Cousin was the orchestrator of the ASMP's reopening in 1832, whose members increased from twelve to thirty, subdivided into five classes (political economy and statistics, philosophy, ethics, law, and history); in addition there were five foreign members (including Sismondi and Malthus) and up to forty overseas correspondents (see Sellière, 1926).

19 Among the various steps taken by ASMP with regard to the social question, it is worth recalling the establishment of the "Beaujour" Award in 1834 and the "Bigot de Morogues" one in 1843, both of which were devoted to research on poverty (cf. Académie des Sciences Morales et Politiques, 1960).

References

Académie des Sciences Morales et Politiques. (1960), *Notices biographique et bibliographique, Règlement, Fondations, Documents divers*, ASMP, Paris.

Baehrel R. (1952), La haine de classe en temps d'épidémie. *Annales. Economies, Sociétés, Civilizations*, 7: 562–593.

Barzun J. (1932), *The French Race: Theories of Its Origin and Their Social and Political Implications Prior to the Revolution*, CUP, New York.

Benoiston de Châteauneuf L.F. (1832), *Rapport sur la marche et les effets du cholèra morbus dans Paris et les communes rurales du département de la Seine*, Impr. Royale, Paris.

Blanc L. (1844), *Histoire de dix ans 1830–1840*, Société Tipographique Belge, Bruxelles.

Boulay de la Meurthe H. (1832), *Histoire du choléra-morbus dans le quartier du Luxembourg, ou précis des travaux de la commission sanitaire de ce quartier*, Renouard, Paris.

Bourdelais P., Dodin A. (1987), *Visages du Cholèra*, Belin, Paris.

Bourdelais P., Raulot J.Y. (1987), *Une peur bleue. Histoire du choléra en France 1832–1854*, Payot, Paris.

Buret E. (1840), *De la Misère des classes laborieuses en Angleterre et en France: de la nature de la misère, de son existence, de ses effets, de ses causes, et de l'insuffisance des remèdes qu'on lui a opposés jusqu'ici, avec les moyens propres à en affranchir les sociétés*, Paulin, Paris.

Castel R. (2003), *From Manual Workers to Wage Laborers: Transformation of the Social Question*, Transaction, New Brunswick, NJ (or. ed. *Les Métamorphoses de la question sociale, une chronique du salariat*, Gallimard, Paris 1995).

Chevalier L. (1956), La statistique et la description sociale de Paris. *Population*, 9(4): 624.

Chevalier L. (1973), *Laboring Classes and Dangerous Classes in Paris During the First Half of the Nineteenth Century*, Howard Fertig, New York (or. ed. *Classes laborieuses et classes dangereuses*, Plon, Paris 1958).

Chevalier M. (1832), *Religion saint-simonienne. Le choléra morbus*, Éverat, Paris.

Chignola S. (2004), *Fragile cristallo. Per una storia del concetto di società*, Editoriale Scientifica, Napoli.

Coleman W. (1982), *Death Is a Social Disease: Public Health and Political Economy in Early Industrial France*, UWP, Madison.

Delaporte F. (1986), *Disease and Civilization, the Cholera in Paris, 1832*, MIT Press, Cambridge and London.

Delpech de Frayssinet J.A. (1833), *Mémoire sur le choléra-morbus, pour servir à l'histoire de cette maladie sur le territoire français*, Pitrat, Lyon.

Dubois C-G. (1972), *Celtes et Gaulois au XVIe siècle. Le développement littéraire d'un mythe nationaliste*, Vrin, Paris.

Dubois F. (1831), *Choléra morbus. Examen des conclusions du rapport de M. Double sur le choléra morbus (adoptées par l'Académie royale de médecine)*, Billière, Paris.

Flachat S. (1832), *Religion saint-simonienne. Le choléra. Assainissement de Paris*, Éverat, Paris.

Foucault M. (2005), *"Society Must Be Defended". Lecture at the Collège de France, 1975–76*, Picador, New York (or. ed. *"Il faut défendre la societé". Cours au Collège de France 1975–76*, EHESS, Paris 1997).
Girardin S-M. (1859), *Souvenirs et réflexions politiques d'un journaliste*, Lévy, Paris.
Gossez R. (1956), Diversité des antagonismes sociaux vers le milieu du XIXe. *Revue économique*, 3: 439–458.
Guizot F. (1828), *Histoire générale de la civilisation en Europe depuis la chute de l'Empire romain jusqu'à la Révolution française*, Pichon et Didier, Paris.
Guizot F. (1853), *Histoire de la civilisation en France depuis la chute de l'Empire romain*, nouvelle édition, Didier, Paris (or. ed. 1829, Masson, Paris).
Hacking I. (1982), Biopower and the Avalanche of Printed Numbers. *Humanities in Society*, 5(3/4): 279–295.
Hacking I. (1990), *The Taming of Chance*, CUP, Cambridge.
Hamlin C. (2009), *Cholera, the Biography*, OUP, Oxford.
Jouanna A. (1976), *L'Idée de race en France au XVIe siècle et au début du XVIIe siècle; 1498–1614*, Champion, Paris.
Lamartine A. de (1864), *Oeuvres oratoires et écrits politiques*, vol. IV, Librairie internationale, Paris.
Larrey D.J. (1831), *Mémoire sur le Choléra-morbus*, Huzard, Paris.
Lazarsfeld P.F. (1961), Notes on the History of Quantification in Sociology. Trends, Sources and Problems. *Isis*, 52(2): 277–333.
Le Mée R. (1998), Le choléra et la question des logements insalubres à Paris. *Population*, 1/2: 379–397.
Leca A-P. (1982), *Et le cholèra s'abattit sur Paris 1832*, Albin Michel, Paris.
Leterrier S.A. (1992), *Les sciences morales et politiques à l'Institut de France, 1795–1850*, thèse de doctorat, Université de Paris 1, Paris.
Longmate N. (1966), *King Cholera: The Biography of a Disease*, Hamilton, London.
Lucas-Dubreton J. (1932), *La grande peur de 1832*, Gallimard, Paris.
Marietti P.G. (1949), *La Statistique générale en France*, PUF, Paris.
Marx K. (1983), Letter to Joseph Weydemeyer, March 5, 1852, in K. Marx, F. Engels (eds.), *Collected Works, Vol. 39 Letters 1852–55*, pp. 60–65 (or. ed. in *Jungsozialistische Blätter*, 1930 and Marx-Engels, *Werke*, vol. xxvii, Dietz Verlag, Berlin, pp. 510–512).
Métral A. (1833), *Description naturelle, morale et politique du cholèra morbus à Paris*, Didot, Paris.
Michel P. (1981), *Les barbares 1789–1848. Un mythe romantique*, PUL, Lyon.
Monfalcon J-B. (1834), *Histoire des insurrections de Lyon en 1831 et en 1834*, Perrin, Lyon.
Morris R.J. (1976), *Cholera 1832. The Social Response to An Epidemic*, Chroom Helm, London.
Pollitzer R. (1960), *Cholera*, OMS, Genève.
Porter T.M. (1986), *The Rise of Statistical Thinking, 1820–1900*, Princeton University Press, Princeton, NJ.
Procacci G., Szakolczai A. (2003), *La scoperta della società. Alle origini della sociologia*, Carocci, Rome.
Rabinow P. (1995), *French Modern: Norms and Forms of the Social Environment*, The University of Chicago Press, Chicago.
Rancière J. (1981), *La nuit des prolétaires. Archives du rêve ouvrier*, Fayard, Paris.
Rémusat C. (1959), *Mémoires de ma vie, t. II: La Restauration ultra-royaliste. La Révolution de Juillet (1820–1832)*, Plon, Paris.

Robinson C. (1983), *Black Marxism: The Making of the Black Radical Tradition*, Zed Books, London.
Roch E. (1832), *Paris malade: esquisses du jour*, Moutardier, Paris.
Rosanvallon P. (1985), *Le moment Guizot*, Gallimard, Paris.
Sellière E. (1926), *Une académie à l'epoque romantique*, Leroux, Paris.
Simon J. (1885), *Une Académie sous le Directiore*, Calmann Lèvy, Paris.
Société des amis du peuple. (1832), *De la Civilisation*, Auguste Mie, Paris.
Tocqueville A. de. (1984), *Oeuvres complètes*, vol. IV, Gallimard, Paris.
Tomasello F. (2015), *La violenza. Saggio sulle frontiere del politico*, Manifestolibri, Rome.
Villermé L.R. (1989), *Tableau de l'état physique et moral des ouvriers employés dans les manifactures de coton, de laine et de soie*, Études et documentations internationales, Paris (or. ed. Renouard, Paris 1840).
Virdee S. (2019), Racialized Capitalism: An Account of Its Contested Origins and Consolidation. *The Sociological Review*, 67(1): 3–27.

3 Liberalism and the science of society

In the previous chapter, we saw how the trauma of the cholera pandemic brought about a new understanding of the issues related to emerging industrial and urban pauperism. The present chapter addresses the way in which these new interpretations and representations of the social question were shaped by the rise of the social research activities that have been already introduced by considering the cholera report (§ 2.5) and the reopening of the *Académie des sciences morales et politiques* (ASMP) in the autumn of 1832 (§ 2.6). We will first take a step back to observe the approach to poverty that had developed in the context of post-revolutionary France, so as to single out the turning point marked by the ASMP's research in the 1830s. By observing the evolution of these social enquiries, we will see how they progressively began to identify specific problems and classify different figures within the dark and hazy universe of subaltern subjects – which were initially represented as a single dangerous class through the metaphor of the "new barbarians" (cf. § 1.2). In such a way, the emergent social research gradually brought the condition of wage labour into focus as a field of knowledge, policy-making, and legislation. By following its evolution in post-revolutionary France, this chapter aims to describe how social investigation on poverty contributed – over the course of the 1830s – to reframing the social question as a labour question.

To retrace this development, we will consider a broad and diverse field of investigations in which it is nonetheless possible to detect a common set of problems marking the origin of the modern social sciences. Focusing our gaze on these sources means tracing a minor and less-explored genealogy for sociological knowledge: one centred not on the invention of concepts, models, and theories but rather on the development of forms of empirical enquiry aimed at identifying political and administrative solutions to the most pressing social issues of the time. In this sense, the following pages retrace the genesis of the modern social sciences as both an intellectual and a *political* process, for two reasons. The first is that the emergence of a new form of scientific knowledge about society was driven by the political need to develop solutions for the governance of the 19th-century social body sprung from political revolutions and reshaped by industrialisation processes that had produced new social subjectivities and issues. The second reason is that the enquiries in question fostered new representations of the social fabric that were bearers of significant political effects – as I will discuss in Chapter 4 – since they

DOI: 10.4324/9781003303497-5

were designed to single out pioneering social policies aimed at reducing the risks highlighted by the epidemic crisis. The combination of these elements produced what we might call a process of "objectivation" of wage labour as a field of study and governance, which unfolded in parallel to the process of "subjectivation" that came to be known as the "labour movement" and that will be the focus of the second part of the book (cf. Chapters 5 and 6).

3.1 The development of social research

To appreciate the turning point marked by the social enquiries carried out under the ASMP's aegis in the 1830s, I will set out to outline the background against which they emerged. To this end, we first need to consider the way in which the interpretation and management of poverty had developed since the watershed of 1789 – specifically, since the revolutionary abolition of guilds decreed by the Le Chapelier laws in 1791 to affirm the principle of the free market. Article 4 of these laws stated that all deliberations and agreements between "citizens belonging to the same professions, arts, and crafts" were "unconstitutional, a threat to liberty and the declaration of the rights of man, and *de facto* null." Such citizens were forbidden from taking part in "deliberations pertaining to their shared interests" or to elect representatives of any sort.[1] By abolishing the guild system, these laws also removed all the traditional social safety nets deriving from it. This fostered the spread and exacerbation of new kinds of poverty that stood in contradiction with the values of equality and brotherhood affirmed by the French Revolution. Besides citizens' civil and political equality, the latter recognised the private property as an "inviolable and sacred right of man" and the budding industrialisation process turned out to be a powerful driving force of inequality in such a domain. The advent of an industrial regime of production and commerce created the conditions for almost limitless inequalities of wealth and fostered the rise of new forms of deprivation. Thus, tension emerged between the egalitarian principles established by the revolutionary process in the legal-political sphere and the spread of poverty among those citizens affected by the end of the social protections that the guilds could ensure in the context of the Ancien Régime.

With the abolition of corporations, the benevolent figure of the beggar asking for charity had been progressively replaced by that of the poor individual requiring a form of aid impacting the public budget and that of the threatening vagrant requiring policing measures. Hence, the first decades of the 19th century were marked by the effort to develop strategies to face the problem of poverty in such a way as to limit its disruptive effects, yet without calling the principle of the free market into question, which is to say without challenging State intervention. Poverty relief measures were thus envisaged which would not conform to the British system of "legal charity" by acknowledging an enforceable right to state assistance that would have indefinitely extended the rather limited French public or semi-public poverty relief system. The latter remained voluntary, entrusted to local authorities, and constituted by *bureaux de bienfaisance*, almshouses, hospitals for poor invalids, and by the few orphanages, madhouses, and institutes for the deaf and blind, while the parish welfare system was equally weak (Castel, 2003; Procacci, 1993). In this context, it was a matter of addressing the problem of poverty while confining it to the moral sphere, so as to limit the consequences of his constant spilling over into the political sphere (Procacci, 1993; Donzelot, 1984).

Classical liberal theory essentially associates poverty with the notions of responsibility, guilt, and individual conduct, thereby ruling out the right to saddle others with the weight of one's existence. In early 19th-century France, the liberal elites' debates on charitable aid reveal an effort to adapt such a theory to a more complex reality and to its concrete challenges. In this regard, Robert Castel speaks of "complex strategies based on the search for non-State answers to the social question," and thus of a *politique sans État* corresponding to the "mobilisation of social elites to exercise a protective power towards those less fortunate and to adopt a charitable function economising on State intervention" (Castel, 2003, p. 374). The proliferation of philanthropic associations constitutes an expression of such policies, which François Guizot (cf. § 1.4) not only theorised but actively championed as president, from 1828, of the *Société de la morale chrétienne.* To grasp the origins of social research on pauperism, we need to set out from these approaches aimed at designing poverty relief measures by ruling out public intervention and confining the question to the moral dimension.

3.1.1 Poverty: work as the limit of charity

> It is charity, in all its various forms, that brings together what chance separates and that, by preserving what is necessary or even useful in inequality, strips it of all that is dangerous and evil within it. Through its peaceful intervention, harmony is maintained. . . . Such is the effect of the benevolent relations that charity introduces; by refining public morals, they consolidate society. . . . The practice of alms-giving creates an art; its theory, a science.
>
> (Tanneguy Duchâtel, 1829, pp. 26–27 and 29)

This interpretation of the practice of charity proposed in 1829 by Tanneguy Duchâtel (who became a member of the ASMP in 1842) reveals a double aim. On the one hand, it expresses the need to stimulate relations and bonds designed to "consolidate society," which is threatened by the problem of poverty. On the other, it confirms the liberal understanding of poverty, but also a tension to lend moral depth to political economy by means of systematic development of the charity. The latter enables philanthropists to reunite what private market and free competition have divided by limiting their more harmful social effects. In this sense, while not bringing the State into play, charity constitutes a kind of *politics* that must be scientifically organised on the basis of "knowledge of the physical and moral laws to which man is subjected" (ibid., p. 18). In this first period, before the activities of the ASMP, social research on poverty is not yet marked by the use of a systematic method, yet reveals a tendency to develop charitable practices as a matter of public interest by not confining them to the individual dimension and furnishing them with an allegedly scientific approach.

The rationale for organising philanthropic practices thus became the object of important debates. A first canonical point of reference in this domain is *Le visiteur du pauvre*, a 1824 text designed to instruct philanthropists as to "the means to recognise true poverty and make alms-giving as useful to the givers as it is to the receivers."[2] The author was Baron Joseph-Marie de Gérando, a linguist, pedagogue, jurist, a member of the ASMP (since its founding) and of the *Société des observateurs de l'homme*, and the founder of the *Société de la morale chrétienne*.[3] Significantly, the aim of his 1824 treatise was to apply to the study of urban poverty the principles developed in 1799, in a pioneering ethnographic text written for the members of a scientific expedition to lands inhabited by "savages" in the Southern Hemisphere (Gérando, 1799). The *charité investigatrice* characterising *l'office du visiteur du pauvre* thus took the form of an "art" but also of a "science," as it consisted in an in-depth ethnographic investigation of the poor people's lives: it "examines before acting; monitors . . .; goes back to the causes, encompassing all circumstances; unites giving with caring, consolation, and advice." It was essentially based on a work of *classement des pauvres*, on a classification designed to avoid any harmful alms-giving directed towards "fake poverty," which deprived the poor and society of the moral and material benefits of work. Philanthropists, therefore, were first to ascertain the existence of one of the three causes of "true" poverty: inability to work, the insufficiency of work's outcomes, or the temporary lack of work. Secondly, they were to study the causes behind such factors to understand what role was played by carelessness, laziness, vices, or dissoluteness. In such a way, charitable aid aimed to deal with poverty not just as a material condition, but also as a *mode of conduct*, and to promote the "treatment of moral illnesses" (Gérando, 1826, pp. 11, 39–40 and 120). The philanthropic activities carried out by literary characters such as Jean Valjean in Hugo's *Les Misérables* and Rudolf of Gerolstein in Sue's *Mysteries of Paris* bear witness to the relevance of such an approach in those years.

Far from confining themselves to alms-giving, philanthropists were expected to develop "exact and in-depth knowledge of the situation of the poor," so as to limit the social costs of fake poverty, which fooled the State and, by promoting idleness, condemned the poor to a future of deprivation. Work, by contrast, promotes "order, perseverance, and temperance; it is a kind of moral gymnastics; it makes each creature used to meekly following the paths laid out by the Creator" (Gérando, 1826, p. 105). Like Tanneguy Duchâtel (1829, p. 18) – who reserved charity for those "wretches who cannot offer anything in return, not even the labour of their arms" – Gerando understands and defines the sphere of work by exclusive opposition to poverty, as the limit and the solution to charitable aid. The latter only comes into play when labour is absent or falls short. In relation to the treatises of these years, Michelle Perrot notes a "difficulty in grasping the specific nature of the problem," in defining the object. Hence the often encyclopaedic character of books on poverty, which invoke and discuss all social ills: the destitute, beggars, orphans, prostitutes, invalids, prisoners, the sick, and madmen. These are the "classical chapters" in a sort of "handicapology" which bases the analysis of poverty on the *incapacity to work* (Perrot, 1972; Leclerc, 1979).

Despite this short-sightedness with regard to the emerging condition of the industrial working poor, the real novelty in these philanthropic treatises is to be found in the tendency to direct traditional alms-giving practices towards the rational planning of "real and active" measures to protect the poor, who "in many respects are like children" (Gérando, 1826, p. 14). Just as with minors, there was a *duty* to help the poor which did not pertain to the sphere of legal relations, but rather to that of morality, and which needed to be somehow institutionalised to re-establish and consolidate social bonds. Society, Gérando writes, "is morally constituted like the family . . . poverty is to wealth what childhood is to adult age": hence, philanthropists need to provide "a kind of adoption" (ibid., p. 9). What we have is the idea of a kind of guardianship agreement, or informal protection contract, that transposes onto the social field of poverty the capacitarian theories that doctrinaire liberalism was advancing in the political field – as described in the first chapter (cf. § 1.4). This is also a kind of *patronage* displayed by the philanthropist towards the poor that foreshadows the patronage of employers towards their workers that we shall see later on (cf. § 3.2.2).

In such a way, philanthropic practices were designed to operate between the individual and the State. This was a space that the French Revolution had deliberately left empty, smooth, and homogeneous, but which actually over the course of the 19th century proved to be filled with subjectivities and problems that needed to be constantly managed to prevent social disorder. Opposition to the extension of State prerogatives was therefore not confined to the adherence to *laissez-faire* theories of economic liberalism. Rather, it also encompassed the development of measures capable of "forging society," of ordering it so as to govern it through the promotion of principles of public morality. The social question was thus essentially understood and represented as a *moral question*. Up until the early 1830s, the liberal approach to it consisted in the effort to push charity beyond the exclusively religious and individual sphere so as to scientifically structure it as a sort of policy, yet one pertaining not to the State sphere but only to the moral one. A drive to rationalise and scientifically organise philanthropic activities already shaped these debates on indigence, in which the sphere of work was nonetheless still only understood as the limit and outer boundary of poverty relief measures.

3.1.2 Pauperism and the British hell

The French intellectual environment and debates we are considering are marked by constant and almost obsessive attention to the British social landscape. This was regarded as the most advanced level of industrialisation and hence as foreshadowing a destiny for France as likely and imminent as it was disquieting. From the 1820s onwards, the immorality of Britain's brand of liberalism, influenced by Malthusian theories, the ineffectiveness and costliness of its welfare system, and the disruptive social effects of its industrialisation became an object of widespread criticism.

"Britain, inflated by trade and all kinds of big industry, has acquired immense treasures; yet these treasures, crammed at the top, have left nothing but the ghastliest poverty for three-quarters of the population, reduced to living off public alms," Baron Bigot de Morogues writes in *De la Misère des ouvriers et de la marche à suivre pour y remédier* (1832, p. 2). From the link between industrialisation and the spread of a new and dreadful kind of poverty, this philanthropist inferred the need for a powerful relaunching of the rural economy, craftsmanship, and family business to oppose the industrial regime and the physical and moral unwholesomeness of the urban environment. His argument rests on an "evident mathematical demonstration" of the connection between property crimes and the development of urban factories to the detriment of the agricultural economy. The extensive and comparative use of statistics on the population, wages, prices, rents, and crime across various geographical areas made this treatise stand out – earning its author a post as an ASMP correspondent. Moreover, it is remarkable that this was one of the first publications to feature the topic of workers' poverty (*la misère des ouvriers*) in its very title. The specific nature of the industrial labour question thus began to emerge through the distinction between rural and urban poverty, along with an effort to bring the relationship between the latter and the phenomenon of crime into focus. These innovations aside, however, Morogues' social research is not yet structured in a systematic way and remains framed within a moral rejection of industrialisation: the author criticises mechanisation, supports protectionism, and does not go beyond a vindication of the countryside's virtues against the new urban industries (Bigot de Morogues, 1832, 1834). "Not only does their method seem questionable or uncertain – Francis Démier (1989, p. 37) writes with regard to treatises of this kind – but the very object they study is viewed within an all too traditional set of problems."

Morogues' contribution must be understood in conjunction with his political effort as a member of the Chamber of Peers (upper house) to promote primary education and his philanthropic work through the *Société des établissement charitables*. He established this society in 1828 together with Alban de Villeneuve-Bargemont, whose *Économie politique chrétienne* (1834) offers the most noteworthy synthesis of the approach under consideration. The author's lengthy career as a prefect in various departments provides the empirical material informing this treatise, which advances a political interpretation of poverty inspired by an Ancien Régime administrative culture shaping an aristocratic criticism of the political economy and of a kind of liberalism that has become divorced from morality. The French labour tradition, rooted in long-standing forms of guild solidarity and centred on agriculture, is thus envisaged as the basis of a paternalistic and charitable economy to be set in contrast with the "baleful influence that the industrial and political system of England" was allegedly exercising throughout the world. Yet, this outlook worthy of a prominent aristocrat is combined with the author's keen awareness of the irreversible transformations triggered by industrialisation. The new forms of poverty engendered by the latter are described by Bargemont through the English term *pauperism*. The latter was first adopted in the French debate in the early 1820s and its uses encapsulated the fear that a similar kind of industrialisation might take hold across the Channel:

> If indigence under the new and unfortunately vigorous name of *pauperism* is spreading across entire classes . . . if it is no longer an accident, but the condition into which most members of the population are forced, then we cannot

> fail to identify these markers of widespread suffering . . . as a close indicator of the most serious and baleful distress.
>
> (Villeneuve-Bargemont, 1834, p. 28)[4]

The gradual semantic shift from *indigence* to *misère*, and finally *paupérisme*, reveals a transformation in the understanding of the experience of poverty. It illustrates how the latter became a social question through an increasingly clear awareness of its relation to industrialisation processes, from which the centrality of the issue of wage labour was to emerge. As we read in the *Dictionnaire d'économie politique*, "pauperism" refers to the "collective, amplified, and general kind of poverty which reduces whole categories of individuals to the condition of indigents in need of aid, as opposed to the accidental kind of poverty deriving from temporary causes or striking, in an isolated way, individuals belonging to entirely different social categories" (Cherbuliez, 1873, p. 574; cf. also Chevallier, 1893). This neologism expresses a mature awareness of the relationship between a series of socio-historical transformations underway and a peculiar condition of indigence affecting growing sections of the population as wealth and technological development increase. Its use reflects a turning point in the investigation of poverty, based on the adoption of a new focus on the way in which industry and wage labour are organised and can foster new forms of deprivation.

Pauperism "does not stand in contrast to wealth, like poverty, but to society, and this gives it a destabilising form" (Procacci, 1993, p. 168). It gives inequalities "physical and moral form," and brings out indigence as a "social question," because – by encompassing whole segments of the population – it raises radical questions about the very permanence of that human form of association we call "society" to designate the social order shaped by the modern political and industrial revolutions. "Today it is no longer a matter of political order, but of the existence of society as a whole," Bargemont writes (1834, p. 2). His words highlight the problem of a kind of poverty which is no longer an individual and contingent destiny, but an enduring, permanent, epidemic, and hereditary condition that exists not at the margins of society, but at its very centre: for it appears to be complementary to the development of civilisation's wealth and progress. This issue thus becomes the focus of new intellectual efforts to develop scientific investigations on society aimed at elaborating strategies to immunise the social body against the risk of its dissolution raised by the spread of industrial pauperism. These philanthropists' treatises are still remote from what will be the method and epistemology of the modern social sciences, yet they already reveal a remarkable tendency towards the definition of their specific object of investigation through the measurement of human phenomena. In doing so, they pave the way for an appreciation of the labour question's importance by establishing a first and crucial distinction between the new, urban form of poverty and the traditional rural one.

3.1.3 Tocqueville and the new "industrial class"

"Villeneuve-Bargemont was the first to raise the labour problem, in all of its complexity, in the French Chamber of Deputies" (Dumont, 2002, p. 116). In the lower house, this author (elected a member of the ASMP in 1845) played a leading role in promoting the 1841 law on child labour, which was to represent the first significant legal-political outcome of the intellectual developments we are retracing (cf. § 4.2). His thought encapsulates the French current known as *économie politique charitable*, which aimed to include the problem of poverty within the scope of political economics by striking a balance between Christian morality and political liberalism. Bargemont's outlook as a noble Legitimist conscious of the irreversible nature of the social transformations underway also made him an influential point of reference for Alexis de Tocqueville's intellectual development, in connection not just to the question of pauperism but also to an Ancien Régime administrative culture (Chignola, 2004, p. 473). This is evident in the *Mémoire sur le paupérisme* of 1835, in which Tocqueville (who was elected a member of the ASMP three years later) engages with the paradox of the exponential growth of both wealth and poverty in modern industrial societies.

This author regards 19th-century poverty as the bitter fruit of the "progress of civilisation," which has brought about a broadening of tastes, needs, requirements, and desires. The emergence of "secondary needs," Tocqueville states, has spawned a stream of new goods, whose production has led to the rise of a *new class* of non-agricultural labourers entrusted with the "special and dangerous mission of securing the material well-being of all others (i.e. all other classes) by its risks and dangers" (Tocqueville, 1997, p. 23). It is the development of civilisation that has created the *ouvriers* (workers) of the "industrial class," making them naturally exposed to the risk of poverty, since the goods they produce are subject to the laws of the market and of competition, and to contingent needs (ibid., pp. 22–24). Hence, the advent of an industrial regime of production and commerce in modern societies is described as having had the following effects: "when one crosses the various countries of Europe, one is struck by a very extraordinary and apparently inexplicable sight . . . on the one hand the number of those living in comfort, and, on the other, the number of those who need public funds to live, growing proportionately" (ibid, pp. 17–18).

These ambivalent social effects of industrialisation especially struck Tocqueville during his journeys to Manchester. The cradle of the Industrial Revolution is described by this author as a "foul drain" from which "the greatest stream of human industry flows out to fertilise the whole world." This "filthy sewer" reveals that modern industrial progress is intrinsically marked by deeply ambivalent features: the simultaneous and unprecedented, parallel and antithetical growth of both wealth and poverty, prosperity and misery, emancipation and subjugation. "Here humanity attains its most complete development and its most brutish; here civilisation works its miracles, and civilised man is turned back almost into a savage" (Tocqueville, 1958, pp. 107–108). Yet, Tocqueville recognises this contradiction as the inevitable consequence of a broader historical development. He understands industrialisation as an effect of the civilisational progress related to the historical movement of equality and sees a "close bond and a necessary connection" among liberty, industry, and commerce (Storey, 2013). Like the egalitarian movement of democracy, industrialisation appears to be a distinctive feature of modern societies, in which the development of commerce and industry has fostered the overcoming of the old hierarchies and structures based on status. Hence, the inexorable and epoch-making march of democracy and that of the Industrial Revolution appear to be linked, although in a way that produces contradictory effects, including the spread of new conditions of deprivation so obscure as to evoke ancient times of wilderness and savagery.

In this reading – influenced by Guizot's courses on the "history of civilisation" (cf. § 1.3) – we come across the Tocquevillian motif of the irreversibility of the new "social condition of the world." This is based on an interpretation that, without praising the new situation, proves its ineluctability, dismissing the prospect of any return to the agricultural, family-based, and traditional past. Although Tocqueville's analysis of pauperism does not draw on statistics, or present any data or empirical survey, it bears witness and actively contributes to the theoretical shift I am here attempting to outline. Based on his direct observations of the British and American industrial contexts, this thinker clearly indicates modern poverty as an issue to be addressed by looking at the labour conditions resulting from both the technological movement of industrialisation and the political developments that had determined the dissolution of long-standing forms of guild solidarity. This corresponds to a shift that, from philanthropic approaches seeking to assess and alleviate the causes preventing the poor from supporting themselves through work, leads to new interpretations of poverty that frame industrial wage labour conditions as the key aspect of the problem of pauperism.

3.1.4 Work as punishment and reward

Tocqueville's understanding of pauperism reflects his concern for the disruptive risks and tendencies towards disintegration underlying the post-revolutionary society, which had been individualised through the unstoppable movement towards equality that marks modern societies. However, he staunchly refuses to entrust State intervention with resolving this problem. Tocqueville firmly opposes the system of public welfare by which "in America, as in England, any man in need has an open right against the State," so that "charity has become a political institution" that shelters "indigents who cannot and those who do not want to profit their life by honest work" (Tocqueville, 1997, p. 36).[5] This principled opposition to the acknowledgement of any "right to welfare" rests on the idea that it would discourage indigents from working, thereby undermining the only virtuous aspect of the growing condition of industrial poverty, which lies precisely in the widespread establishment of the discipline of wage labour as a material necessity. This is a sort of "ethics of work" that shapes Tocqueville's social theory as a whole, including his analysis of punishment. By considering how this author conceptualised the latter in relation to labour and the criminal question, it is possible to introduce a second crucial distinction that was about to be established within the blurred universe of the subaltern classes – in addition to the juxtaposition between rural-agricultural and urban-industrial poverty – and which played a crucial role in the emergence of the modern idea of the working class. This is the distinction between "labouring" and "dangerous" subjectivities.

In April 1831, together with Gustave de Beaumont, Tocqueville was sent on a government mission to conduct a study of the penitentiary system in the USA, the country which had been the first to apply the modern principle of the sheer deprivation of freedom as a general form of punishment. In the report resulting from this nine-month journey – *Du système pénitentiaire aux États-Unis et de son application en France* (Tocqueville & Beaumont, 1833) – the two young magistrates compared the solitary confinement of the "Philadelphia system" with the more "communitarian" one of Auburn. In the name of a "scientific" perspective intended to ensure the "defense" of society against the soft approach distinguishing the "false philanthropy" of authors such as Charles Lucas, Tocqueville and Beaumont endorsed the solitary confinement model. In their view, the latter sets the inmate "alone against society as a whole," making him yearn for work, and projecting its effects of control and prevention onto the entire social body. This issue continued to be present and relevant in Tocqueville's thought at least until 1843, when, as an advocate for the law on solitary confinement, he stressed the need for – and the benefits of – labour among prisoners (see Tocqueville, 1884b). "What leads almost all men to crime is laziness. There aren't many thieves among good workers," Tocqueville writes (1884a, p. 97), arguing for a model of imprisonment in which the loneliness that comes with solitary cell-confinement has the advantage of "making prisoners eager" to work, producing a disciplining of their conduct. Thus, a work ethic is forcibly promoted within prison walls, while outside fear is instilled in potential criminals and rigorous punishment is ensured for the benefit of honest citizens (ibid.). "Imprisonment," states Pellegrino Rossi (1829, p. 169), the leading juridical champion of doctrinaire liberalism, "is punishment par excellence in civilised societies. It has a moralising influence, since it is accompanied by the obligation to work." We can thus recognise an emerging tendency to attribute a strong moral value to the discipline of wage labour, a value that is defined by opposition to the conducts and circumstances that lead deprived individuals towards criminal activities.

In the debate on the prison system and the criminal question we come across several topics and categories that are also central to the debate on the social question. The reason for this is that these two topics intertwine in relation to the emergent distinction between "labouring classes" and "dangerous classes." This is an opposition between workers and criminals – between poor yet honest labourers and the kind of delinquent marginal subjects that prison was expected to reform through the disciplines of the cell and of work – that began to emerge in the judicial and penitentiary spheres, and soon produced a deep influence on the analyses and representations of the social question. Such a distinction constitutes a key turning point in the process investigated in this chapter and was the focus of one of the first competitions launched by the Academy of Moral and Political Sciences (AMPS) in 1833 – as we will see soon (§ 3.2). This was the moment "in which the opposition between the worker and the delinquent was beginning to crystallize," Michel Foucault writes, identifying in the process of reform of punishment and of the prison system an effort to isolate the phenomenon of "delinquency" as a specific field of knowledge-power. Hence, he indicates the rise of a "strategic opposition" between "illegalities and delinquency" that made it possible to erect a "barrier to separate delinquents from all the lower strata of the population" (Foucault, 1995, pp. 277, 285).[6]

The creation of this specific distinction/opposition between the labour world and the marginal/criminal one probably constitutes the most delicate and crucial step in the process of production of the notion of "working class" I aim to retrace – that is to say, in the progressive transformation of those representations of the radical otherness of the subaltern classes which I set out from by examining the metaphor of new barbarians. As we have seen, the philanthropic treatises carried out by the *économie politique charitable* partly laid the foundations for this transition, insofar as they singled out one first and crucial distinction between traditional rural poverty and that emerging in cities affected by industrialisation and the urban crime that came with it. Based on this distinction, an awareness gradually took root – crystallising into the category of pauperism – that urban poverty was no longer to be viewed in an exclusive and oppositional relation with the domain of work. Instead, its new, major, and growing form was to be grasped in conjunction with industrial labour conditions, which thus needed to be included at the very heart of any analysis of the social question. Another crucial distinction that was subsequently to emerge is the one between male factory work and female workers' conditions, which we will consider by addressing the early development of the French labour movement and the gendered character of the "making of the French working class" (cf. § 6.3 and Scott, 1988). Based on the scenario retraced so far, I can now introduce the social research activities carried out under the ASMP's aegis to further delve into the dialectical opposition between dangerous classes and the labour world to which social and intellectual historians have quite rightly assigned considerable importance in studies on the genesis of the French working class.

3.2 The dangerous class and the working one: producing a labour force

The whole course of the July monarchy was marked by punishment-related debates and initiatives that intertwined the "criminal question" with the social one – including the debates on prison labour, which throughout the 1840s drew opposition from workers' associations. During the epidemic outbreak, Parliament was busy discussing a reform of the penal and criminal procedure code that represents one of Orléanism's major legislative measures. It envisaged detention as a general punishment for all crimes not entailing a death sentence, removed the latter from nine instances of crime, and abolished corporal punishment. This was consistent with the measure which – again in 1832 – removed the guillotine from the Place de Grève, where public executions had been staged for the previous five centuries. Moreover, the reform introduced the crucial institution of extenuating circumstances, which allowed judges to arbitrarily reduce a sentence based on elements such as the defendant's life, profile, motives, and conduct. This regulation made it possible to judge the subject even before and apart from his crime by considering his habits and attitudes – starting from his willingness to work – to assess his profile as a "delinquent" and evaluate it within the framework of emergent knowledge about the criminal world.[7] It is therefore unsurprising that one of the first competitions launched by the AMPS shortly after its reopening was devoted to research aimed at

> identifying . . . the elements that make up . . . that part of the population which constitutes a *dangerous class* in terms of its vices, ignorance, and poverty; and to identify the means which the government, wealthy or well-to-do men, and intelligent and industrious workers could use to improve this dangerous and depraved class.[8]

Announced in 1833, the award was assigned five years later to a civil servant from the Seine prefecture, Honoré-Antoine Frégier, for a treatise that was then published in 1840 and is usually credited with having defined the expression *classes dangereuses* and introduced it into the 19th-century debate.

3.2.1 Separating the wheat from the chaff

"To govern the social body, it is necessary to know it, and to know it, it is necessary to study it as a whole and in its parts, to learn what role each part plays in relation to the whole," writes Frégier (1840, p. 370). The author is here enunciating the idea that the government must promote social research practices capable of establishing an "alliance between power and science" based on an organicist conception of society. The chief instrument for this alliance is identified as a "statistical description of administrative facts" that is made increasingly detailed through the development of those "records of administrative power" represented by police archives (ibid., p. 6). These offer the quantitative documentary basis for the author's treatise, which intertwines it with the qualitative empirical material deriving from conversations and interviews with prefects and police commissioners. The first part of *Des classes dangereuses de la population dans les grandes villes, et des moyens de les rendre meilleures* is thus devoted to "annotated statistics" pertaining to the population segment under consideration: a numerical and sociological estimate of the "dangerous class" present in the French capital. This effort to statistically define the object of the research, while at the same time discussing the criteria and procedures for such a classification and definition, illustrates the methodological turn marked by the enquiries conducted under the aegis of the ASMP. This turn consists in the systematic and unprecedented use of statistics and, more broadly, in the tendency to establish a scientific approach capable of giving these surveys a normative character. Such features supported the transposition of the research findings into administrative and legislative measures: an outcome already implicit in the way these public competitions were framed and promoted.

Frégier describes his treatise as "an administrative and moral work": while the first term confirms its ambition to intertwine social science and governance practices, the reference to morality embodies what still distinguishes these enquiries from the epistemology of the modern social sciences. The political sciences of the ASMP were always – and primarily – *moral* sciences because the spirit of the Academy conformed not so much to 18th-century Enlightenment ideas as to Guizot's formula of the *gouvernement des espirts* – which typically represents this climate marked by the attempt to graft morality onto politics so as to free it from the passions unleashed by the paradigms of popular sovereignty and general will (cf. § 1.2). Researches conducted on popular strata were thus increasingly designed to assess their "moral" as well as "physical" conditions. Hence, Frégier advances a taxonomy of the dangerous class that is based first of all on the moral dimension of "vice" and includes gamblers, drunks, *maîtresses*, prostitutes and their clients, vagabonds, ex-convicts, swindlers, thieves, receivers of illicit goods, and a whole range of "idle and vagrant" individuals who, in the urban environment, constantly "reached out to the corrupt part of the working class" (ibid., pp. 1–17). Idleness is envisaged as the other side of vice, "since the poor, when given over to bad passions, stop working and establish themselves as the enemy of society, since they disavow its highest law, which is work." Addressing this problem thus means first of all developing and organising the distinction and opposition between "the class of poor yet honest and industrious workers" and "the vicious, depraved, and dangerous class." Therefore, this treatise appears to be designed not so much to define the "dangerous" segment of society as to build, develop, and spell out the criteria for this distinction between the bad social conduct of the immoral and idle classes and the humble yet honest poverty of "intelligent and industrious workers" (to quote the words used in the very call by the ASMP). Once he has identified the "alliance between vice and poverty" as the heart of the problem – according to the hypothesis that the "suspect and dangerous" class is almost entirely sprung out of the "poor and depraved part of the working classes" – Frégier focuses on the quantitative and qualitative definition of the Parisian *working classes* to single out the depraved segment that is susceptible to becoming dangerous.[9]

Upon closer scrutiny, then, this treatise on the *classe dangereuse* actually seems destined to bring out the specific figure of the *classe laborieuse* by distinguishing it from the threatening and nebulous range of subjects and problems in which it is immersed in the social descriptions and representations of the 1830s.[10] It is precisely this magmatic combination that we find in Victor Hugo, Eugène Sue, and the great popular novels of French Romanticism. By contrast, the term *Lumpenproletariat* used by Marx to describe the 1848 revolution bears witness to the established *partage* between working classes and dangerous ones (cf. Conclusion). This distinction emerged both through that process of subjectivation of labour embodied by the "workers' movement" (cf. Chapters 5 and 6), and through this sticky process of "objectivation" of the wage worker as a focus of knowledge and administration that we are describing here and by which the nascent social sciences began to develop their method.

3.2.2 From charity to patronage

The first factor capable of "re-establishing moral conditions" was identified by Frégier in the "human virtue" of work. Much of his text is thus devoted to the *preservatifs* that make it possible to "prevent and banish poverty through work," which is not "a purely material agent," but a real "virtue" capable of "preventing bad passions" (Frégier, 1840, pp. 278–281). Hence, the core of this treatise on the "dangerous classes" ultimately turns out to be a broad reflection on the organisation of labour and its transformations. "The manufacturing industry exercises a powerful influence over the urban population, the study of which is the object of our research," writes Frégier (1840, p. 288), who significantly was later to specifically focus his attention on the working class' conditions (see Frégier, 1851).

We find some classic ingredients of philanthropic treatises – such as the need to promote Christian morality among workers, of supporting the education of subaltern classes, and of rationally organising charitable aid – along with other elements that mark a substantial discontinuity with previous treatises – and sometimes even foreshadow the labour movement's claims. First of all, an effort is made to define an "equitable salary" and fair factory rules. Second, the author voices his support for popular savings banks and even praises mutual aid societies, which were the main form of workers' organisation in these years – yet on condition that they do not advance any claims but simply provide assistance, accepting the involvement of bourgeois philanthropists. These views mark a turning-point with respect to the previous distrust of manufacturing (cf. § 3.1), which Frégier instead describes as "the most fruitful, rich, and varied form of labour," the organisation of which must however be redefined also "for the benefit of the material advantage and morality of the industrious classes." Against any form of agricultural nostalgia, "the strong and regular organisation of industry" is presented as a solution to existing social problems as long as that solidarity and commonality of interest between employers and workers is ensured – as it is in the administration and the army – that is already intrinsic to the mechanisms of market competition.[11] "This system can be called *patronage*," which is the system best-suited to "promote a taste for work, order, frugality, and good manners" by combining the material support and moral education of workers (Frégier, 1840, pp. 288–311). Such a focus on patronage as an avenue to rethink the organisation of industrial work is the hallmark of this treatise on the dangerous classes, which actually takes the form of an enquiry into the labour world that even delves into the professional relationship between employers and workers within factories.

Through the idea of patronage, Frégier reframes the perspective of the philanthropists' protection of the poor – typical of treatises on *charité investigatrice* (cf. § 3.1.1) – within the labour relationship between the employer (no longer *maître* but *patron*) and the worker. The aim of patronage is to lead the worker to adhere to, identify with, and be incorporated into a business through a guarantee of *social protection*. The latter consists of the employer's willingness to take charge of his employee's socio-biological needs both within and without the business. This system is based on an exchange between the worker's loyalty, regularity, and devotion and the employer's willingness to take on the cost of the latter's social reproduction as manpower: support in the event of illness, attention towards the conditions of the whole family unit (including in the event of pregnancies), willingness to take on workers' children as apprentices in view of generational continuity within the business, assistance to elderly workers with no sons to care for them, and so on. Such is the fundamental logic underlying that "informal protection contract" that takes the name of employers' *patronage*. It embodies a social integration strategy that is based on the centrality of wage labour, is envisaged as independent from State intervention and anticipates the translation of certain aspects of this informal duty to protect into laws via the juridical codification of labour relations.

> My sole aim is to develop and extend patronage. . . . Those who have undertaken a careful study of workers' habits do not hesitate to think and say that the prospect of reforming them largely depends on entrepreneurs' actions. . . . I would be wonderfully repaid for my research . . . if this work contributed to a reform of industry capable of ensuring a less turbulent, less precarious, and sweeter condition for the industrious classes.
>
> (ibid., pp. 296, 309 and 347)

Thus writes Frégier, illustrating the paradox of a demand for social reform coming from the liberal camp in an effort to develop strategies to deal with the social question that is driven by the conservative ambition to "defend society" and "moralise" the subaltern classes. Whereas in *Organisation du travail* Louis Blanc (1840) proposed a State-led social reform, these liberal milieus promoted business organisation as the driving force for a "reform of the mores" of the popular classes led by entrepreneurs. Patronage practices thus encouraged employers to take responsibility for their workers, establishing this principle on the political-moral level before the emergence of labour law started enshrining it on the juridical level through the codification of wage labour relations. This perspective found its fullest formulation in Frédéric Le Play's work *Les ouvriers européens* (1855), which marked a new turning point in the history of labour studies as the first real sociology of work treatise.[12] Moreover, it was in the strongholds of employers' patronage that, from the 1860s, the great workers' strikes were to break out (Castel, 2003, pp. 417 ff.).

By encouraging workers to remain with a business so as to promote the intertwining of factory life and everyday life, the principles of patronage played a significant role in the establishment of the modern system of employment in France. They constitute a first attempt to attack the condition of job insecurity and instability characterising the new labour market as a result of the abolition of guilds and the increasing intervention of private capital. They contributed to overcoming the widespread distrust of large manufactures which marked the dawn of industrialisation in France and the first enquiries on pauperism. "Manufacturing discipline" thus began to be regarded as the primary means to accomplish a "pacification" of the subaltern classes through the "wage regularity it enables, the fixing of the population, and the possibility to easily assess sanitary conditions" (Donzelot, 1977, p. 71). While large productive units continued to be portrayed as receptacles of promiscuousness, poverty, and hence social hazards, the enactment of supervision, moralisation, protection, and control measures by entrepreneurs began to emerge as an antidote to the constant mobility of people searching for work and higher wages that characterised the traditions and practices of *compagnonage* (cf. § 5.2).

The *nomadism* associated with small trades, seasonal labour, and precarious occupations was increasingly perceived as a key problem related to the new industrial poverty, which needed to be addressed by ensuring job security and stability to consolidate the border separating the working and the dangerous class. Indeed, nomadism constituted the main link between the metaphor of barbarism and the 19th-century proletarians who were immigrating into manufacturing cities en masse. Limiting this pervasive nomadic condition paved the way towards new social representations, including the representation of what came to be known as the "working class" (in the singular). The patronage system interpreted this logic by fostering conditions of compatibility between the ways of life of wage workers and the new production regime that was emerging through the increasing economic power and pervasiveness of private capital. Such a logic consisted of promoting the establishment of a segment of the subaltern classes as *workforce* through their attachment to individual businesses and manufacturers. In other words, it was a matter of *turning the barbarian into a worker* by getting him to submit to the discipline and benefits of modern wage labour. Frégier provided a contribution in this direction by developing a representation that made it possible to "sift out" of the farrago of the social question a working class that clearly distinguished itself from the ways of life typical of the dangerous classes. This crucial distinction was thus added to that between traditional or rural poverty and modern industrial pauperism laid out in the previously considered treatises (cf. § 3.1). As illustrated in Chapter 6, the distinction between male and female labour conditions was to become a further element in this process of definition – or "objectivation" – of the modern working class.

3.3 Doctor Villermé and the epistemology of the social sciences

In November 1834, the political economy branch of the ASMP promoted and funded a major enquiry into France's biggest manufacturers to evaluate "the physical and moral conditions of the working classes in the most exact possible way." This was an internal direct appointment, entrusted to Louis-François Benoiston de Châteauneuf – an economist and social demographer who had been in charge of the official report on cholera – and Louis-René Villermé – a physician who had been a leading voice in the debates on the epidemic and a member of the official committee of enquiry on cholera (cf. § 2.5). While the former studied the west and rural areas, the latter focused on more industrialised textile regions, carrying out a broad investigation that marked an important turning point in the developments we are exploring and in the process of redefining the social question as a specific labour question. Villermé's *Tableau de l'état physique et moral des ouvriers* (1840) offers an unprecedented description of industrial work conditions as the central challenge that post-revolutionary 19th-century society had to face to ensure its very destiny. It is worth considering the whole intellectual path that led this author to publish the *Tableau*, as his trajectory crosses the entire range of topics we have considered so far and, in the next chapter, will allow us to set these topics in relation to the history of administration and legislation.

3.3.1 The public health movement and the "work" of cholera

Villermé began his career as a military surgeon, serving in Napoleon's army for a decade. His interest then turned to public health, particularly in relation to criminal and incarceration issues. In 1820, he embarked on a study of "prisons in relation to hygiene, morality, and political economy," which was based on visits to gaols, as well as on quantitative evaluations, and earned him a place at the Academy of Medicine. He then focused his work on the causal patterns emerging from an analysis of death rates, first in prisons and later within the French population as a whole (Villermé, 1820, 1828, 1830, 1831). Villermé concluded that social conditions had to be recognised as a crucial variable in such an analysis and this triggered his interest in those poor classes that consistently displayed significantly higher mortality rates. The way in which this physician formulated the problems at issue, his concern with ensuring salubrious conditions, and his systematic use of statistics in relation to medicine immediately place his work in that strand of medical science which in those years was emerging with the name of "public health movement" or, in French, "*hygiénisme*" (Coleman, 1982; La Berge, 1989, 1992). His intellectual connection with Adolphe Quételet further contributed to fuelling his interest in statistics, which makes Villermé one of the founders of social demography in view of his constant efforts to intertwine medicine and the investigation of population data (Mireaux, 1962; Lecuyer, 2000; Julia & Valleron, 2011).

In 1828 he founded the *Annales d'hygiène publique et de medicine légale* together with the anatomopathologist Alexandre Parent-Duchâtelet, another hygienist and pioneering social investigator who authored a famous enquiry into prostitution in Paris and a treatise on public sanitation in relation to the various professions (Parent-Duchâtelet, 1836, 1838). The main feature of this journal was an unprecedented effort to institutionalise a form of scientific knowledge intertwining the systematic use of statistics, the medical study of hygiene, and the analysis of the social realm. In the *Preamble* to the first issue of *Annales* (vol. I, 1828, p. 2), we read:

> The medical tendency is the necessary complement to the industrial tendency, since the influence which the latter has exerted on salubriousness is unquestionable in the sense that it has multiplied the hazards to which industrial populations are generally far more exposed than agricultural populations.

The main aim of this approach was therefore to develop social immunisation strategies against the multiplication of hazards that marked emergent industrial societies. The public health movement presented itself as the "art of preserving the health of men gathered in a society" through a redefinition of medicine's epistemological framework in the industrial age, starting from a new understanding of sanitary issues based on the use of population statistics. This "party of public health" (Coleman, 1982) explicitly aimed to inform government measures and public policies by establishing an "association" with "philosophy and legislation" to fight "social pathologies" (Villermé, 1830, p. 294). Through the notions of "milieu" and of the "social environment," and an organicist conception of society, the hygienist perspective oriented the development of the epistemological framework of the budding social sciences, directing its research practices towards the "evaluation of the physical and moral conditions" of the urban subaltern classes. "By developing a *physiological approach* to the study of society centred on social pathology," understood as the negative side capable of revealing the positive side of possible administrative and legislative initiatives, hygienists promoted "a kind of medicine which, on account of its empirical and methodological bases, aspired to become a social science" (Procacci, 1993, pp. 156–157). The trauma of the 1832 epidemic stimulated and justified the penetration of this approach into public debate, political discourse, and social research practices. We have already seen how the difficulties in coming up with a diagnosis and treatment for cholera made the latter an obscure and protean object, just like the social question: the strength of the public health movement lay precisely in its capacity to connect these two elements – epidemic risks and pauperism as a social pathology – by promoting a form of medical knowledge that was structurally intertwined with a scientific look at society and an analysis of the "social body."

It is therefore evident that the cholera outbreak immediately established Villermé at the centre of public debate, not least because the epidemic's dynamics evoked the contents of his research on unequal mortality rates across social classes. In opposition to the theories of cholera as a contagious disease, which emphasised the need for isolation, he endorsed "health measures" that envisaged the social environment as the strategic sphere for preventing the epidemic's spread. He thus promoted hygienic-sanitary interventions in those urban milieus where the infection was likely to emerge (Villermé, 1833). Villermé then joined the public committee of enquiry on the epidemic led by Châteauneuf, which adopted the method of the hygienic-sanitary assessment of places deemed insalubrious, emphasising the problem of the subaltern classes' conditions (cf. § 2.5). For the first time, the urban social milieu was approached as an object that could be systematically investigated to promote welfare practices for the safeguarding of the social body. In such a way, the pandemic experience pushed the empirical method of medicine beyond its boundaries and – through the public health movement – projected it towards a new and broader subject: the scientific analysis of industrial society. This overlap between medicine and social investigation enabled hygienists to establish their own perspective within the epistemological framework of the budding social sciences. The latter came to envisage pauperism as the primary object for testing an empirical method for the scientific analysis of society that would appear to have been largely borrowed from medicine. These developments sketch out a kind of "minor history" of the origins of the social sciences which intertwines the traditional history of ideas – the construction of concepts and paradigms which in those years gained traction through the work of authors such as Saint-Simon and Comte – with the invention and implementation of social research *practices*. Adopting this lens allows us to appreciate the political dimension of the genesis of modern sociology, since the rise of these research practices was driven by the urge to find responses to pressing social events. Besides, this perspective also reveals the diverse roots of sociological knowledge, resulting from the contingent combination of approaches and personalities from the fields of medicine, anthropology, governance, law, and political economy. Thus, the treatises we are considering may be regarded as an "impure archive" of the modern social sciences, understood as a sphere of empirical investigation practices in which different disciplines became intertwined in relation to a key issue, the social question of urban pauperism, turning it into a scientific object to develop social security and risk reduction policies.

Starting from "a biological-ecological model drawing on physiology and anatomy for its concepts," Villermé was "seeking to develop an understanding of society as a whole composed of interrelated and interrelating functional parts" (Rabinow, 1995, p. 61). Hence, this author "was led to approach the social sciences because of his experience as a physician" (Démier, 1989, p. 37). His career illustrates the crystallising of a political-intellectual approach that interpreted the trauma of cholera as proof of the need to scientifically organise knowledge of the urban social strata deemed responsible for the disease's spread. Hence, the urgency to articulate political responses to the range of problems most dramatically epitomised by the pandemic made the morass of pauperism the object of an increasingly organised method of observation, which primarily pursued its *classification*. The newly reopened AMPS offered one of the most striking examples of this political-intellectual rationale (cf. § 2.6). Thanks to his leading role in the debates on the disease, Villermé was immediately elected as one of its members, drafted its first *Mémoire* – concerning the French population's composition (Villermé, 1837) – and became its president in 1849, not least by virtue of the success of his *Tableau de l'état physique et moral des ouvriers employés dans les manufactures de coton, de laine et de soie*, published in 1840 and destined to set the standard for all labour enquiries to come.

3.3.2 The "physical and moral conditions" of the working class

The 4,000-franc grant offered by the ASMP in 1834 to "evaluate the physical and moral condition of the working classes" reflects the progressive focusing of the analysis of the social question on industrial labour conditions, and the way in which the latter had been gradually assumed as a general perspective to understand and manage the problem of pauperism. In turn, the intellectual path that led Villermé from the study of public health in relation to the subaltern classes' conditions to the investigation of the organisation of labour in large factories exemplifies the way in which wage work was established as a central subject of knowledge and administration. In February 1835, in the Lyon region, this physician began the investigation he was to complete in the northern departments two years later:

> I followed the workman from his workshop to his home. I walked in with him, and studied him within his family; I attended his meals. I did even more: I saw him in his labour and in his household; I wanted to see him in his pleasures, observe him in his social activities. There, listening to his conversations, sometimes participating, I became, without his direct assent, a

> confidant of his joys, his pains, his regrets, and his hopes, and a witness to his vices and virtues.
>
> (Villermé, 1840, Vol. 1, p. vi)

We find here the ethnographic approach marking philanthropic treatises on poverty (cf. § 3.1), yet this time within the context of a systematic investigation conducted on the basis of what is conceived as a "positive" method focusing on a specific and well-defined subject: workers in that industry "which takes up most of the manpower," namely the textile industry.[13] Villermé distinguishes between its three sectors – cotton, wool, and silk – and then between the various departments, cities, and factories. An unprecedented amount of information is collected, organised, and presented: for each locality, data is provided pertaining to manufacturing methods, workers' tasks, working hours, wages, housing costs, and the prices of food and other consumer goods. The *Tableau* is therefore usually regarded as the first genuine work enquiry, an influential cornerstone in labour studies that laid the foundation for the birth of the sociology of work. With this treatise – William Reddy (1984, p. 369) argues – social research on labour conditions acquires "a definite form, to which all future practitioners of this art will be expected to conform."

Much space is devoted to the Lyonnais *fabrique* and to the *canuts* (cf. § 1.1 and 5.1), who according to Villermé (1989, p. 369), "far from being morally degraded and of meagre intelligence as has been said, are on the contrary more advanced in true civilisation . . . than many men raised by their wealth or social status above the workers' rank." In this apology for textile workers based on the notion of "true civilisation" we can glimpse a polemic against those who, like Girardin in the early 1830s, had "degraded" them to the rank of new barbarians (cf. § 2.1). The gap between Villermé's description of Lyonnais workers and that provided by the *Journal des débats* in 1831 bears witness to the transformation of the liberal elites' representations of subaltern subjects that this chapter and the previous one have retraced and interpreted: the shift from the metaphor of barbarism to the emergent image of the honest and industrious worker. Like Girardin, Villermé was a champion of political and economic liberalism. Yet, he believed that liberalism ought to promote a kind of positive knowledge that would make it possible to "diagnose" those social pathologies for which it was necessary to take governmental and administrative action to safeguard the social body. Indeed, in his view what distinguished the liberal order from the Ancien Régime was precisely this diagnostic faculty, this capacity of society to tell the truth about itself. It was therefore to ensure the development of liberal society that the *Tableau* provided a portrayal of industrial pathologies of unprecedented rawness and depth, revealing the distortions and excesses which needed to be corrected to ensure the bourgeois civilisation's destiny – starting with the major issue of child labour, as we shall see in the next chapter.

The vivid and scathing denunciation of some baleful aspects of work in large factories – sources of promiscuousness, alcoholism, and a more general "corruption of morals" – does not lead Villermé to question the need for capitalist development. Instead, the *Tableau*'s general premise is that the latter brings unquestionable improvements to the living conditions of the whole population.[14] The analysis of the industrialisation process is so detailed that it reveals the latter's complex character, the various ways in which it had penetrated into the countryside, and the positive effects of the alternation between agricultural and manufacturing work, which mitigates the effects of economic crises. There is no longer any room for outdated criticisms of the industrial era based on an apology for the traditional and rural economy. On the contrary, it is precisely with the aim of ensuring industrial and economic development that Villermé focuses on the social pathologies stemming from the exploitation of manpower to advance moderate, specific, and circumscribed proposals for reform (cf. §§ 4.1 and 4.2). Hence, his perspective clearly differs from and overcomes the agricultural, artisanal, and family-centred tendency characterising the "Christian political economy" we have considered above (cf. § 3.1), yet without subscribing to the political economy's orthodoxy of British liberalism.

The first volume of the *Tableau* presents the results of the investigation conducted across the various sectors and localities, while the second one discusses elements common to the whole textile industry, the main problems associated with its work conditions, and political, social, and legislative strategies to deal with them. Regular use is made of statistics while the data from previous social enquiries conducted in the 1830s within the framework of the *économie politique charitable* are frequently employed as a documentary basis (cf. § 3.1.2). But the fundamental piece of empirical evidence is drawn from first-hand observation, modelled after the ethnographic methods of philanthropists' treatises from the 1820s (cf. § 3.1.1). Statistical evaluation and empirical investigation are intertwined and interpreted from a medical-hygienist perspective aimed at assessing workers' physical-sanitary conditions; their food, hygiene, and sexual habits; and their dwellings and work places' climatic-environmental conditions. As in the previous treatises, here too we find a strong moralising tendency whereby "forgetfulness of moral principles" is regarded as a major cause of workers' poverty. Thus, Villermé (1989, p. 378) indicates a "fair" salary as that which does not exceed the basic level required for the social reproduction of the labour force, arguing that "the more workers earn, the more easily they can satisfy their depraved tastes."[15] Yet to this elitist conservative view, a medical approach is now added that focuses on elements such as the temperature and quality of the air in factories, and more generally on labour's consequences in terms of workers' physical constitution, which makes Villermé one of the fathers of occupational medicine.

The mantras of improvidence, irreligion, alcoholism, dissoluteness, and concubinage were thus downplayed in favour of other reflections of an "ecological" nature, so to speak, which placed *security* policies before moralising. This gaze on social security, the work environment, and the governance of industrial labour is the most innovative and original aspect of the *Tableau*. The very detailed and moderate reform proposals it offers reflect an emergent tendency towards pioneering welfare policies that made the wage labourer's condition into the strategic pivot for the integration and governing of industrial pauperism. The fact that they were subsequently translated into legislative measures reveals the political vocation and effects of the empirical investigations which marked the genesis of the modern social sciences. The next chapter considers these outcomes to describe the impact of the *Tableau* in terms of legislation and policies for workers' protection and, more broadly, the way in which the practices of social enquires considered so far contributed to the genesis of the modern principles of welfare, starting from the regulation of labour relations.

Notes

1 On 14–17 June 1791, the Constituent Assembly unanimously voted in the laws proposed by Isaac Le Chapelier, the founder of the Feuillants, later guillotined in 1794. Subsequently, under the Napoleonic Empire, the law of 12 April 1803 renewed the prohibition to form coalitions and established the employment record book (cf. § 4.1). In 1804, art. 1781 of the civil code ruled that an employer's word was to be taken over that of his employee in salary disputes; in 1810, art. 415 of the penal code made the establishment of coalitions for the purpose of collectively suspending or preventing work a punishable crime (in 1825–52 over 11,000 sentences were delivered in relation to it). Workers' unrest in the early 1830s was one of the causes that led to the issuing of a law on 10 April 1834 that increased penalties for associations and contributed to sparking the second *révolte des canuts* (cf. § 5.1). The juridical picture remained unchanged for many decades, until the Ollivier law of 2 May 1864 abolished the crime of coalition and the Waldeck-Rousseau law of 21 March 1884 legalised trade unions, abolishing the Le Chapelier law (see Burstin, 1990, 1997; Le Crom, 1998).

2 These words come from the call for investigations launched by the Lyon Academy, and on the basis of which Gérando's work won the award in 1820. This was first published, after significant revision, four years later (on the following developments of this author's approach to poverty, see Gérando, 1839, 1841).

3 In 1821 Gérando established this society together with Rochefoucauld-Liancourt (the former president of the Revolutionary Committee for the Extinction of Mendicity and then of the first French savings bank); leading French philanthropists then entered the *Société de la morale chrétienne*, including Constant, de Broglie, Lamartine, Guizot, and Tocqueville.

4 Along these lines, see also Fodéré (1825). The "Christian economists" often referred to Sismondi, while their most frequent targets were Charles Dupin's industrialism and Charles Dunoyer's liberalism: see Duroselle (1951) on this current of thought.

5 See also Rémusat (1840) for a similar perspective on public welfare.

6 Specifically, Foucault (1995) states that punishment reforms had the effect of creating and isolating a particular form of illegality, namely "delinquency," which could be made use of against other popular illegalities, particularly those of the workers (absenteeism, theft, vagrancy, frauds, etc.). By "popular illegalities" (or working-class illegalism) he means the spontaneous "resistance" put up by the subaltern classes against the socio-economic transformations underway, which often intertwined with workers' struggles and Republican movements, triggering the "great fear" of the subaltern classes.

7 The reform law, issued on 28 April 1832, abolished corporal forms of punishment such as stocks, the pillory, branding, and the cutting of hands; it made terms of imprisonment for debt shorter; it introduced a distinction between political crimes and ordinary ones; it treated recidivism lighter; and it limited deportation in favour of detention. The death penalty was abolished for the crimes of conspiracy, the counterfeiting of coins and signets, and all forms of theft. Extenuating circumstances were described as "undefinable and unlimited"; among the most commonly invoked factors were the defendant's good conduct before the offence, his or her poor education, age, signs of regret, motive, influence from accessories to the crime, ignorance of the law, poverty, and lack of premeditation (Garçon, 1901). In this period, the morality and law branches of the ASMP focused on the debate on the prison system, with contributions from two leading voices in this debate, namely Lucas and Bérenger.

8 On the ASMP competitions, see Picot (1901). This 3,000-franc award was offered by the ASMP morality branch and assigned, after an extension, in 1838, based on a report by the economist Charles Dunoyer.

9 The use of data is substantial, yet their interpretation seems questionable and arbitrary: it gives the idea that the author is trying to use this data to justify a specific social picture rather than carry out any actual investigation. Frègier aims to estimate the numerical consistency of the working-class population in Paris in order to deduce from it the size – equal to "one-third" – of the depraved and potentially dangerous segment. This quantitative description is then followed by a qualitative one of the mores and habits of the "depraved portion" of male and female workers and ragmen.

10 "It is only as the effect of a whole procedure of selection, in which the penal system is a cornerstone, that around 1840 we see a whole series of discourses appear that are both the effect of the division and have the function of overturning it. Thus, Frégier's text-fiction constructs the *category of dangerous class*," writes Foucault (2015, p. 172) in a text that offers a reading of the similarities between the prison-based punitive system and the disciplinary regime of work, between "wage-form" and "prison-form," between "crime and punishment" and "work and salary."

11 Frégier also states that agriculture and public works should be promoted not in opposition to industry, but as a way to absorb excess manpower in times of crisis, and decries both businessmen's greed and the "tyranny of workers' secret societies" aimed at "dictating wage prices" through blackmail.

12 This author was long neglected on account of his conservative perspective and then reappraised due to his significant methodological contribution to sociology's development (see also Le Play, 1864). Based on extensive research conducted in factories and mines, Le Play's work aimed to provide the material foundations for a positive method of investigation of labour conditions, and to systematically define the principles of patronage, which had acquired considerable importance over the course of the Second Empire. In relation to the latter, it is also worth mentioning the development of the first *cités ouvrières* – or company towns – like the Cité Ouvrière de Mulhouse, which was promoted by a dozen entrepreneurs, partly thanks to public funding from Napoleon III, and aimed at providing workers with modest yet comfortable housing with basic sanitation. The town was built in several phases from 1853 to 1897 until there were 1,243 single and family houses, each with an independent entrance and garden.

13 In 1839, the French cotton industry employed roughly 900,000 workers (including 100–150,000 children), the wool industry 20,000, and the silk industry 180,000.

14 "Since our Revolution, we have seen poverty . . . decrease significantly. Furthermore, among us wealth and its advantages are less the exclusive privilege of only one class than ever before: everyone lays claim to them today, which is why the poor see themselves as being more unfortunate than before, even though in fact their condition has improved" (Villermé, 1989, p. 367).

15 The "moralisation of workers" is described as a great "necessity in the present epoch," and extensive space is devoted to an investigation of workers' "vices" with the aim of distinguishing poor yet honest workers from the dangerous classes: "this separation between the good and the bad, in different neighbourhoods, is an important fact," Villermé writes with regard to Lille. Alcoholism is presented as the workers' greatest scourge, so much so that the author suggests that employers should agree not to hire workers who drink too much (Villermé, 1989, pp. 367–378). Even when it comes to the *canuts*, Villermé praises their wisdom yet denounces "their passion for expensive pleasures, their profligacy, and their excessively free, at times dissolute mores" (ibid., p. 363). These considerations are combined with a scrutiny of the entrepreneurs' conduct, because – in accordance with the classical liberal perspective – it is deemed responsible for any reform of workers' conditions: the entrepreneurs "alone can accomplish it; without them it is impossible" (ibid., p. 407).

References

Bigot de Morogues P.M.S. (1832), *De la Misère des ouvriers et de la marche à suivre pour y remédier*, Uzard, Paris.

Bigot de Morogues P.M.S. (1834), *Du Paupérisme, de la mendicité, et des moyens d'en prévenir les funestes effets*, Dupré, Paris.

Blanc L. (1840), *L'organization du travail*, Prévot, Paris.

Burstin H. (1990), *Un itinerario legislativo: le leggi Le Chapelier del 1791*, in id (ed.), *Rivoluzione francese. La forza delle idee e la forza delle cose*, Guerrini, Milano.

Burstin H. (1997), Problèmes du travail à Paris sous la Révolution. *Revue d'histoire moderne et contemporaine*, 44(4), October–December: 650–682. https://doi.org/10.3406/rhmc.1997.1891

Castel R. (2003), *From Manual Workers to Wage Laborers: Transformation of the Social Question*, Transaction, New Brunswick, NJ (or. ed. *Les Métamorphoses de la question sociale, une chronique du salariat*, Gallimard, Paris 1995).

Cherbuliez A. (1873), Pauperisme, in *Dictionnaire d'économie politique*, Cocquelin-Guillaumin, Paris, p. 574.

Chevallier É. (1893), Paupérisme, in L. Say, J. Chailley (eds.), *Nouveau Dictionnaire d'économie politique*, Guillaumin, Paris, pp. 449–455.

Chignola S. (2004), *Fragile cristallo. Per una storia del concetto di società*, Editoriale Scientifica, Napoli.

Coleman W. (1982), *Death Is a Social Disease: Public Health and Political Economy in Early Industrial France*, UWP, Madison.

Démier F. (1989), *Le Tableau de Villermé et les enquêtes ouvrières du premier XIXe siècle*, foreword to Villermé (1989), pp. 1–49.

Donzelot J. (1977), *La police de familles*, Minuit, Paris.

Donzelot J. (1984), *L'invention du social. Essai sur le déclin des passions politiques*, Fayard, Paris.

Dumont J. (2002), *L'Eglise au risque de l'histoire*, Éditions de Paris, Paris.

Duroselle J.B. (1951), *Les débuts du catholicisme social en France*, PUF, Paris.

Fodéré F.E. (1825), *Essai historique et moral sur la pauvreté des nations*, Huzard, Paris.

Foucault M. (1995), *Discipline and Punish: The Birth of the Prison*, Vintage Books, New York (or. ed. *Surveiller et punir. Naissance de la prison*, Gallimard, Paris 1975).

Foucault M. (2015), *The Punitive Society: Lectures at the Collège de France 1972–1973*, Pagrave Macmillan, New York (or. ed. *La Société punitive. Cours au Collège de France 1972–1973*, Gallimard-Seuil, Paris 2013).

Frégier H-A. (1840), *Des classes dangereuses de la population dans les grandes villes, et des moyens de les rendre meilleures*, Baillière, Paris.

Frégier H-A. (1851), *Solution nouvelle du problème de la misère, ou Moyens pratiques d'améliorer la condition des ouvriers des manufactures et en général des classes laborieuses*, Amyot, Paris.

Garçon E. (1901), *Code pénal annoté*, Larose & Tenin, Paris.

Gérando J.M. de (1799), *Considérations sur les diverses méthodes à suivre dans l'observation des peuples sauvages*, Société des observateurs de l'homme, Paris.

Gérando J.M. de (1826), *Le visiteur du pauvre*, Renouard, Paris (3rd ed.).

Gérando J.M. de (1839), *De la bienfaisance publique*, Renouard, Paris.

Gérando J.M. de (1841), *Des Progrès de l'industrie, considérés dans leurs rapports avec la moralité de la classe ouvrière*, Renouard, Paris.

Julia C., Valleron A-J. (2011), Louis-René Villermé (1782–1863), a Pioneer in Social Epidemiology: Re-analysis of His Data on Comparative Mortality in Paris in the Early 19th Century. *Journal of Epidemiology and Community Health*, 65(8): 666–670.

La Berge A.E.F. (1989), *Public Health in France and the French Public Health Movement, 1815–1848*, UMI, Ann Arbor.

La Berge A.E.F. (1992), *Mission and Method: The Early Nineteenth-Century French Public Health Movement*, CUP, Cambridge.

Le Crom J.P. (ed.) (1998), *Deux siècles de droit du travail. L'histoire par les lois*, l'Atelier, Paris.

Le Play F. (1855), *Les ouvriers européens: étude sur les travaux, la vie domestique et la condition morale des populations ouvrières de l'Europe*, Imp. Impériale, Paris.

Le Play F. (1864), *De la Réforme sociale en France*, Plon, Paris.

Leclerc G. (1979), *L'observation de l'homme. Une histoire des enquêtes sociales*, Seuil, Paris.

Lecuyer B-P. (2000), L'argent, la vie, la mort: les recherches sociales de Louis-René Villermé sur la mortalité différentielle selon le revenu (1822–1830). *Mathématiques et Sciences Humaines* (149) ISSN: 0987–6936 Online ISSN: 1950–6821.

Mireaux É. (1962), Un Chirurgien Sociologue: Louis-René Villermé (1782–1863). *Revue Des Deux Mondes*, 2, 15 January: 201–212.

Parent-Duchâtelet A. J-B. (1836), *De la prostitution dans la ville de Paris, considérée sous le rapport de l'hygiène publique, de la morale et de l'administration*, Baillière, Paris.

Parent-Duchâtelet A. J-B. (1838), *Hygiène publique, ou Mémoires sur les questions les plus importantes de l'hygiène appliquée aux professions et aux travaux d'utilité publique*, Baillière, Paris.

Perrot M. (1972), *Enquêtes sur la condition ouvrière en France au XIXe siècle*, Hachette, Paris.

Picot G. (1901), *Concours de l'Académie: sujets proposés, prix et récompenses décernés, liste des livres couronnés ou récompensés, 1834–1900*, Institut de France, Paris.

Procacci G. (1993), *Gouverner la misère. La question sociale en France 1789–1848*, Seuil, Paris.

Rabinow P. (1995), *French Modern: Norms and Forms of the Social Environment*, University of Chicago Press, Chicago.

Reddy W.M. (1984), *The Rise of Market Culture: The Textile Trade and French Society, 1750–1900*, CUP, Cambridge.

Rémusat C. de. (1840), *Du paupérisme et de la charité légale*, Renouard, Paris.

Rossi P. (1829), *Traité de droit pénal*, vol. III, Saultelet, Paris.

Scott J.W. (1988), *Gender and the Politics of History*, Columbia University Press, New York.

Storey B. (2013), Tocqueville on Technology. *The New Atlantis. A Journal of Technology and Society*, October 1: 48–71.

Tanneguy Duchâtel C.M. (1829), *La charité dans ses rapports avec l'état moral et le bien-être des classes inférieures de la société*, Mesnier, Paris.

Tocqueville A. de. (1884a), *Écrit sur le système pénitentiaire en France et à l'étranger* (*Journal des Vallons*, 30 September 1838 and *Moniteur Universel*, 1 October 1838), in Id. *Oeuvres Completes d'Alexis de Tocqueville*, tome IV, vol. 2, pp. 94–100.

Tocqueville A. de. (1884b), *Rapport fait à la Chambre des députés au nom de la commission chargée d'examiner le projet de loi sur les prisons (séance du 5 juillet 1843)*, in id (ed.), *Oeuvres Completes d'Alexis de Tocqueville*, tome IV, vol. 2, pp. 127–142.

Tocqueville A. de. (1958), *Journeys to England and Ireland*, Yale University Press, Cambridge, MA.

Tocqueville A. de. (1997), *Memoir on Pauperism*, Civitas, London (or. ed. *Mémoire sur le paupérisme*, éd. Société académique de Cherbourg, Cherbourg 1835).

Tocqueville A. de, Beaumont G. de. (1833), *On the Penitentiary System in the United States and Its Application in France: With an Appendix on Penal Colonies*, Philadelphia, Blanchard (or. ed. *Du système pénitentiaire aux États-Unis et de son application en France*, Gosselin, Paris 1832).

Villeneuve-Bargemont A. de. (1834), *Économie politique chrétienne, ou Recherches sur la nature et les causes du paupérisme en France et en Europe, et sur les moyens de le soulager et de le prévenir*, Paulin, Paris.

Villermé L-R. (1820), *Des prisons telles qu'elles sont et telles qu'elles devraient être, par rapport à l'hygiène, à la morale et à la morale politique*, Méquignon-Marvis, Paris.

Villermé L-R. (1828), *Mémoires sur la mortalité en France dans la classe aisée comparée à celle qui a lieu dans la classe indigente*, vol. 1, Mémoires de l'Académie royale de Médicine, Paris, pp. 51–98.

Villermé L-R. (1830), De la mortalité dans les divers quartiers de la ville de Paris. *Annales d'hygiène publique et de médicine légale*, III: 294–342.

Villermé L-R. (1831), Note sur la mortalité parmi les forçats du bagne de Roquefort. *Annales d'hygiéne publique et de médicine légale*, VI: 113–127.

Villermé L-R. (1833), Des épidémies sous le rapports de l'hygiène publique, de la statistique médicale et de l'économie politique. *Annales d'hygiène publique et de médicine légale*, IX: 5–54.

Villermé L-R. (1837), *Mémoire sur la distribution de la population francaise par sex et par état*, Académie des sciences morale et politiques, Paris.

Villermé L-R. (1840), *Tableau de l'etat phisique et moral des ouvriers employés dans les manifactures de coton, de laine et de soie*, Renouard, Paris.

Villermé L-R. (1989), *Tableau de l'état physique et moral des ouvriers employés dans les manifactures de coton, de laine et de soie*, Études et documentations internationales, Paris (or. ed. Renouard, Paris 1840).

4 Towards the "citizen-worker"

So far, we have retraced a transformation in the social representations of subaltern subjects in the emergent industrial context, whereby the initial images of the new barbarians and dangerous classes were progressively replaced by more complex ways of understanding the social fabric. The previous chapter has described the role played by the development of practices and methods for the empirical investigation of society, especially those promoted by the Academy of Moral and Political Sciences (ASMP). By analysing such investigations, I have tried to outline a minor and less widely explored history of the rise of the modern social sciences. This history does not focus on the emergence of major concepts, theories, and models. Rather, it delves into the political factors that underpinned this intellectual process by stimulating the rise of unprecedented activities of social enquiry according to the urge to single out strategies and tools for governing industrial pauperism. The present chapter focuses on the legal-political outcomes produced by the social investigations considered so far – or, we might say, on their "truth effects." It adopts the perspective of legal and administrative history to describe how the social enquires of the 1830s were translated into legal-political measures that inaugurated a social reform project based on wage labour conditions as the strategic area for the governance of the social question. Through this angle, we will see how the initiators of social investigation inspired the rise of pioneering welfare measures focused on the figure of the wage worker as a central subject of new emerging social rights.

These legal-political outcomes were somehow implied in the very epistemological framework shaping the social treatises examined so far. We have seen, indeed, that this framework was largely inspired by the public health movement – or *hygiénisme* – that emerged from medical science and explicitly aimed to produce an impact in terms of legislation and administration (cf. §§ 2.4, 2.5, and 3.3.1). To exemplify this pattern, I have retraced the intellectual path of one of the founding fathers of this movement, Louis-René Villermé, whose investigation gradually shifted from clinical medicine to medical statistics and the search for a science of society based on medical principles. This shift also corresponded to a redefinition of his research focus from the whole French population to the subaltern classes and eventually to the specific domain of industrial wage workers. Hence, Villerme's *Tableau* of 1840 epitomises the reframing of the "social question" as a "labour

DOI: 10.4324/9781003303497-6

question," which happened through a sort of "objectivation" of industrial work conditions as a specific field of enquiry, policy, and legislation. The second volume of this treatise is indeed devoted to the definition of the major common issues affecting work conditions in big French manufactures and of the legal-political measures to be implemented for mitigating those issues: circumscribed reform proposals that were subsequently adopted by French legislators. The present chapter examines such measures, particularly those regarding the employment record book (§ 4.1) and child labour (§ 4.2), to describe the rise of the modern principles of labour law and social protection. After analysing these topics and their translation into the legislative sphere, we will consider another investigation awarded by the ASMP in 1840 (§ 4.3) that will allow us to shift our gaze towards the socialist field – which will be the subject of the following chapters.

4.1 The employment record book and the governing of manpower

Villermé devotes the sixth chapter of the second volume of the *Tableau* to the employment record book and to its consequences on the condition of wage workers. His remarks on this subject contributed to the reforms introduced in the early 1850s regarding this legal and administrative device, which embodied a major method for governing manpower in France throughout the 19th century (Sauzet, 1890; Plantier, 1900; Kaplan, 1979; Gaudemar, 1982; Cottereau, 2002; Le Crom, 2003; Dewerpe, 2010; Sacchi Landriani, 2019). It is now worth considering first the genesis and juridical rationale of the institution of the *livret ouvier* (§ 4.1.1) and then its meaning and contribution to the processes of "objectivation" of the labour realm under investigation (§ 4.1.2).

4.1.1 A passport within national borders

The employment record book was first established as a tool to guarantee and stabilise the new labour relationships based on the principle of free access to work sanctioned by the abolition of professional guilds in 1791 (cf. § 3.1). It was introduced in 1803 in the wake of a report by the Council of State fuelled by employers' complaints about workers' tendency to exploit the competition for salaries – which became possible in the post-revolutionary "free" labour market – by moving from one business to another without fulfilling their commitments and contracts.[1] Hence, Germinal law 22 of year XI established that "no one can . . . hire a worker, unless the latter is provided with a book containing a certificate of release from his commitments, issued by those [employers] he left." With the *Arrêté du 9 frimaire an XII*, the Minister of the Interior, Chaptal, officially regulated such a book, making it mandatory and turning it into a sort of worker's *passport* to be validated by the authorities at every change of residence. Art. 3 of this decree states: "every worker travelling without an approved book will be deemed a vagrant and be liable to be arrested and punished as such."[2] The book was issued upon submitting one's apprenticeship license, a request by one's employer, or the testimony of two citizens who already had one. Upon the termination of a worker's employment, the employer was required to register the worker's discharge and the fact that he had fulfilled his obligations and paid his debts. To leave the city, the worker needed to receive the discharge document approved by the mayor and to state the place he wished to move to. Employers hiring a worker without a book in proper order were subject to fines.

By recording labour relations and certifying workers' fulfilment of their commitments towards their employers, the book served as a means of contractual regulation and as a guarantee – but *only for one side*, that of the employer. This was also an ambiguous document from a penal perspective, because no specific sanction was implemented for not having a book, except for its identification with the crime of vagrancy. Yet, the Court of Cassation, with its ruling of 9 July 1829, invalidated this legal identification between one's lack of a book and the vagrancy felony arguing that it was not consistent with the *Arrêté du 9 frimaire*. This ambiguity is reflected in the intermittent and inconsistent application of the institution across both time and space: the law was almost never applied in the countryside, whereas it was reinforced by municipal regulations and prefects' decrees in manufacturing cities (Le Crom, 2003). Villermé (1989, p. 440) himself stresses that many workers "do not have it, particularly in certain places, because the law does not oblige them to obtain one (this being a loophole in its provisions)." Precisely by virtue of this ambiguity and flexibility, the employment record book would appear to have served primarily as a dynamic dispositif used to police and govern manpower.

Significantly, by describing the *livret* as "the best means of all . . . to make workers show commitment, to predispose them to find employment, and to have a guarantee of their loyalty," Villermé credits the employment record book with "the good system of policing that now governs our factories" (ibid.). Nevertheless, he also stresses how "the natural course of events" may have revealed some loopholes in this law, of which he offers a sustained critique aimed at promoting its reform to improve the workers' condition. In particular, the *Tableau* stresses the connection between the book regulation and the way employers abuse it through advances in workers' salaries. Some "manufacturers unworthy of the name" take advantage "in an unmerciful and unscrupulous way" of the right to record debts in the book and to withhold the latter until these debts are cleared to carry out "a disgusting form of exploitation" based on deplorable work conditions and wages. "The system of giving workers' advances is a form of plunder, a crime . . . that invokes the very letter of the law to distort its spirit," a "particular kind of slavery" that deprives workers of their freedom by abusing the prohibition of hiring them if they lack a book attesting to their debts being cleared. With outrage, Villermé describes this dynamic of indebtedness as "the most active cause of weavers' poverty and demoralisation" in several cities (ibid., pp. 435–440), calling for the kind of reform measures that were to be fully introduced with the reform laws of 14 May 1851 and 22 June 1854.

This legislation addressed the employment record book's juridical ambiguities by establishing a more equitable relationship between the two parties – that is, by abolishing employers' right to withhold the book and prohibiting the recording of debts. At the same time, however, these measures confirmed and reinforced the institution of the *livret*, also extending it to women and labourers working from home, and introducing a specific sanction for workers lacking a book and for any employers hiring them (Cère, 1853; Arnaud, 1856; Sacchi Landriani, 2019). By transforming the use of the employment record book and stripping it of its juridical ambiguities, this reform enabled the *livret ouvrier* to remain in place along the whole 19th century (until 1890), bearing witness to the delicate functions assigned to it with respect to the governing of manpower. The new reform also illustrates the way in which the social investigations examined so far generated "truth effects," not only on the level of the production of world images and social representations, but also on that of policy and legislation.

4.1.2 Policing workers' mobility

Established to safeguard the two parties in an employment relationship, the book was thus stripped of its privatistic function and strengthened from the point of view of its administrative function by turning it into a sort of workers' "identity card" or "passport." Even though it was not fully enforced, the association of one's lack of a book with the crime of *vagrancy* was particularly significant. In the wake of the guilds' abolition, the nomadic attitudes associated with vagrancy had become characteristic of "the worker still poorly *degagé* from past habits and/or disoriented by the transformation underway," and whose "geographical and moral instability" constituted both a socio-political problem and a "serious obstacle to the development of a mode of production that strictly required *regularity and stability*" (Le Goff, 1985, pp. 61, 31–32). Indeed, vagrancy implied the idea not merely of movement across space, but also of avoidance of the discipline of work and the family. Hence, the instability and mobility of manpower was among the main problems to be addressed for the development of a widespread industrial regime in France (Castel, 1995, p. 412; Campesi, 2009, pp. 150 ff.; Foucault, 2013, p. 197). In serving as a passport to be stamped at every change of residence, the book made workers' mobility the object of a form of administrative control designed to force each worker to settle in one place and get rid of a range of nomadic behaviours and attitudes associated with the problem of vagrancy. The metaphor of the new barbarians crystallised the perception of vagrancy as a social hazard while the *livret ouvrier* offered a legal device to reduce the risks associated with it. Villermé (1989, p. 402) argues that "everywhere, nomad workers, folks alien to the local community, *compagnons*, bachelors, people who are not tied to the family hearth, are those who generally have the worst mores." With reference to this kind of "nomad" worker, he writes that:

> the book gives him a domicile, so to speak; . . . it is through his book, i.e. through its records and attestations about his life as a worker, provided by the bosses who have hired him, that the worker attests to his own integrity and good conduct; hence, good workers, honest workers, are very attached to their book.
>
> (ibid., p. 440)

The *livret*, therefore, embodies an administrative technology designed to "fix" the worker not just geographically, but also morally and socially. An "honourable certification of his moral standing and skill" (Plantier, 1900, p. 68), the book qualifies the individual, the poor person, the subaltern, and the proletarian *as a worker* – and thus, potentially, as a citizen. It attests to his industriousness and good conduct and prevents his mobility, indiscipline, insolvency, and any other barbarous, savage, vagrant, and vicious inclinations. This institution thus operates in the field of those strategies designed – in the name of "moralisation" – to draw a line between the poor yet honest worker and the marginal – and typically nomadic and deviant – proletarian. It fixes, or "objectivises," a segment of the subaltern classes as a productive force by promoting discipline and regularity. By serving as an identity card for employees, the book identifies the worker as such, that is, it qualifies the specific subjectivity of the worker within the broader field of proletarian and subaltern forms of life, territorialising it to socialise it and frame it within the duties and rights of an industrial workforce (Ewald, 1986). As a means of contractual discipline, of policing, of moralisation, and of exercising administrative control over mobility, this dispositif embodies an overall strategy for the governing of manpower that was developed over the course of the 19th century: significantly, the authorities' main response to the 1831 *révolte des canuts* was precisely to revoke and reissue all the workers' employment books in the city.

What "truly matters" for workers – we again read in the *Tableau* – "is having stable wages, even more so than high wages, and to be able to purchase what they need at fixed prices rather than cheaply, yet only for some time" (Villermé, 1989, p. 374). It was precisely on account of its capacity to promote stability and regularity that Villermé supported the use of the record employment book, along with other social and administrative measures contributing to these processes of production and "objectification" of a stable workers' subjectivity as the central focus for new welfare policies. In addition to the book and the aforementioned patronage principles (cf. § 3.2), from the 1820s popular savings banks became another crucial element in this liberal discourse on the "institutions regarded as most apt to prevent workers' poverty" (ibid.). We then have popular kindergartens, primary education, boards of arbitration and conciliation between employers and employees (*conseils des prud'hommes*), and mutual aid societies providing support in the event of illness – which were accepted, as long as they kept to their specific focus and did not enter into the field of politics. Villermé praises these societies, bearing witness to a desire to co-opt them in relation to strategies for the prevention and moralisation of poverty based on work after they had been *de facto* prohibited by the Le Chapelier laws, and then barely tolerated – if not vigorously opposed – whenever they turned into an instrument of the workers' struggle.

4.2 The birth of labour law

In the history of labour, ideas, and legislation, the *Tableau de l'état physique et moral des ouvriers* is usually also – and especially – associated with the 1841 law on *child labour*, in relation to which Villermé is generally regarded as having a sort of political and moral authorship. This was the primary issue that, in his view, had emerged from the investigation of workers' conditions commissioned by the ASMP he had started in 1834, and, as early as 1837, he presented two reports on child labour and discussed the topic in the *Annales d'hygiène publique* (Villermé, 1837, 1843a, 1843b). In this way, Villermé added his influential voice – and that of the ASMP and public health movement – to a campaign first launched by industrialists from the Upper Rhine and later strengthened by a petition submitted to the Parliament in 1837 by the *Société pour l'encouragement de l'instruction primaire parmi les protestants de France.*[3] Thus, what began to emerge was a "coalition of convenience between humanitarian liberals and conservative believers" (Weissbach, 1989, Ch. 2) who had witnessed how the use of steam or coal machinery in factories – by making workers' physical strength less of a requirement – had fostered the widespread hiring, at lower wages, of children – whose small, nimble hands proved particularly useful in the textile sector. From being a problem initially described as serious yet marginal, the issue of child labour gradually established itself as a general matter "of humaneness" thanks to the agency of these elites who brought together paternalistic philanthropic industrialists and religious social conservatives belonging to both the public and the private sector. This was a circle of notables still too small to be described as "civil society" and it included many of the philanthropists and pioneers of social investigation considered in the previous chapter. Most prominent among them was Villermé, a staunch supporter of "a humane law" intended "to reconcile opposing interests, those of the manufacturers and those of the workers" (Villermé, 1989, p. 423). In 1837–41 this issue gained growing traction and became the focus of heated discussions which were to become the first real national debate on the effects and tendencies of an industrialisation process that was still at a nascent stage in France.

It was not a matter "of preventing children from working, but of ensuring that their health is not spoiled," Villermé writes, attesting both to its medical-hygienist approach to the matter and to the moderate nature of his proposal. However, insofar as it necessarily required political intervention in industrial and labour relations, this proposal had a potentially disruptive impact with regard to the dogma of "freedom of enterprise" that had been at the centre of the Orleanist political economy and of post-revolutionary liberalism. Villermé was aware of this, but in the face of the "barbarous use" and "murderous abuse" of children in factories, he did not hesitate to criticise certain *laissez faire* clichés. His non-negotiable argument was that "the remedy for the deterioration of children . . . could only be found in a law" setting "a limit on daily working hours" (Villermé, 1989, pp. 416–431): a circumscribed and moderate law that would nonetheless mark a symbolic extension of state intervention in the economic field. The debates which repeatedly raged in Parliament reflect a vivid awareness of the break that this issue could potentially bring about; Gustave de Beaumont argued in the Chamber:

> it is an unprecedented experience; of which the new law is but a taste . . . it is the first step that we are taking on a path which is not devoid of dangers: it is

> the first action towards the regulation of enterprise, which requires freedom in order to operate.
>
> (*Le Moniteur Universel*, 23 December 1840)

In the Senate, Victor de Broglie emphasised that the proposed new measures "threaten society's most vital interests" by suggesting "for the first time to curtail paternal authority and labour freedom" (*Journal des Débats*, 6 March 1840). The law that was eventually approved in March 1841 is usually regarded as the first piece of welfare legislation in France, sometimes even as the beginning of modern labour law. Let us consider this law's political origins and juridical rationale in order to frame it as a provisional landing place for the investigation conducted in these chapters, given that it marks the beginning of wage labour's juridical codification and hence of the transposition of the political-intellectual processes examined so far into the realm of legislation and administration.

4.2.1 The law on child labour

In the wake of the growing attention to this matter, in 1837 the Minister of Trade ordered an enquiry into the subjects "involved" in or "affected" by child labour, that is an "official survey" of the most relevant entrepreneurs, chambers of commerce, employers' associations, and local institutions and authorities dealing with this matter.[4] The resulting *Rapport du Bureau des manufactures sur les réponses à la circulaire du 31 juillet 1837 relative à l'emploi des enfants dans les fabriques* presented data and information regarding the average age at which children started working (8–9 years), the usual duration of the work day (12–14 hours), wages, night shifts and work on Sundays, moral conduct, and education. The conclusions stated that factories were "if not a school which teaches mores, at least a school which teaches order, work, and submission" (Bureau des Manufactures, 1837). Two years later, the first parliamentary debate on the issue chiefly revealed a profound and widespread reluctance to question or jeopardise the principles of liberalism, even in the face of the universally acknowledged and deplored scourge of child exploitation. The urgency of the matter was unanimously recognised, largely on account of a – so to speak – "biopolitical" concern: the spread of rickets among the working-class population had a negative impact on military recruitment to the point that it came to constitute a national defence problem of general concern. "Here is one indisputable outcome: the manufacturing population is, in general, weaker and more feeble," argued deputy Billaudel, who nonetheless echoed the predominant tone by then adding: "one must blame those wretches whose lack of reason and foresight casts them into such a baleful condition; it is not industrialists who are to blame" (*Le Moniteur Universel*, 16 June 1839).[5] In this case too, then, the tendency was to reframe the problem within the field of discourses on the subaltern classes' moralisation. In the Chamber, Barbet argued:

> You have been told that *the race was being bastardised in the spinning mills*.... But it is not the mills alone that must be blamed for the population's

> rickets; it is parents' poor behaviour, excessive imbibing of strong drink, improvidence. . . . Seeking to establish the age at which children can start working in an absolute way, for the whole of France, would be a serious attack on industry and on paternal will.
>
> (*Le Moniteur Universel*, 16 June 1839, emphasis added)[6]

The need to face the health problems caused by child labour is therefore acknowledged yet seen as subordinate to the need not to undermine the principles of "freedom of trade and enterprise," of respecting "paternal authority," and fathers' rights to provide for their family even by sending their children off to work. This principled scepticism translates into a – typically liberal – political-juridical discourse on the inappropriateness of regulating the matter through a general national law that would "establish an absolute principle" regardless of the multiple factors that make the various areas of the country differ in terms of business, environment, climate, minors' health, etc. This law would "injure individual freedom as well as that of the head of family, and would exceed the boundaries of society's power,"[7] since – as jurist Pellegrino Rossi argues – "there are no social facts more diverse, more varied, than those pertaining to childhood; and yet they want to take these facts and generalise them in a peremptory way through a law" (*Journal Des Débats*, 5 March 1840, p. 3; similar arguments were also expressed by Gay-Lussac). Thus, as a result of the 1839 debate, Parliament merely committed the government to draft a project delegating the regulation of the matter to local authorities.

Several members of Parliament appealed to Villermé's enquiry, "the work of an impartial academic," often quoting him so inopportunely that he felt compelled to rectify their statements and explicitly side with the supporters of national law (Villermé, 1989, *Supplément* IV, pp. 595–619). These included philanthropists and Christian social theorists such as Villeneuve-Bargemont among the deputies, and Bigot de Morogues and Gérando among the peers (cf. § 3.1). Since it had already regulated the matter in 1833 – with a bill limiting the working day of minors under 13 years of age to eight hours – Britain was now presented as a "model" to be followed by the champions of the law in France (who also referred to the Prussian and Austrian cases), while opponents stressed the bill's limited application (on which see Kirby, 2003). The national law was also endorsed by the *Journal des débats*, which defended the rights of "young workers who die as victims of this excess of barbarism" (March 1840): the metaphor of barbarism, which Girardin had first introduced in this very newspaper a decade earlier to describe the workers involved in the Lyon insurrection (cf. § 2.1), was now applied to the employer side of the industrial world.

Relying on these position statements, and particularly on the commitment of Charles Dupin – a member and president-to-be of the ASMP – the parliamentary commission managed to radically change the government's project and to impose a new debate on the possible legislation. During the latter, a new prevalent orientation in favour of the national law gradually emerged. Eventually, on 22 March 1841, Parliament approved the *Loi relative au travail des enfants employés dans les manufactures, usines ou ateliers* (Dupin, 1840; Renouard, 1840). "The development of reports and debates in the Chamber of Deputies between 1837 and 1840 is remarkable," Claire Lemercier (2003) writes, stressing the role of treatises such as that by Villermé in this "acceleration" of the urgency perceived in the issue. The 1841 law echoes and addresses the points issued by the *Tableau*, thus revealing the way in which the social investigations of those years, which made the worker's condition an object of scientific enquiry, contributed to making it the focus of new welfare policies based on the broadening of the sphere of rights to that of labour.

4.2.2 The juridical codification of wage labour

The law of 22 March 1841 set age and working hour limits for children employed in factories with over twenty workers, in the textile sector and all other mechanised industries – that is, ones involving steam plants or mechanised furnaces. The minimum working age was set at eight years, while a maximum number of working hours per day was established depending on age (eight up to the age of twelve, twelve up to the age of sixteen). Work on Sundays, feast days, and at night was prohibited (with some rare exceptions for workers over the age of thirteen). The employment record book was now made mandatory also for child workers, as was education up to the age of twelve. Employers were forbidden from hiring children older than twelve who lacked an elementary diploma. Local authorities were allowed to change the law only in a restrictive sense, and fines – which increased for repeat offenders – were set for violations ascertained by *inspecteurs*. Yet, this aspect resulted in a very limited and intermittent application of the law, since at the end of the parliamentary procedure – and against the rapporteur's own advice – it was established that these inspectors were to be selected from among the *propriétaires* or *exploitants des établissements* (Guénau, 1927; Cabantous, 1842).

Entrusting entrepreneurs themselves with the task of checking for possible violations evidently meant reducing the impact of the law. Hence, for quite some time, the problem of the ineffectiveness of this bill has catalysed the attention of social, legal, and administrative historians. The history of welfare legislation has long focused on the law's limited application, not least based on an 1846 ruling by the Court of Cassation stating that a factory owner could not be held accountable for the absence from school of the children he employed. Furthermore, employers claimed that it was often workers themselves who hired children to help them with specific tasks – which reveals how employment was still largely informal and reminiscent of previous family and artisanal forms of labour. However, precisely with regard to this point, art. 9 of the 1841 law marked an important break insofar as it made it mandatory for employers to display the legislative text, along with the factory regulations, in their plants. Through the delimitation in art. 1 of its own field of application, the law further contributed to the definition of hitherto hazy notions such as *manufacture*, *usine*, *atelier*, and other crucial elements of the emergent industrial regime in France. As two reform bills were blocked by the 1848 revolution and the war of 1870, *loi 22 mars 1841* remained in force up until 1874 when it was replaced by an equally weak one: only in 1892 was a law finally introduced to make inspections systematic (Le Goff, 1985; Le Crom, 1998).

The limited application of the 1841 bill should not overshadow its radical symbolic significance. This lies in the fact that, for the first time in the post-revolutionary context, employment relationships became a field of legislation – that is, through the lawmaker, the state took the initiative and intervened for the first time *within* such a realm. The Le Chapelier laws of 1791 operated in the very opposite direction (cf. § 3.1), since they established a system where employment relationships were governed solely by private contracts – which the civil codes made legally binding – and the equality of citizens meant formal civil equality between the contracting parties. The law that Chaptal promoted in 1803 regarding the employment record book (cf. § 4.1) only concerned matters of debts and mobility that fell outside or beyond the employment relationship. Hence, the profound break marked by the 1841 law – from a political-juridical standpoint and in terms of the emergence of modern social protection measures – corresponds to the very act of legally regulating a sphere that had hitherto been deemed to fall outside the purview of political power. In the name of public interest, for the first time, the State pushed its sphere of regulation within the professional relationship between two individuals (and the relationship between family members), setting a legal limit to the principles of freedom of enterprise (and paternal authority) to defend the weakest part of society. Thus, political power entered the realm of industrial labour through legislation aimed at safeguarding a segment of the workforce and "immunising" a section of the population that the industrial regime was exposing to a socio-biological risk.

This constituted a small yet highly symbolic rift in the relationship between political liberalism and the principles of economic freedom. By imposing limits on daily working hours, night shifts, and labour on feast days, the 1841 law caused minors' status as wage labourers to become the object of pioneering welfare policies. To attain their juridical goal of protecting citizens, these policies had to affect and regulate the realm of employment relationships, which since the Great Revolution had been considered a private sphere inaccessible to state intervention. "For the first time since the abolition of guilds . . . in 1791, the government had taken it upon itself to outlaw trade in certain kinds of labour" (Reddy, 1984, p. 171). If only in the first part of his life, each worker came to enjoy a kind of "legal protection" specifically connected to his status as a wage labourer. In doing so, the law drew a primary formal distinction between a wage worker and the traditional figure of the semi-independent craftsman. It thus paved the way for a process of *juridical codification* of the wage labourer's condition destined to shape the development of industrial capitalism in Europe.[8]

In such a way, the law of 1841's rationality inaugurated the principles of modern *labour law*, paved the way for emerging policies of social protection, and foreshadowed a process of social integration based on a broadening of the juridical sphere to that of work. The strategies for the "immunisation," "defence," and hence "conservation" of society thus came to be redefined as an *integration* project that caused wage labour to become the chief means to access public protection systems and the main support for individuals' integration into the rights and duties of citizenship. Donzelot (1977, p. 57) speaks of a "spirit for the conservation of liberal society" which, starting with the contributions of the public health movement, encouraged "the State to step in through measures in the sphere of private law" by turning "the industrial sphere" into a focus of application and "support" for a system of "integration of citizens."

4.2.3 The "objectivation" of the working subject

"Generally speaking," deputy Corne argued in support of regulating child labour, "there is no weaker population that is more subject to rickets and more exposed to diseases – including some unknown to other social classes – than those making a living from manufacturing work" (*Journal des Débats*, 22 December 1840). In the debates on the 1841 law, we once again find the medical-hygienist approach to the social question that we have seen emerge and become crystallised in relation to the 1832 epidemic (cf. § 2.4 and 3.3.1). Yet, from the complexity of the urban subaltern classes, it was now transposed to and refocused on the specific domain of wage labour: this shift corresponded to a redefinition of the social question as a distinctly working-class one – that is, as a labour question. Social researchers actively took part in this shift because they did not merely describe society, but somehow contributed to "producing" it through allegedly scientific representations. Their investigations produced "truth effects" by conveying images of the world capable of influencing public opinion and driving public debate by virtue of their scientific vocation and the authoritativeness deriving from the use of public statistics and the mechanism of official competitions.

The figure of the (male) wage labourer gradually emerged at the centre of these representations, as the key subject in the diverse realm of the subaltern classes. This process developed in parallel with a semantic change in the word *ouvrier*, which – as we shall see in the next chapter – initially carried such a broad meaning as to include a range of professional figures simply sharing the manual nature of their work, and which later progressively came to be associated with a condition of industrial wage labour that was clearly distinguished from traditional crafts (cf. § 5.2). This condition became the object of growing investigations that laid the foundations for the "invention" of labour law. Hence, the working subject was to be established as the focus of emerging strategies of social protections, welfare policies, and citizenship rights designed to include the social and industrial realm into the sphere of governance in order to mitigate the "pathologies" and risks resulting from industrialisation.

The gradual focusing of enquiries into the social question on paid employment established the worker's condition as the object of a kind of knowledge that was to turn labour law into a specific discipline – at times intertwining it with those claims advanced by the nascent labour movement. It is from this perspective that we must understand the law on child labour as the first break with the dogma of State non-intervention in the field of economic relations and as a crucial step in the process of "objectivation" of the wage worker as a subject of policies, rights, and legislation. The 1841 bill inaugurated the juridical codification of employment relationships by which the condition of the wage labourer – a radically new role compared to the traditional crafts and long associated with job insecurity, exclusion, poverty, and marginality – became the linchpin of the modern welfare and social rights system centred on work. This juridification process went hand-in-hand with the semantic transformation of the term "worker," which now came to describe a specific condition of paid employment and no longer a wide range of different social and professional figures merely sharing the manual nature of their work (cf. § 5.2). This legal, political, and social definition of work subjectivity contributed to a paradigm shift whereby the strategy of "making the proletarian an owner" – which characterised the liberal discourse on the social question in the 1820s and 1830s – was progressively replaced by that of "fixing" and giving stability to workers so as to make wage labour the focus of public policies designed to reduce the social hazards resulting from industrialisation (Ewald, 1986, p. 206). This shift opened up the possibility for *property* – which had become the main means to exercise the rights and liberties established by the great Revolution – to be partly and progressively replaced by *labour* as the main avenue to access citizen rights. This meant that the figure of the *bourgeois citoyen* as property-owner could be complemented with that of the *citizen-worker*, making them the twin pillars of the new architecture of rights that was to emerge over the course of the 19th century.

The regulation of child labour paved the way for new welfare policies that made wage labour the pivot of an integration project based on the broadening of the juridical sphere through its penetration into the employment relationships of the industrial realm. This step laid the foundations for turning such relationships into the primary focus of modern social citizenship rights. This "translation" of the employment relationship into a juridical relationship was destined to acquire a central role in the aftermath of the 1848 revolution in France, namely in the emergence and spread of the claim to the *right to work* for all citizens and in the clash on the *ateliers nationaux* that determined the course of the revolutionary process (cf. Conclusion). Over the second half of the 19th century, then, the kind of safeguards granted to child labourers in 1841 were progressively granted to all wage labourers, establishing the worker as the specific subject of welfare and social security policies stemming from the complex intertwining between the labour movement's struggles and institutional strategies aimed at governing manpower and the inequalities produced by industrialisation.

4.3 From liberal enquiries to working-class and socialist ones

By regulating children's work on feast days and night shifts, the 1841 law foreshadowed key claims in the politics of the nascent labour movement. This leads us to the links between the developments we have observed so far in the institutional and liberal spheres, and those concerning the socialist and workers' field. "The history of the investigations into workers' conditions between 1830 and 1848 is the history of social reform," Hilde Rigaudias-Weiss writes (1936, p. 234), stressing the paradoxical character of this outcome with respect to the conservative aims originally driving these investigations.[9] Throughout the 1840s, the investigation practices initially developed in liberal and government milieus were progressively adopted by the labour, socialist, and social-republican opposition. In 1840, *L'Atelier* – a *Journal addressé aux ouvriers par des ouvriers* of Catholic inspiration – launched an enquiry into "workers' conduct," and similar initiatives were subsequently taken up by the *Journal du Peuple* in 1841, by Étienne Cabet's *Le Populaire* in 1842, and by Victor Considerant's *La Démocratie pacifique* in 1845.[10] This practice thus also became a means to support democratic and working-class claims. This was the case, for instance, with the major petition promoted by Ledru-Rollin, and published by *La Réforme* on 3 November 1844, in favour of an official parliamentary enquiry into the conditions of French workers. One hundred thirty thousand signatures were collected, but no deputy was willing to uphold the petition in Parliament.

Sprung from the search for new strategies to "defend society" and protect the bourgeois order, the practice of social investigation was therefore also adopted in contexts aimed at social emancipation and transformation. Yet, it never became exclusively used in the latter contexts, as is shown by the enquiry promoted by the government in 1848 to respond to social unrest. "Given the consequences of the revolutionary turmoil, the executive authorities asked the Academy of Moral and Political Sciences for its contribution": hence the ASMP's section of political economy entrusted to Adolphe Blanqui (1849, pp. 5–6) the task of "evaluating the exact situation of the working classes" for the purpose of "re-establishing moral order."[11] Later in that same year, however, on 10 May 1848, the National Assembly also voted for the establishment of a 36-member "commission of inquiry on the improvement of agricultural and industrial labour" that was charged with preparing the questionnaire for the inquiry and planning its implementation (Vidalenc, 1948).

These developments reveal that the genesis of empirical sociology in 19th-century France was marked by a tendency to make this emergent form of knowledge also a tool to be used in the political arena and in public debates – as had been the case with historiographical knowledge in the past (cf. § 2.1). A revealing element with respect to this dynamic is the public competition for the Beaujour prize launched by the Academy of Moral and Political Sciences shortly after the mission entrusted to Villermé and devoted to research aimed at "determining what poverty consists in and in what way it manifests itself." In 1840, the year in which the *Tableau* was published, the ASMP awarded the prize to Eugène Buret's research on *The Poverty of the Working Classes*, while criticising some of its socialistic tendencies.[12] "While Villermé's *Tableau* somehow marks the end of the 1830s, Buret's socialistic book, which Villermé was entrusted with presenting to the Academy, inaugurated the period of disquietude in social thinking in the 1840s," when "a powerful ideological opposition to liberalism . . . swept through the very sphere of intellectual power" (Demier, 1989, pp. 65–66).

Buret answered the Academy's call through a study on "the widespread, permanent, and progressive impoverishment of working-class populations" in France and Britain, thereby reasserting the specifically working-class character of the social question: "it is within this population's ranks . . . that pauperism, this threatening enemy of our civilisation, is recruited" (Buret, 1840, Vol. I, p. 69). A pupil of

Sismondi's, this author advances a historical criticism of capitalism that differs from that associated with the "Christian economics" of prominent philanthropists insofar as it denounces the inability of private philanthropy to make a significant impact on pauperism. By contrast, he affirms the need to "give all the victims of poverty, not public or private alms, but the means to emancipate themselves through work" (ibid., p. 88). Hence, the treatise develops an "apology for work" and of "redemption through work" by stressing its status as the only source of wealth, and hence the only legitimate foundation of property (ibid., p. 91). The problem of modern poverty would thus stem from the fact of having reduced labour to a mere "exchange value," by having failed to acknowledge its "moral value" and having subjected it "to all the whims of competition, without any safeguards." The solution, therefore, does not lie in charity, but in ensuring the dignity, protection, and stability of work (ibid., pp. 44 and 86–88).[13]

By adopting a historical perspective, this treatise develops a distinction between modern poverty and traditional poverty by highlighting the replacement of family-based work by factory work, which is marked by insecurity and de-skilling: "in the current regime, work lacks any security, safeguard, and protection" (Buret, 1840, Vol. I, p. 70). Distancing himself from Villermé's approach in this respect, Buret highlights the radical contradictions of industrial capitalism and thus explicitly criticises the ideology of economic liberalism. In his view, recurrent devastating crises represent an intrinsic feature of this system rather than an exception. Far less notable from the point of view of empirical and methodological research than Villermé's *Tableau*, this treatise chiefly stands out on account of its theoretical-political perspective, whose scientific character Buret affirms to support a plan for "peaceful, positive reforms." This plan points to the contradiction between the economic regime governing industry and the principles underlying the development of civilisation. By highlighting this tension, he points to the shortcomings of that "social science which, under the name of political economy, has sought and believed to have found the laws of nations' prosperity" (ibid., p. 11). In Buret's view, political economy had – after Smith – exclusively focused on wealth, neglecting the governing of men and the organising of their happiness, which was this discipline's original aspiration (Ricardo is indicated as the chief representative of this tendency to turn economics into a science akin to mathematics, by detaching it from ethics). Against this "ontology of wealth," Buret upholds a "physiology of society" as a science studying the social fabric in its living functioning, including the relations between social classes, where poverty and wealth feed each other. This science also considers and studies the other factor associated with wealth, namely poverty; hence, Buret champions a *social economy* capable of transcending and reframing the political economy's main assumptions (even in its charitable-Christian version). What lies at the centre of this perspective is the criticism of an economic doctrine that "has always limited its object to the point of being little more than an abstract theory of production and values" (ibid., p. 5), thereby concealing its intrinsically historical and political nature through its claim to have a scientific status.

This investigation of economic principles, methods, and concepts thus foreshadows the critique of political economy which was to acquire a central role in the nascent socialist discourse, particularly as developed by Marx. Significantly, when the latter author arrived in Paris in 1843, he obtained a copy of *La misère des classes laborieuses en Angleterre et en France*, which he quoted three times in his *Economic-Philosophical Manuscripts* of 1844.[14] Buret's reflections on how political economists do not "acknowledge" workers "as men but only as a means of production" (1840, p. 68) would appear to have largely influenced this text by Marx. This is particularly the case with the concept of wages as an exchange value that measures labour as good in an abstract way, and with the description of the alienated representation of man provided by political economy.

This leads us to the topic of the next chapter, as it reveals how any genealogy of wage labour's subjectivity in 19th-century France must pay attention to the intersections and relations between the representations of the social question that emerged in the liberal-institutional field and in the nascent social sciences, and those which took shape through the emergence of a working-class and socialist discourse. The establishment of wage labour as the pillar of modern social citizenship also emerge from the mutual influences and interplays between, on the one hand, the processes of "objectivation" of the figure of the worker as a focus of knowledge and administration that we have observed so far and, on the other, those "subjectivation" processes that came to be known as the "labour movement" (which will be the focus of the next chapters). In other words, to retrace the way in which labour acquired a major position in the systems of citizen rights that emerged over the course of the 19th century, we must grasp the combined effects of the development of strategies to govern the social question centred on wage labour's juridical codification and the growth of a discourse focusing on the subaltern classes' emancipation that came to revolve around the figure of the wage labourer. It is this latter side, concerning the processes of political subjectivation and emancipation of labour, that we will now turn to examine.

Notes

1 The report by the Council of State reads: "In decreeing the absolute freedom of enterprise, the Constituent Assembly could not foresee fraud. The habit of breaching one's work commitments has become so universal among workers that it is impossible to rely on their cooperation; hence, it emerges that manufacturers are prevented from drawing up employment contracts out of fear that they might be forced to relinquish them before their fulfilment," cit. in Bernard (1903, p. 11).

2 Ewald (1986, p. 113) stresses how Chaptal, who served as Minister of the Interior in the years 1800–04, was the first to envisage industry as a national matter of public interest starting with the problem of the relations with Britain's trading power: "hence the creation . . . of a device [the book] destined to structure government action, industrialists' enterprise, and workers' labour into a harmonious whole, a system of mutual support." Antecedents of the employment record book can be found in medieval guilds; their use was then regulated by the Royal Council of State in 1740 and by an edict in 1776. Hence, it was only between 1791 and 1807 that workers enjoyed full freedom to move

from one factory to another. On the laws of 1791 and other measures against labour associations, cf. § 3.1.

3 Catholics too played a role, albeit a minor one (Abbé Ferry of Nancy promoted a similar petition). Among industrialists, a crucial contribution was provided, from as early as the late 1820s, by the *Société industrielle de Mulhouse*.

4 This kind of survey of "interests" is reminiscent, on the one hand, of the kind of expertise practices that had long been introduced in Britain, and, on the other, of those self-reflective practices involving the government and society that were typical of the capacity-based theories of the doctrinaires (cf. § 1.4). It is worth noting that the workers themselves were not included among those "affected."

5 Similar arguments are also found in the 1837 enquiry conducted by the Ministry of Trade: "even if children were not employed in factories, they would suffer the same kind of ill-treatment. This is due to their misfortune at birth and to the bad habits of the popular class to which they belong. Therefore, one must not blame industry alone. One must chiefly rely on the progress of mores for the disappearance of these forms of ill-treatment, as well as most of the ills affecting the working-class population" (quoted in Villermé, 1989, p. 429). On these debates, see Lynch (1988) and Sueur (1989). The "corruption of mores" stemming from the concentration of minors of either sex in manufacturing plants constituted as much of a concern as their physical deterioration and lack of education.

6 Racial metaphors are widely used in the debate, where child labour is described as "white slavery" and Montalember states: "if agriculture destroyed bovine or equine breeds to such a degree, an attempt would immediately be made to improve its operational methods" (*Journal des Débats*, 5 and 6 March 1840).

7 Cf. Deputy and Minister Cunin-Gridaine's address in *Le Moniteur Universel*, 16 June 1839 and Taillandier's address in *Journal des Débats*, 2 December 1840. The speakers further invoke demographic reasons as well as those pertaining to the new production methods that, they claim, make free access to child labour essential. In accordance with the classic liberal approach, the opponents of a bill on this matter called for the promotion of public recognitions and awards for industrialists committed to improving child workers' conditions, while rejecting the idea of a reform imposed by law.

8 In 1910 the establishment of the first real labour code in France was to mark a crucial outcome of such a project: see Dolléans (1936), Dehove (1955), Le Goff (1985), Cross (1989), and Le Crom (1998).

9 Rigaudias-Weiss identifies popular uprisings as a central factor that, as a reaction, led the Academy of Moral and Political Sciences to carry out investigations into workers' conditions. She stresses the importance of Buret's and Villermé's investigations in relation both to future socialist theories (particularly as documentary sources) and the nascent labour legislation.

10 Among the very first investigations into workers' conditions launched by the labour or socialist movement, we must recall – in addition to the famous writings on *compagnonnage* (cf. § 5.2) by Agricol Perdiguier (1841, 1854) – a succinct enquiry into the "condition of the various social strata" published by *L'Artisan* as early as 1830, as well as Louis Blanc's *Organisation du travail* (1839), which draws upon data collected from 830 factories.

11 Hence the treatise *Des classes ouvrières en France pendant l'année 1848* by Adolphe Blanqui (1849), who was Louis-Auguste's brother (cf. § 6.2) and J. B. Say's successor as the chair of Political Economy.

12 The 5,000-franc quinquennial "Beaujour" award was introduced in 1834 – in the wake of the *canuts'* second insurrection – and eventually split into three different prizes in 1840 on Villermé's recommendation. Only a section of Buret's treatise won the award (Picot, 1901).

13 "Our fathers have gloriously rehabilitated work . . . after this magnificent apology for work, which is not opposed by anyone in the civilised world," mankind "is now left with the task of . . . rehabilitating work in practice, as it has already been rehabilitated in theory" (Buret, 1840, Vol. I, p. 48).

14 Buret's work is also referred to in the notebooks that Marx drafted in Brussels between February and June 1845 (Rigaudias-Weiss, 1936, pp. 134–157). Note, however, that Buret states his hostility towards both Communism and class conflicts, presenting industrial poverty as a necessarily transitory condition, just like slavery.

References

Arnaud C. (1856), *Du livret d'ouvrier*, Camoin, Marseille.

Bernard H. (1903), *Le livret ouvrier. Thèse pour le doctorat devant la Faculté de Droit de l'Université de Lyon*, Rousseau, Lyon.

Blanc L. (1839), *L'organisation di travail*, Administration de librairie, Paris.

Blanqui A. (1849), *Des classes ouvrières en France pendant l'année 1848*, Paulin, Paris.

Bureau des Manufactures. (1837), *Rapport du bureau des manufactures sur les reponses à la circulaire du 31 juillet 1837 relative a l'emploi des enfants dans les fabriques*, Imprimerie Royale, Paris.

Buret E. (1840), *De la Misère des classes laborieuses en Angleterre et en France: de la nature de la misère, de son existence, de ses effets, de ses causes, et de l'insuffisance des remèdes qu'on lui a opposés jusqu'ici, avec les moyens propres à en affranchir les sociétés*, 2 vol., Paulin, Paris.

Cabantous L. (1842), *Instructions pratiques sur la loi relative au travail des enfants dans les manufactures*, Corbeil, Crétéil.

Campesi G. (2009), *Genealogia della pubblica sicurezza. Teoria e storia del moderno dispositivo poliziesco*, Ombre Corte, Verona (Eng. trans. *A Genealogy of Public Security. The Theory and History of Modern Police Powers*, Routledge, London and New York 2016).

Castel R. (1995), *Les Métamorphoses de la question sociale, une chronique du salariat*, Gallimard, Paris (Eng. trans. *From Manual Workers to Wage Laborers: Transformation of the Social Question*, Transaction, New Brunswick, NJ 2003).

Cère P. (1853), *Livret d'ouvrier, précédé d'un petit Manuel à l'usage des ouvriers*, Libraire du Conseil d'État, Paris.

Cottereau A. (2002), Droit et bon droit. Un droit des ouvriers instauré, puis évincé par le droit du travail. *Annales. Histoire, Sciences Sociales*, 57(6): 1521–1557.

Cross G.S. (1989), *A Quest for Time. The Reduction of Work in Britain and France, 1840–1940*, University of California Press, Berkeley.

Dehove G. (1955), *Histoire du travail en France. Mouvement ouvrier et législation sociale, vol. 1: Des origines à 1919*, Domat-Montchresten, Paris.

Demier F. (1989), *Le Tableau de Villermé et les enquêtes ouvrières du premier XIXe siècle*, prefazione a Villermé (1989), pp. 1–49.

Dolléans É. (1936), *Histoire du mouvement ouvrier*, vol. I, Collin, Paris.

Donzelot J. (1977), *La police de familles*, Minuit, Paris.

Dewerpe A. (2010), En avoir ou pas. À propos du livret d'ouvrier dans la France du XIX siècle, in A. Stanziani (ed.), *Le travail contraint en Asie et en Europe. XVIIème – XXème siècles*, Éditions de la Maison de Sciences de l'Homme, Paris, pp. 217–239.

Dupin C. (1840), *Du travail des enfants qu'emploient les ateliers, les usines et les manufactures*, Bachelie, Paris.

Ewald F. (1986), *L'État providence*, Grasset, Paris.

Foucault M. (2013), *La Société punitive. Cours au Collège de France 1972–1973*, Gallimard-Seuil, Paris (Eng. trans. *The Punitive Society. Lectures at the Collège de France 1972–1973*, ed. A.I. Davidson, Palgrave Macmillan UK 2015).

Gaudemar J-P. de. (1982), *L'ordre et la production. Naissance et formes de la discipline d'usine*, Dunod, Paris.
Guénau L. (1927), La législation restrictive du travail des enfants: La loi française du 22 mars 1841. *Revue d'histoire économique et sociale*, 15: 420–503.
Journal des Débats. (1814–1944), Paris. Retrieved from: https://catalogue.bnf.fr/ark:/12148/cb39294634r
Kaplan S.L. (1979), *Réflexions sur la police du monde du travail (1700–1815). Revue historique*, cclxi, 17 gennaio-marzo: 17–77.
Kirby P. (2003), *Child Labour in Britain, 1750–1870*, Macmillan, Palgrave.
Le Crom J.P. (dir.) (1998), *Deux siècles de droit du travail. L'histoire par les lois*, l'Atelier, Paris.
Le Crom J.P. (2003), Le livret ouvrier au XIXe siècle entre assujettissement et reconnaissance de soi, in Y. Le Gall, D. Gaurier (dir.), *Du droit du travail aux droits de l'humanité. Études offertes à Philippe-Jean Hesse*, PUR, Rennes, pp. 91–100.
Le Goff J. (1985), *Du silence à la parole. Droit du travail, société, état (1830–1985)*, Calligrammes, Quimper.
Le Moniteur Universel. (1811–1901), Paris. Retrieved from: https://catalogue.bnf.fr/ark:/12148/cb344523379
Lemercier C. (2003), La chambre de commerce de Paris, acteur indispensable de la construction des normes économiques. *Genèses*, 50(1): 50–70.
Lynch A. (1988), *Family, Class, and Ideology in Early Industrial France: Social Policy and the Working-Class Family 1825–1848*, UWP, Madison.
Perdiguier A. (1841), *Le Livre du Compagnonnage*, Pagnerre, Paris.
Perdiguier A. (1854), *Mémoires d'un Compagnon*, Duchamp, Paris.
Picot G. (1901), *Concours de l'Académie: sujets proposés, prix et récompenses décernés, liste des livres couronnés ou récompensés, 1834–1900*, Institut de France, Paris.
Plantier A. (1900), *Le livret des ouvriers. Thèse de droit*, Jouve et Boyer, Paris.
Reddy W.M. (1984), *The Rise of Market Culture: The Textile Trade and French Society, 1750–1900*, CUP, Cambridge.
Renouard A.C. (1840), *Rapport fait au nom de la Commission chargée de l'examen du projet de loi relatif au travail des enfants*, Henry, Paris.
Rigaudias-Weiss H. (1936), *Les Enquêtes ouvrières en France entre 1830 et 1848*, Elix Alcan, Paris.
Sacchi Landriani M. (2019), Rethinking the Livret D'ouvriers: Time, Space and 'Free' Labor in Nineteenth Century France. *Labor History*, 60(6): 854–864. doi: 10.1080/0023656X.2019.1645318
Sauzet M. (1890), *Le Livret obligatoire des ouvriers*, Pichon, Paris.
Sueur P. (1989), La loi du 22 mars 1841. Un débat parlementaire: l'enfance protégée ou la liberté offensée, in J-L. Harouel (dir.), *Histoire du droit social. Mélanges en hommage à Jean Imbert*, PUF, Paris, pp. 493–508.
Vidalenc J. (1948), Les résultats de l'enquête sur le travail prescrite par l'Assemblée Constituante dans le département de l'Eure, in *Actes du Congrès du centenaire de la révolution de 1848*, PUF, Paris, pp. 325–341.
Villermé L-R. (1837), Discours sur la durée trop longue du travail des enfants dans beaucoup de manufactures. *Annales d'hygiène publique*, t. 28: 164–176.
Villermé L-R. (1843a), Quelques considérations sur la taille, la conformation et la santé des enfants et des adolescents dans les mines des huile de la Grande-Bretagne. *Annales d'hygiène publique*, t. 30: 28–43.

Villermé L-R. (1843b), Du travail et des condition des enfants et des adolescents dans les mines de la Grande Brétagne. *Journal des économistes*, February: 35–70.

Villermé L-R. (1989), *Tableau de l'état physique et moral des ouvriers employés dans les manifactures de coton, de laine et de soie*, Études et documentations internationales, Paris (or. ed. Renouard, Paris 1840).

Weissbach L.S. (1989), *Child Labor Reform in Nineteenth-Century France: Assuring the Future Harvest*, LSUP, Baton Rouge.

Part II

Subjects: Work as politics

5 The rise of the working class

"As every social historian knows, in Lyon in November 1831, the proud *canuts* brought the working class onto the stage of universal history," Jacques Rancière (1985, p. 34) writes, pointing to the field of tension that will be our focus in the following pages: the field that opens up between a specific *event* – "Lyon in November 1831" – and the emergence of a *conceptual structure* – "the working class" – destined to become entrenched in everyday language and to exercise powerful "truth effects" for almost a century and a half. This second part of the book focuses on the genesis – or "invention" – of such a conceptual structure. It retraces the way in which the *working class* became a "collective singular" (Koselleck, 1975, 1979), that is, a single consistent notion able to encompass and include the various representations that were previously associated with the complex universe of the subaltern classes. To do so, the next two chapters investigate the rise of the modern labour movement, understood as the process of "subjectivation" of wage workers as a political collective actor, or subjectivity: a process that unfolded in parallel with the "objectivation" of the labour world as a field of knowledge and administration that I have described in the first part of this book.

To explore the *political subjectivation of labour*, we will return to the 1831 uprising of the Lyonnais weavers – *la révolte des canuts* – from which this investigation set out in the first chapter. As we will see, historians have envisaged this event as the symbolic point of origin for the modern labour movement in Europe. Since the definition of its origin has always shaped the way in which the very nature of subjectivity is understood, the present chapter observes how different historical interpretations of the Lyon insurrection have nurtured different conceptions of the very notion of the working class and of its political ontology. It will, therefore, establish a field of tension between the 1831 event, to be grasped within its specific context, and the representations that have sought to assign it a position and meaning in history. Among these, I will first consider the canonical interpretation provided by *Marxist historiography* (§ 5.1) to retrace how the Lyonnais insurrection was constructed as the moment of "birth" of the modern labour movement, that is, as the watershed event that determined the emergence of a new social and political subjectivity destined to change the course of history. Subsequently, I will investigate the way in which this interpretation was challenged and transformed by different ways of understanding the ontology of the working class, such as those

DOI: 10.4324/9781003303497-8

produced first by the *new social history* school (§ 5.2) and then by the impact of the so-called *linguistic turn* in social and labour history research (§ 5.3). It is in the light of these interpretations that the next chapter analyses the way in which the Lyon insurrection was understood and represented by its contemporaries – namely by 1830s and 1840s sources belonging to the working-class, republican, and socialist field – to provide an original reading of the genesis of the labour movement in the 19th century. In the conclusion, I will then consider how an architecture of rights revolving around the citizen-worker – that is, a model of citizenship and a system of social recognition based on labour – emerged through the interaction between the processes of "objectivation" and "subjectivation" of labour work described in the two parts of this book.

5.1 The labour movement's first word?

As early as 1827, forty-odd Lyonnais weavers took the pioneering initiative of establishing a mutual aid association (*Association Mutuelle*) to defend themselves against commercial crises and international competition. More than anyone else, it was Pierre Charnier who had made the Lyonnais waivers (the *canuts*) aware of the "need and art of becoming associated," by creating – in the footsteps of guild traditions and *compagnonnage* – a secret society divided into small lodges to find a way around the coalition bans imposed by the Le Chapelier Laws in the aftermaths of the 1789 revolution (cf. § 3.1). Within a short time, mutualism in Lyon gave rise to 122 lodges, which by the end of 1833 had 2,400 members – almost half of the city's *chefs d'atelier*, or master weavers (cf. § 5.2). By drawing upon this mutual aid experience, in the autumn of 1831, the associated weavers mobilised to demand a minimum price (*tarif au minimum*) for works commissioned from them by silk merchants (*fabriquants*), committing themselves not to accept any commissions below this rate. To this end, they each paid the *Association Mutuelle* a fee to ensure that "the *chef d'atelier* may receive a franc a day for each loom left vacant" as a consequence of rejecting a work offered at a lower rate.[1] However, the *fabriquants* refused to negotiate and denounced the workers' violation of the principle of the freedom of enterprise by submitting a *Mémoire* to the Chamber (Baron, 1832, pp. 37–55). Hence, by mid-November over 4,000 looms had become inactive:

> Seeing that all their efforts to make it out of the abyss of poverty into which they had been cast had borne no fruits, [the *canuts*] tried one last course of action. After a consultation, they decided to bring all looms to a halt. . . . they sought to stop working until the merchants, tired of the delays with their commissions, would finally agree to pay for them according to the *tarif*; but the possibility also remained open that the workers themselves, driven by necessity, would be forced to return to work and submit to the victors' law.

Thus write weavers Bernard and Charnier (n.d., p. 7) in their report for the government, enunciating principles destined to give rise the modern right to strike: a right based on the test of strength between two "equal rights," "both equally bearing the seal of the law of exchanges," to use the expressions by which Marx's *Capital* (1967, pp. 235 and 301) was to describe the "protracted civil war, more or less dissembled, between the capitalist class and the working class." But on 21 November 1831, when the workers' smocks found themselves facing the national guard uniforms donned by the merchants on the Grande-Côte, this "dissembled" conflict actually took the form of a violent battle that lasted three days and in which 170 people were killed and several hundred wounded.

When the first clash cost eight workers their lives, the *canuts* picked up shovels, sticks, pitchforks, and a few rifles, melted cutlery down into bullets, demolished pavements, and raised barricades. Women and children stood at the windows armed with rocks and tiles, repelling all incursions and pushing the army and civilian militia away from the Croix-Rousse area – which was the economic centre of Lyon's silk industry almost entirely inhabited by weavers. Lieutenant Rouget then summoned the national guard, but only a few hundred men out of 15,000 answered the call. The order, however, sparked a reaction from the workers, who set fire to the toll houses on Pont du Concert, attacked and ransacked garrisons, and erected barricades on city bridges. The resistance in Croix-Rousse then turned into a general offensive on Lyon when the working-class suburbs of Brotteaux and Guillotière joined in. As the din of battle grew louder, over a barricade in Croix-Rousse a black flag was raised emblazoned with the words *Vivre en travaillant ou mourir en combattant*: the name *canuts* was to become inextricably linked to this catchphrase. Was this the labour movement's "first word' in Europe?

In The Fourth Annual Report by the General Council of the International Workingmen's Association (1869), Marx recalled this slogan to celebrate the growing support which the association was enjoying in Lyon "among that heroic population which more than thirty years ago inscribed upon its banner the watchword of the modem proletariat" (Marx, 1869). Ten years later, Paul Lafargue indicated the Lyon insurrection as the first struggle exclusively waged by the working class: "it goes to the everlasting credit of the working-class population of Lyon that they were the first to raise the flag of proletarian struggle: *either live and work or die fighting*."[2] Likewise, in 1913 Lenin regarded "the uprising of the Lyons weavers" as "the embryonic class struggle of the proletariat, which was only just beginning to emerge as something different from the common mass of the petty-bourgeois "people" (Lenin, 1913, Eng. transl. 1977, p. 295). Hence, after the 1917 revolution, the Soviet authorities promoted historical research on this matter, starting from the 1929 work in which E.V. Tarle (1929, p. 133) described "the Lyon insurrection of 1831" as "marking a turn in the history of the working class, not just in France but in the whole world."[3] The relevance of these references fully accounts for the importance that Marxism and the historiography of the labour movement have attributed to the 1831 events as a point of origin and foundational moment. The Lyon insurrection thus came to be "generally considered to mark the beginning of the modern labour movement" (Rudé, 1984, p. 184).

A relevant role in the development of this general opinion would appear to have been played by Engels' analysis of the effects of the Lyon events on the history of ideas. "In 1831, the first working-class rising took place in Lyons," he writes,

who ranked it among the facts "which led to a decisive change in the conception of history":

> The class struggle between proletariat and bourgeoisie came to the front in the history of the most advanced countries in Europe, in proportion to the development . . . of modern industry. . . . But the old idealist conception of history . . . knew nothing of class struggles based upon economic interests. . . . The new facts made imperative a new examination of all past history. Then it was seen that *all* past history was the history of class struggles.
>
> (Engels 2006, p. 51)

The subsequent developments of the historiography of the labour movement would appear to have been extensively influenced by this framework, which identifies *industrialisation* – "the development of the modern industry" – as the driving force for historical discontinuity, to which the emergence of the first specifically working-class struggles should be attributed. From this angle, the 1831 insurrection is thus represented as the "endpoint of one period and the starting point of another," which marked the irruption of "a new social force, the working class," to quote Fernand Rude (1944, pp. 22, 43), who devoted several works to the *révolte des canuts* and Lyonnais mutualism, stressing its "truly modern spirit, akin to contemporary trade unions" (Rude, 2007, p. 187).[4] In the wake of Engels' theses and Soviet historiography, the 20th century brought an understanding of the 1831 insurrection as the "first appearance on history's stage of proletarians as a class" (Thorez, 1974, p. 13), which stimulated theoretical developments by "ushering in a new generation of socialists" (Droz, 1972, p. 361) and revealing "the slow evolution of the working-class masses parallel to industrial growth" (Aguet, 1954, p. 47).[5]

Up until the 1970s, historiographical analysis was dominated by this approach, which assigned meaning to the Lyon events by emphasising that it embodied a double break. On the one hand, there was a discontinuity with previous *social* uprisings, such as *jacqueries*, food riots, and the ransacking of bakers" ovens, which chiefly appeared as "irrational" and "unpolitical" acts. On the other, there was the break with previous *political* unrest, such as the 1789 and 1830 revolutions in France, which had always been marked by the bourgeoisie's presence and prominent role. By stressing this double discontinuity, Marxist historiography made it possible to envisage the Lyonnais insurrection of 1831 as a point of origin, that is to say: as a watershed moment that provides a polarised representation of the "old" and the "new" according to a teleological trajectory which assigns a direction to history and a meaning to events, a trajectory culminating in the image of the organised industrial working class. By being assigning the status of a point of origin, the 1831 events are framed within a destiny of "maturity" coinciding with the configuration of the 20th-century labour movement: "certainly, nothing was ripe yet, but everything was there in embryonic form" (Rude, 1944, p. 736). In this interpretation, the features of the working class in the mature industrial era shape the image of the past and, with it, that of the *révolte des canuts* as the "birth," "baptism," and "first word" of a new socio-historical subjectivity sprung from the Industrial Revolution.

5.2 *Ouvriers*

The fact that *ouvriers*' (workers) is the term which the *canuts* used to refer to themselves and by which they were described in public debates has no doubt favoured and justified the interpretation considered so far. However, from the 1830s sources it is clear that this term carried a different meaning from that it was to acquire during the history of the labour movement, and by which it shaped the notion of "working class" as it became part of contemporary political vocabulary. Largely synonymous with craftsman, *ouvrier* would appear to have been used in those years simply as a rough definition of the manual labourer as anyone who makes a living through his or her physical work. For instance, the 1835 edition of the *Dictionnaire de l'Académie française* (vol. 2, p. 323) defines the *ouvrier* as someone "who usually labours with his hands and produces some kind of work to earn a living," and, significantly, does not list the expression "working class" among the common usages of the term "class" (vol. 1, p. 327). Rey (1992, pp. 2511–2512) underlines that *ouvrier* "has been used in its modern sense since 1155," as a term to describe any provision of manual labour that served as a 'synonym' for craftsman up until the 17th century. In other words, as Gossez stresses (1956, p. 442), "by 'worker' [we are to] understand a manual labourer, this term being merely an approximation of his social condition."

In its generic polysemy the term *ouvrier* would therefore appear to encapsulate and express the wide range of figures and factors constituting the labour world of the early 19th century, to which the use of the term "working class" *in the singular* still remained quite foreign. For instance, in the wake of the insurrection the Mayor of Lyon addressed "workers of all classes" (Baron, 1832, p. 36), and the Orléanist newspaper *Le Temps* described the event by speaking of the "sum of Lyonnais working classes" (2 December 1831), and Jean-Baptiste Monfalcon (1834, p. 80) described it as "the general insurrection of workers of all classes." The plural form of these expressions conveys not just the polysemy and broad meaning of the word *ouvirer* and the heterogeneity of the labour world of the time, but also the specific condition of the *canuts* insofar as, in the weavers' milieu, the term *ouvriers* designated at least three different figures.

The first was that of the *maîtres* or *chefs d'atelier* (master weavers), who promoted mutualism and led the conflict that culminated in the insurrection. These were artisans proud of their profession who worked independently on their own looms, in laboratories which they either owned or rented, and which were often also the homes in which they lived with their family, who usually played some role in the manufacturing process. Jules Favre, the lawyer defending these craftsmen and self-employed workers against the charge of "industrial conspiracy," argued that the article of the penal code concerning this crime "only applies to the workers' class, which does not include *chefs d'atelier*" (Favre, 1833, p. 22). This conclusion was based on the observation that, even if they personally work on looms, *chefs d'atelier* cannot be considered "manpower," that is, workers who sell their manual labour.[6]

The manpower *strictu sensu* instead includes, first of all, *compagnons*, who were recruited, on a more or less temporary basis, to work on the *maîtres*' looms.

Their condition was marked by job insecurity, spatial mobility, and often an alternation between farming and industry.[7] Therefore, "the term *ouvrier* continued to be used to refer to both *maîtres* and their employees, and it was only in our century that an *ouvrier* became, by definition, not only someone performing manual labour, but employed by an entrepreneur" (Rudé, 1984, pp. 214–215). *Compagnons*, moreover, often lived in the *atelier* where they worked, which is to say on the *maîtres*' property. They entertained a professional relationship with the latter based on paternalism and received wages from them in the form of a fixed quota on the price paid by the silk merchants for the finished product. Thus the bond of solidarity between *maîtres* and *compagnons* de facto outweighed the conflicts entailed by the relation of subordination: indeed, the two categories immediately became close allies in the 1831 insurrection.

Alongside these two main figures of the silk industry – *chefs d'atelier* and *compagnons* – we also find boys between the ages of 15 and 20 who were hired as apprentices; women, who would carry out less taxing tasks such as packing for lower wages; and children, who were employed to cast the silk thread shuttle in the manufacturing of composite fabrics. The surrounding activities performed by *ouvriers* in charge of folding, dyeing, or washing the fabric complete the picture of this industry in Lyon. Here, the textile sector employed over 80,000 workers – 30–40,000 *compagnons*, 8–10,000 *chefs d'atelier* (each owning six-eight looms on average), and almost 800 merchants – making it the largest manufacturing centre on the Continent. Its economic fabric was marked by a high level of industrialisation, which nevertheless did not yet coincide with the concentration of production into big factory units with a high degree of mechanisation, but rather took the form of a range of small manufacturing enterprises.

The outline just provided gives us an idea of the crucial fact that, for most of the 20th century, the labour movement's historiography identified its object's symbolic point of origin with an initiative that was actually taken by subjects who were still clearly artisan figures. These were small loom *owners* operating within a socio-economic context that had yet to undergo many of the transformations grouped under the label of "Industrial Revolution," which gave shape to the way in which the concepts of labour and social class were defined in the contemporary political vocabulary.[8] In other words, these figures display crucial differences with respect to the established idea of the worker, which is primarily defined on the basis of its place within the system of division of work and of the ownership of the means of production. "A citizen working from home on looms he owns, and not a proletarian, as political passions or interests would have it," writes Monfalcon (1834, p. 31) to describe *chef d'atelier*'s condition and its formal independence from the *fabriquant*. Similar issues also concern the idea of the capitalist, insofar as the insurgent workers' "counterpart," the silk merchants, were the owners only of silk emporia, whose work consisted in receiving commissions for finished goods, purchasing the raw material, and handing it in – together with the designs to be realised – to *chefs d'atelier* hired on the basis of a *prix de façon* for each delivery. They embodied a very different figure from that of the capitalist owner of the means of production, not least because *fabriquants* did not directly employ anyone (except for pattern designers). Like the term "worker," that of "entrepreneur" did not yet have a clear, unambiguous meaning in these years: in France terms such as *patron* and employer only became common legal terms after 1848, while the previous debates were still dominated by the words *chef*, *propriétaire*, and *exploitant de la manifacture*.

We can thus see that the economic conflict which led to the 1831 revolt was not marked by any employment relationship or direct subordination to entrepreneurs' orders. Those credited with having uttered the "first word" of the labour movement – with the "first typically working-class insurrection" (Lefranc, 1957, p. 286) – were social figures whose defining features predate the establishment of the industrial system of the division of labour and the ownership of the means of production by which the very notion of working class was to acquire intelligibility and political significance. From this perspective, it may be argued that the *labour movement* was born *before* the *working class*, because it had already emerged in an artisan context that was predominantly domestic and family-based, and founded on a wide range of workshops scattered throughout the urban fabric, according to a "technical composition" of labour to which the equation involving industrialisation and the concentration of production in factory units was still wholly foreign.[9] What Marxist historiography has long described as the birth of the labour movement, then, was the initiative of artisans operating from their own home workshops, and not of factory workers who would sell their own manpower to a capitalist. This simple yet crucial contingency suggests the opportunity to rethink the genesis of the labour movement and of the very notion of working class by shifting the main analytical framework from the technical-industrial domain to that of social, political, and cultural factors.

5.3 The artisans' last stand

Villermé's *Tableau* devotes considerable space to the *fabrique* and *canuts* of Lyon, stressing their shared professional identity, civic spirit, fair degree of education, and eagerness to assert their independence from merchants. The latter only establish rates and delivery times, but "do not have a workshop of their own, do not own any plant in which workers work under their eyes or those of their employees." Therefore, "between the *fabriquant* and the workers he employs, there is no real patronage relationship" Villermé (1989, pp. 353–354 and 356; cf. pp. 341–399 on the silk industry in Lyon). Since it was the weavers who established the pace and form of their own work, we do not find the kind of subordination that specifically defines the relationship of employed labour and, with it, our contemporary notions of worker and entrepreneur. However, one of the aspects which vividly emerges from Villermé's enquiry is precisely the "fraying" of this artisan fabric through the growing encroachment of capital and mechanised industry. Highlighting this aspect, Charles Tilly (1986) also emphasised the pressure exercised by silk merchants to broaden their authority by using capital to limit artisans' autonomy.[10] This pressure was chiefly exercised by legal means, for instance, by using rent debts to gain possession of looms and drive *canuts* into a condition close to that of wage labourers. This contributed to reducing the artisans' power to decide what to manufacture and in what quantities, and increased their subordination to and state of dependence on the merchants – who were already the owners of the raw material and at times even of the workshop that was being let.

In the light of these elements, from a given moment onwards, some historians began to frame the 1831 mobilisation not so much as the first specifically working-class insurrection as a staunch display of artisan resistance against the effects of capital's impact on traditional craft professions. Through this angle, the Lyon events can be seen as a struggle in defence of one's own professional independence and against the change of one's condition into that of a wage labourer: against, we might say, the growing pressure to *become-the-working-class*, or become wage workers.

This perspective was chiefly developed from the 1960s onwards by a kind of historiography seeking to free the understanding of the modern working class' genesis from the determinism that had led it to be regarded as one of the necessary effects of an economic process, the Industrial Revolution, envisaged as a force generating a radically new subjectivity: the industrial worker "sprung" from the factory system. Starting with Edward Palmer Thompson's "new social history," this deterministic idea was challenged by rethinking the concept of class in terms of a "socio-historical formation" resulting from a variety of events that cannot be confined to the economic-industrial sphere, but which significantly also reflect political and cultural processes.[11] Hence the growing interest in sources constituting an expression of the labour world which bear witness to its political cultures, forms of sociability, everyday life, and urban experiences. Such elements have led this historiography to assign a crucial role to *guild traditions* as a factor shaping the mobilisations that mark the emergence of the modern labour movement, highlighting their continuity with the artisan struggles of the past in terms of claims, language, world-views, and forms of organisation. The search for a point of "origin" is thus replaced by the investigation of the "provenance" – or "filiation" – of this movement. Such a perspective reverses the genealogical trajectory between working-class subjectivity and its history by focusing on the role played by long-standing professional traditions and organisations.[12] Alongside factors associated with the Industrial Revolution, political phenomena and cultural formations thus come into play and become crucial to understand the labour movement's genesis. These elements indeed seem to be particularly relevant in the French case, where the rapid rise in workers' mobilisations would appear to reflect more the fast pace of political events than the industrialisation process, which only accelerated and became widespread in the second half of the 19th century. The slow pace of this process militates against the assigning of any ontological priority to economic events when it comes to explaining the processes of working-class subjectivation that had already prominently emerged before 1848.

Retracing those historical continuities already highlighted by Tocqueville in *L'ancien régime et la Révolution*, "new social history" research has revealed the shortcomings of any readings of the genesis of the modern labour movement centred on those rifts and novelties deemed to have determined the emergence of an entirely new subjectivity brought into being by the Industrial Revolution.

Conversely, this research has retraced and highlighted the thread of a thematic and organisational continuity which extends from ancient professional guilds – via *sans-culottes*, *compagnonnage*, and mutualism – to the new forms of labour association that began to emerge in the early 1830s and then found their full expression in the 1848 events. From this perspective, the Lyon uprising of 1831 can be understood as an "insurrection of the labour world against the new order" (De Francesco, 1983, p. 373; Johnson, 1975; Moss, 1976). This perspective reverses the coordinates orienting our understanding of the Lyon insurrection, and such an inversion coincides with – and nourishes – a different conception of the very notion of the working class. The latter can now be conceived of as a socio-historical formation which actively takes shape through political, social, and cultural events, at least as much as it does via transformations in manufacturing processes and the organisation of labour.

Besides, the forms taken by the weavers' mutual association, which laid the foundations of the mobilisation culminating in the 1831 insurrection, would appear to have been directly derived from the guild and *compagnonnage* traditions. To avoid the restrictions on the right to coalition set by the post-revolutionary legislation, the *canuts* initially got together in a secret society divided into "lodges" of twenty members each. Its primary purpose was to safeguard against injuries and sickness, and uphold professional claims similar to those advanced by the old craft guilds.[13] Even the events culminating in the insurrection would appear to have been governed by a logic inherited from the Ancien Régime, as shown by the workers' request for the prefect to act as an intermediary and to regulate the labour market, which reflects the traditional idea of local authorities' paternalistic duties towards the subaltern classes. "The working class . . . itself calls you a protector and father," the *canuts* wrote to the prefect in the appeal by which they began their mobilisation on 16 October 1831. When announcing the creation of a *commission des ouvriers* charged with defining a reasonable *tarif au minimum*, they asked the prefect – in the name of the "harmony which must exist in relations between all social classes" – to act as an impartial mediator in the negotiation they planned to begin with the merchants (Baron, 1832, p. 34). In the following weeks they repeatedly shouted "vive le Préfet, vive le pére des ouvriers" ("Long live the prefect, long live the workers' father!"), without ever refusing to acknowledge his authority, even after the expulsion of the army and other government forces from the city. This way of understanding the role of public authority clearly echoed the administrative culture of the Ancien Régime and the function it assigned to political power and craft guilds in regulating the local economy. Alongside this guild legacy, what also appears relevant on the political level is the continuity with the French revolutionary tradition, in particular with the republican imagery of the great Revolution. This is illustrated by the very demand for a minimum rate – which was brought forward along with the accusation that merchants were aspiring to the old privileges of the aristocracy – and by the fact that the *canuts*' motto implicitly echoed the revolutionary one *vivre libre ou mourir*.[14]

Many studies focusing on elements of this kind – that is, on the role of past social and political events in shaping the forms of mobilisation that marked the rise of the modern labour movement – have thus sought to investigate the "birth of class consciousness" among artisan groups defined by an identity drawn from the traditions of the previous century. This has been considered as the crucial element marking a substantial historical discontinuity. Hence, it is by analysing the development of a new class consciousness – understood as a process unfolding from within the labour world – that several "new social history" scholars have tried to reinterpret the birth of the labour movement by overcoming the socio-economic determinism that had framed the development of class struggles as a result of industrialisation. Such contributions have undoubtedly ensured great advancements in the understanding of these matters. Yet, in more recent years, the heuristic value of categories such as "class consciousness" has been increasingly called into question. Scholars have stressed that this kind of notion necessarily presupposes the existence of a "class structure" with *objective* interests and needs, which workers and subalterns can come to know through some process of self-awareness. The very existence – or knowability – of such a structure has been challenged by a further shift in social and labour history studies that have emerged since the early 1980s.

This new wave of studies has shifted the research focus to the way in which the representations and perceptions of class interests and needs were produced on the political-discursive level and defined in *political languages*. Hence, the latter has come to be framed as the fundamental level to understand the development of new collective identities, such as that of the working class. From the 1980s onwards, in the wake of the so-called "linguistic turn," these assumptions have led authors such as William H. Sewell (1980), Gareth Stedman Jones (1983), and Johann Wallach Scott (1988) to highlight the need to "study the production of interests, identification, grievance, and aspiration within political languages themselves," and to trace the formation of specific "class languages" structuring and organising the understanding of one's own condition, that is, of workers' needs and interests.[15] In the same years, the philosopher Jacques Rancière (1981) also embarked – yet from a different perspective – on a remarkable study of workers' languages in the 1830–40s, with the aim of developing a different interpretation of the working-class and socialist tradition in contrast to the "scientific Marxism" of the Althusserian school (cf. §§ 6.3; 6.5).

5.4 Fragments of a working-class discourse

Once we have established the significance of continuity with the past, with the guild tradition and the revolutionary one, a question can be raised. If from a certain moment onwards scholars came to envisage the *révolte des canuts* as a struggle of artisan resistance inspired by a traditional logic, why did they nonetheless confirm its fundamental position as a symbolic point of origin in the labour movement's history? If the reversing of the genealogical trajectory led historians to understand the 1831 insurrection in the light of the impact of guild traditions and struggles, why did it not also lead to a different understanding of the event's place in the genesis of the labour movement?

Questions of this kind certainly bring into play the break marked by the transition towards new forms of "association," such as mutualism, in the labour world. Yet, they also touch upon a broader dimension, which has to do with social representations, images of the world, political languages, and the nature of the public debate engendered by the events that shook France in the first half of the 19th century. The analysis of this dimension requires us to leave aside the role assigned to the Lyon insurrection by the labour movement's historiography and to return to the way in which it was understood at the time of its occurrence. We have already seen that contemporaries perceived it as an event that challenged the very meaning of the lengthy post-revolutionary phase of transition, as was shown by its representation – first proposed by an editorial published in the influential *Journal des débats* – as the symptom of a "new barbaric invasion" (cf. § 2.1). When viewed in its singularity, the insurrection can chiefly be seen to mark a major rift in the way in which French society perceived itself and its inner divisions, since – as discussed in the first chapter – it exacerbated the feelings of *political* disquietude that already marked the age by adding new concerns about the *social* realm. "The great liberal historians of the European Restoration, such as Augustin Thierry and Guizot, had only highlighted the "social antagonism between the Franks and the Gauls," writes Fernand Rude (1944, p. 378), stressing a crucial point: "now, the *Trois Glorieuses* had just sealed the 'Franks' defeat and the 'Gauls'' triumph, when a split occurred in the victors' ranks. A third antagonistic class made its appearance." By bringing about this "appearance" at the centre stage of subjects previously confined to the shadows of subalternity, the Lyon insurrection – combined with the events of the following months (cf. § 1.1) – raised the question of their place in representations of post-revolutionary French society. This was, first of all, the question of their definition as social and political actors and therefore of the way in which they should be *named* in public debates. The hypothesis I wish to formulate here and test in the next chapter through the analysis of 1831 sources is that the significance and break of the Lyonnais event from the point of view of labour history essentially lies in the way in which the weavers sought to make themselves heard in the public sphere in post-revolutionary France, shaken by the emergence of the social question.

The break I wish to highlight, then, is chiefly of a political-discursive nature. It springs from the workers' effort to express their demands as artisans – demands of a corporative nature – through a language suited to the new socio-political context, that is, capable of finding a place in the discourses dominating the bourgeois France of the Orléanist period. The ability to engage with the latter's liberal language was a precondition for the weavers' assertion of their claims in the public arena and, at the same time, for their effort to challenge the principles of bourgeois individualism, which came to be opposed through the catchword of *association* as the meeting point between guild traditions and the social and political language of post-revolutionary France (Sewell, 1980, pp. 280 ff., 1981). The *canuts*' appeal to the prefect, which marked the beginning of the mobilisation for the *tarif*, vividly illustrates this will to draw upon the language of Orléanism and use it to support their own claims:

> The working class that is being enlightened, day after day, by the torch of civilisation is not ignorant of the fact that it is only through order and tranquillity that it will be able to obtain the kind of trust which, as the fundamental basis of trade, ensures – through work – the satisfaction of its everyday needs and gives it the means to provide for itself in its old age.
>
> (cit. in Baron, 1832, pp. 31–32)

In the labour field – but also in republican and Saint-Simonian discourse, as we shall see in the next chapter – a growing effort was made to define and represent the workers' world and its struggles by developing a language that opened up new avenues for collective identity and recognition. It is in the light of this interweaving of names and languages that we can make sense of some of the patterns of subjectivation of labour and of the processes leading to the formation of the collective singular "working class" as the precondition for a unitary movement of French workers. Rather than taking the notion of class as an established social reality with specific interests and needs – on the basis of which it is possible to follow the development of a "class culture" and/or a "class consciousness" reflecting them – we can therefore investigate how the dominant representations and conceptions of such interests and needs were produced. Hence, it is a matter of observing how the experiencing of these interests and needs was expressed, structured, and made intelligible through certain signifiers, terms, and names within specific discursive contexts.

The linguistic-discursive dimension of the break marked by November 1831 finds a striking embodiment in its coinciding with the founding of the first workers' newspaper of some relevance and duration in European history. On Sunday 30 October 1831, the *canuts* published the first issue of *L'Écho de la fabrique. Journal industriel de Lyon et du département du Rhône*: an eight-page Sunday paper that served as the mouthpiece of the *Association générale et mutuelle des chefs d'atelier de la ville de Lyon et des faubourgs*. Each lodge was required to purchase at least one share of this journal, which was first established to support the dispute that was to culminate in the insurrection. Hence, the *Prospectus* of the first issued decried the fall of the *prix de façon* below subsistence rates, blaming the merchants' greed, and making an appeal to the public authorities. Here the *canuts* showed vivid awareness of what was at stake on the political-discursive level insofar as they identified their "weapon" as the deployment of the workers' own words and discourse: "the public voice demands a different order . . ., as a weapon to defend their rights, the unfortunate workers have chosen publicity."[16] In the next chapter, I will draw upon this working-class source, and intertwine it with others belonging to the republican and socialist fields, to outline an original interpretation of the genesis of the labour movement and of the modern notion of working class.

Notes

1 Cf. Association des Tisseurs Lyonnais (1831). For the sources from which I am deriving my account of these events, cf. note 1 in § 1.1.

2 This is an article commemorating the Commune, published in the mouthpiece of the French Workers' Party, *L'Égalité* (2 June 1880, p. 2): "the revolution of 18 March [1871] did not have, like the 1831 Lyon rising, exclusively the character of a class struggle."

3 "In this insurrection, workers were not the main participants, as during the July revolution, but the only participants; not followers, but initiators. . . . It has been said that the Russian worker after 9 February 1905 and before 9 February are two different men, who do not even resemble each other. The same can be said about the French worker before and after the Lyon insurrection," Tarle (1929, p. 133). This is the last chapter – which was translated into French and published in *La Revue Marxiste* – of the book issued in 1928 by the Marx-Engels Institute of Moscow with the title *Rabotchii klass vo Frantsii v pervye vremena machingo proizvodsta ot kontsa Imperii do vosstaniia rabotchike v Lione* (The Working Class in France at the Beginning of Mechanised Production, from the End of the Empire to the Workers' Insurrection in Lyon). Similar views were subsequently expressed by F. Potemkine, *Lioniske vosstania 1831 i 1834* (The Lyon Insurrections of 1831 and 1834), published by the *Academy of Sciences* of the Soviet Union in 1937.

4 Rude started working on the *révolte des canuts* after he realised – during his Russian sojourn in 1933–35 – what keen interest this subject had elicited in the Soviet Union. Hence, the landmark study of 1944 inaugurated his forty-year work on this topic (Rude, 1944, 1953, 1977, 2007), which was chiefly aimed at stressing the foundational role that the *canuts* had played in the history of the European labour movement: "In mutualism lay the seeds of trade-unionism . . . in the Volunteers of the Rhône those of a 'workers' political party. . . . The Lyon events nourished the essential ideas of historical materialism" (Rude, 1944, p. 736).

5 Thorez served as Secretary of the French Communist Party in the years 1930–64. For a similar interpretation of the revolt of the *canuts*, see Lefranc (1957), Bron (1968, pp. 61 ff.), and Perdu (1974); on the Parisian labour movement, see the landmark study Gossez (1967). Among other pioneering works on the history of the French labour movement, see esp. Festy (1908), Dolléans (1936, pp. 57–69), and Lasserre (1949, pp. 56 ff.).

6 "In its academic and legal sense, a worker is someone who only sells his manual labour. He is also referred to as manpower, a term which encapsulate my thought. Now, the *chef d'atelier* is not manpower. . . . Besides, it matters little that he occupies a loom; his function is to employ *compagnons*; he is no more a worker than the fabricants who have someone weave valuable patterns in their homes, and sometimes weave them themselves" (Favre, 1833, p. 22).

7 *Compagnon* comes from the tradition of *compagnonnages*, whereby already in the Middle Ages workers in the same profession would travel around France in search of work to be negotiated collectively, but also for the sake of training and apprenticeship, mutual assistance, and "moralisation." These associations would also organise strikes and controlled all employment in certain centres, where they could stop people from working for certain employers – to the point of leaving whole cities without manpower. The most important associations, which were always in violent contrast with one another, were the "Saint devoir de Dieu," the "Devoir de liberté," and the "Compagnons du devoir." The founding of the Société des Ferrandiniers in Lyon in February 1832 as the first mutual aid association of *compagnons* in the silk-weaving sector is an important event because it bears witness to the decline of traditional *compagnonnage* organisations. Their decline in the 19th century was due to internal violence, rigid hierarchies, the weight of rituals and mysteries, the savage bullying of apprentices, and the fact that they only included nomad workers. The texts by Agricol Perdiguier (1839, 1854) are

certainly the most important source on this phenomenon in the 19th century, on which also see Icher (1989, 2010).

8 As is widely known, the modern concept of "social class" has been largely influenced by Marx, who nonetheless never completed the planned *Das Kapital*'s chapter on classes: the incomplete draft, only a few lines long, was posthumously published as Ch. 152 of *Capital*'s third book. Yet, his legacy has inspired a widespread use of the notion of class by thinkers and scholars, who have used it as an analytical tool to frame the way in which the transformation triggered by the Industrial Revolution led to the formation of the industrial proletariat and modern social cleavages (cf. Cavalli, 2004). Concerning the history of the concept of class, see De Mauro (1971), who highlights Guizot's crucial role in the incorporation of this term into modern political language.

9 I am using the notion of "technical composition of labour" in the sense assigned to it by the Italian journal *Classe operaia* in 1964–66 and then developed by 'workerist' theorists such as M. Tronti, A. Negri, S. Bologna, and L. Ferrari Bravo.

10 Tilly (1986, pp. 274 ff.) stresses that merchants certainly imposed exacting standards on the goods they bought from workers, and argues that much of the day-to-day bickering between merchants and ostensibly independent artisans concerned such questions as whether the finished goods met the standards for full payment, whether the workers had taken some of the raw materials the merchants had given them, and whose measure should be used in gauging the quantity of goods produced.

11 See Thompson (1963, p. 213): "The making of the working class is a fact of political and cultural, as much as of economic, history. It was not the spontaneous generation of the factory-system. Nor should we think of an external force – the 'industrial revolution' – working upon some nondescript undifferentiated raw material of humanity, and turning it out at the other end as a 'fresh race of beings'." "New social history" thus switches from a techno-industrial genealogy of working-class subjectivity to a political-cultural one. The centrality it assigns to an anthropological concept of culture has led to studies on the aspect of "experience" reminiscent of ethnography: see also the pioneering works by Rudé (1959, 1984), and later Cobb (1970) and Agulhon (1984).

12 I am using the terms "origin" (*Ursprung*), "provenance" (*Herkunft*), and later "emergence" (*Entstehung*) as these have been discussed and defined by Foucault (1971).

13 Silk-weaving was a well-established tradition, stretching back to the 15th century in Europe. This makes the *canuts*' history one of struggles and great professional pride (see Godart, 1899). The first *mutual* association of *canuts* was established by Pierre Charnier in 1827. It was aimed at the defence of the professional category and, set minimum age of 25 and the ownership of four looms as membership criteria – meaning that it was only open to the wealthier weavers. Lyon's first "Société de secours mutual" was actually established by hatters in 1804. Others were set up over the course of the following three decades, but the *canuts*' mutual aid groups were far the most numerous and enduring ones.

14 To further stress how the revolutionary experiences of the past shaped *canuts*' claims, it is worth quoting an editorial published in their journal (on which cf. § 5.4 and Chapter Six): "What is the third estate? Everything. What has it been in the political order until today? Nothing. What does it demand? To be something. Instead of third estate, give it the name proletariat, and you will find that these questions are still on the agenda. Now we recall what happened when they were posed for the first time," (*Écho de la fabrique*' no. 23, 9 June 1833) On the other hand, in defending the legitimacy of the *tarif*, prefect Bouvier-Dumolard (1832, p. 12) insisted on precedents during the Revolution.

15 Concerning the debate which accompanied these new orientations in social and labour history, see La Capra (1983), Berlanstein (1993), Guilhaumou (1993), Joice (1995), Eley (2005), and Eley and Nield (2007).

16 Prospectus of the *Écho de la fabrique*, p. 1. On the history of this newspaper, see Frobert (2010), head of the project of digitalising the Lyonnaise workers' press from the years 1831–34, now available online in full at the URL http://echo-fabrique.ens-lyon.fr/index.

php. Before the *Écho de la fabrique*, other workers' newspapers had been published in Paris in 1830 – i.e. *L'Artisan, Journal des Ouvriers*, and *Le Peuple* – but none of them had lasted more than three months (Godechot, 1966; Popkin, 2002).

References

Aguet J-P. (1954), *Contribution à l'histoire du mouvement ouvrier français: Les grèves sous la Monarchie de Juillet (1830–1847)*, Droz, Genève.

Agulhon M. (1984), Working Class and Sociability in France Before 1848, in P. Thane, G. Crossick, R. Floud (eds.), *The Power of the Past. Essays for Eric Hobsbawm*, CUP, Cambridge, pp. 37–66.

Association des Tisseurs Lyonnais (1831), *Extrait de l'acte social*, Bibliothèque municipale de Lyon – Fonds ancien, MS_RUDE_376_f41 (cf. also Association générale et mutuelle des chefs d'atelier de la ville de Lyon et des faubourgs, Acte d'association, in Fernand Rude (ed.), *Les révoltes des canuts 1831–1834*, La Decouverte, Paris, p. 189).

Baron A. (1832), *Histoire de Lyon pendant les journées des 21, 22 et 23 novembre 1831*, Baron, Lyon.

Berlanstein L.R. (ed.) (1993), *Rethinking Labor History: Essays on Discourse and Class Analysis*, Unversity of Illinois Press, Chicago.

Bernard C., Charnier P. (n.d.), *Rapport fait et présenté à M. le président du Conseil des ministres, sur les causes qui ont amené les événemens de Lyon, par deux chefs d'ateliers*, Impr. de Charvin, Lyon.

Bouvier-Dumolard L. (1832), *Compte rendu des événemens qui ont eu lieu dans la ville de Lyon au mois de novembre 1831*, Tenon, Paris.

Bron J. (1968), *Histoire du mouvement ouvrier français, tome I: Le droit à l'existence du debut du XIXe siècle à 1884*, Éditions Ouvrières, Paris.

Cavalli A. (2004), Classe, in N. Bobbio, N. Matteucci, G. Pasquino (a cura di), *Il Dizionario di politica*, UTET, Torino, pp. 109–114.

Cobb R.C. (1970), *The Police and the People. French Popular Protest 1789–1820*, OUP, Oxford.

De francesco A. (1983), *Il sogno della repubblica. Il mondo del lavoro dall'Ancien Régime al 1848*, Franco Angeli, Milano.

De Mauro T. (1971), Storia e analisi semantica di 'classe' (1958), in Id (ed.), *Senso e significato*, Laterza, Bari.

Dictionnaire de l'Académie française, Firmin-Didot, Paris 1835.

Dolléans É. (1936), *Histoire du mouvement ouvrier*, vol. I, Collin, Paris.

Droz J. (dir.) (1972), *Histoire générale du socialisme*, vol. I, PUF, Paris.

Écho de la Fabrique. (1831–1834), Lyon. Retrieved from: http://echo-fabrique.ens-lyon.fr/index.php

Eley G. (2005), *A Crooked Line: From Cultural History to the History of Society*, University of Michigan Press, Ann Arbor.

Eley G., Nield K. (2007), *The Future of Class in History: What's Left of the Social?* The University of Michigan Press, Ann Arbor.

Engels F. (2006), *Socialism: Utopian and Scientific*, Mondial, New York (or. ed. in F. Engels, *Herrn Eugen Dührings Umwälzung der Wissenschaft*, Genossenschafts, Leipzig 1878).

Favre J. (1833), *De la coalition des chefs d'atelier de Lyon*, Babeuf, Lyon.

Festy O. (1908), *Le mouvement ouvrier au début de la monarchie de juillet (1830–1834)*, Cornely, Paris.

Foucault M. (1971), Nietzsche, la généalogie, l'histoire, in Suzanne Bachelard et al. (eds.), *Hommage a J. Hyppolite*, PUF, Paris, pp. 145–172 (Eng. trans. Nietzsche, Genealogy, History, in Michel Foucault, *Language, Counter-Memory, Practice. Selected Essays and Interviews*, ed. Donald F. Bouchard, Cornell University Press, Ithaca, NY 1977, pp. 139–164).

Frobert L. (2010), *L'Echo de la fabrique: naissance de la presse ouvrière à Lyon*, ENS, Lyon.

Godart J. (1899), *L'ouvrier en soie, monographie du tisseur lyonnais. Etude historique, économique et sociale*, Bernoux & Cumin, Lyon and Paris.

Godechot J. (1966), *La presse ouvrière 1819–1850*, Bibliotheque de la Revolution de 1848, La Roche sur Yon.

Gossez R. (1956), Diversité des antagonismes sociaux vers le milieu du XIXe. *Revue économique*, 3: 439–458.

Gossez R. (1967), *Les ouvriers de Paris, vol. 1: L'organisation*, Bibliothèque de la Révolution de 1848, La Roche sur Yon.

Guilhaumou J. (1993), Analyse de discours: les historiens et le "tournant linguistique". *Langage et société*, 65: 5–38.

Icher F. (1989), *Le Compagnonnage*, Grancher, Paris.

Icher F. (2010), *Les compagnons du tour de France*, La Martinière, Paris.

Johnson C.H. (1975), Economic Change and Artisan Discontent: The Tailors' History 1800–1848, in R. Price (ed.), *Revolution and Reaction: 1848 and the Second French Republic*, Barnes & Noble, New York, pp. 87–114.

Joice P. (1995), The End of Social History? *Social History*, 20(1): 73–91.

Koselleck R. (1975), Geschichte, Historie, in Otto Brunner, Werner Conze, Reinhart Koselleck (eds.), *Geschichtliche Grundbegriffe: lexikon zur politisch-sozialen Sprache in Deutschland*, vol. 2, Klett-Cotta, Stuttgart, pp. 647–717.

Koselleck R. (1979), *Vergangene Zukunft: Zur Semantik geschichtlicher Zeiten*, Suhrkamp Verlag, Franfurt am Main (Eng. trans. *Futures Past: On the Semantics of Historical Time*, Columbia University Press, New York 2004).

La Capra D. (1983), *Rethinking Intellectual History: Texts, Contexts, Language*, Cornell University Press, Ithaca, New York.

Lasserre G. (1949), *Histoire du syndicalisme ouvrier*, vol. I, Domat-Montchrestien, Paris.

Lefranc G. (1957), *Histoire du travail et des travailleurs*, Flammarion, Paris.

Lenin V.I. (1977), August Bebel, in *Lenin Collected Works*, vol. 19, Progress Publishers, Moscow, pp. 295–301 (or. ed. in *Severnaia Pravda*, no. 6, 8 August 1913).

Marx K. (1869), *Report of the Fourth Annual Congress of the International Workingmen's Association, Held at Basle, in Switzerland*, The International Workingmen's Association, Basle. Retrieved from: http://hiaw.org/defcon6/iwma/documents/1869/basle-report.html.

Marx K. (1967), *Capital*, vol. 1, International Publishers, New York (or. ed. *Das Kapital. Kritik der politischen Oekonomie*, Verlag von Otto Meissner, Hamburg, 1867).

Monfalcon J-B. (1834), *Histoire des insurrections de Lyon en 1831 et en 1834*, Perrin, Lyon.

Moss B.H. (1976), *The Origins of the French Labor Mouvement 1830–1914. The Socialism of Skilled Workers*, UCP, Berkeley.

Perdiguier A. (1839), *Le Livre du Compagnonnage*, Pagnerre et Perdiguier, Paris.

Perdiguier A. (1854), *Mémoires d'un compagnon*, Duchamp, Genéve.

Perdu J. (1974), *La révolte des canuts 1831–1834*, Spartacus, Paris.

Popkin J.D. (2002), *Press, Revolution, and Social Identities in France, 1830–1835*, PUS, University Park, PA.

Rancière J. (1981), *La nuit des prolétaires. Archives du rêve ouvrier*, Fayard, Paris (Eng. transl. *The Nights of Labor: The Workers' Dream in Nineteenth-Century France*, Temple University Press, Philadelphia 1989).

Rancière J. (1985), Savoirs hérétique et émancipation du pauvre, in Jean Borreil (ed.), *Les sauvages dans la cité. Auto-émancipation du peuple et instruction des prolétaires au XIXe siècle*, Seyssel, Champ Vallon, pp. 34–53.

Rey A. (dir.) (1992), *Dictionnaire historique de la langue française*, vol. II, Le Robert, Paris.

Rude F. (1944), *L'insurrection lyonnaise de novembre 1831. Le Mouvement ouvrier à Lyon de 1827 à 1832*, Domat-Montchrestien, Paris.

Rude F. (1953), *C'est nous les canuts*, Domat-Montchrestien, Paris.

Rude F. (1977), *Le Mouvement ouvrier à Lyon*, Fédérop, Lyon.

Rude F. (2007), *Les révoltes des canuts 1831–1834*, La Decouverte, Paris (or. ed. 1982).

Rudé G. (1959), *The Crowd in the French Revolution*, Clarendon, Oxford.

Rudé G. (1964), *The Crowd in History 1730–1848*, Wiley, New York.

Scott J.W. (1988), *Gender and the Politics of History*, Columbia University Press, New York.

Sewell W.H. (1980), *Work and Revolution in France: The Language of Labor from the Old Regime to 1848*, CUP, Cambridge.

Sewell W.H. (1981), La confraternité des prolétaires: conscience de classe sous la monarchie de Juillet. *Annales. Économies, Sociétés, Civilisations*, 36(4): 650–671.

Stedman Jones G. (1983), *Languages of Class: Studies in English Working Class History, 1832–1982*, CUP, Cambridge.

Tarle E.V. (1929), L'insurrection ouvrière de Lyon. *La Revue Marxiste*, 2, March.

Thompson E.P. (1963), *The Making of the English Working Class*, Vintage books, New York.

Thorez M. (1974), *Préface*, in M. Moissonier (ed.), *La révolte des canuts. Lyon, novembre 1831*, Éditions Sociales, Paris.

Tilly C. (1986), *The Contentious French*, Harvard University Press, Cambridge, MA.

Villermé L-R. (1989), *Tableau de l'état physique et moral des ouvriers employés dans les manifactures de coton, de laine et de soie*, Études et documentations internationales, Paris (or. ed. Renouard, Paris 1840).

6 The political subjectivation of labour

While the previous chapter analysed the 1831 insurrection in Lyon from the standpoint of the meaning and position that it has been assigned in the history of labour, the present chapter considers this same event in its singularity, that is, in his specific historical context. It delves into the way in which the *canuts*' revolt was perceived and understood by its contemporaries to propose an interpretation of the rise of the labour movement and its historical-political significance. We have already seen that the Lyon revolt coincided with the birth of the first enduring working-class publication in Europe – *L'Écho de la fabrique* (ÉDF – cf. § 5.4). We can now refer to this source to retrace the genesis of a working-class discourse and its development in connection with other discourses belonging to the opposition to Orléanist liberalism, that is, to the *republican* field and the nascent *socialist* one. In relation to the former, our focus will be first on the newspaper *Le National* (LN) edited by Armand Carrel, which at that time was the eighth French newspaper in terms of the number of copies and circulation, and which grew closer to republicanism after having played a leading role in the mobilisation against the curtailing of press freedom that culminated in the revolution of July 1830. Then, we will consider the *Société des Amis du Peuple* (SAP) – founded by Auguste Blanqui, Vincent Raspail, and Armand Barbès on 30 July 1830 to influence the course of the revolution – and its effort to innovate the republican discourse by incorporating social themes. As for the nascent socialist field, the focus will be on the *Saint-Simonian movement*, which was particularly relevant in the political scenario of this period and revolved around the Parisian community of Menilmontant, led by Prosper Enfantin, and the newspaper *Le Globe*, edited by Michel Chevalier. What this chapter tries to single out in relation to these sources is their common effort to name and define the social figures which burst upon the public stage through the 1831 insurrection. This effort brought about a new representation of the subaltern classes based on the terms "workers," "people," "class," and "proletariat": a representation which engendered processes of semantic transformation of such categories that set the ground for the advent of the "collective singular" *working class* (Koselleck, 1975, 1979).

The following pages first retrace the reception of the concept of social class – affirmed in the French public sphere by liberal bourgeois historians such as Guizot and Thierry – within working-class, republican, and socialist publications. We will thus see how the latter appropriated the word *class* and assigned it a new social

DOI: 10.4324/9781003303497-9

meaning by setting it in relation to other signifiers such as *people*, *proletariat*, and *workers*, bringing about processes of mutual resignification between these terms, and producing a new constellation of meaning to describe and define the subaltern subjects. The aim of the present chapter is to point out the role that this discursive dynamic played in fostering the subjectivation of the labour world as a political actor, because it is within this dynamic that the collective singular "working class" gradually emerged as a unitary representation within which the still-heterogeneous universe of the subaltern classes was able to identify and envisage itself as a collective subjectivity. Such a representation set the conditions for the emergence of the modern workers' movement, which this chapter aims to frame as a subjectivation process developed first of all on the level of political discourse. The argument that will be ultimately put forward is that the genesis of the modern labour movement can be understood as a "discursive formation and practice" aimed at redefining the boundaries of the political field and the very meaning of politics.

6.1 Republican-social discourse: the "popular class"

To frame the 1831 insurrection in the discursive context of its time, we should, first of all, observe the way in which this event was put in relation to the "July Revolution" that had occurred sixteen months before. One of the most striking effects of the *révolte des canuts* was indeed the fact that it recalled the Parisian popular uprisings of 1830, which had led to the fall of the Restoration regime and to the establishment of the Orléanist one, thereby evoking the issue of the collective subject which had enabled this transition and of its position in post-revolutionary society. "What lies at the heart of the debate between liberals and republicans is, therefore, the challenge of the representation of the people," writes Michèle Riot-Sarcey (1998, pp. 95–97): "the conflict is primarily a semantic conflict because each [party involved] adheres to the same fundamental principles." The tensions that the Lyonnais insurrection of November 1831 produced by recalling the Parisian revolution of 1830 revolved around the effort to affirm an authentic meaning of the signifier "people," on which the representation of the July events was built. Hence, the internal structural ambiguity of the idea of people – which designates both the political *unity* of the people-nation and the social subjects that constitute the lower stratum, or segment, of that unity – nurtured a vibrant debate on the link between the weavers' insurrection and the 1830 revolution, and on the nature and meaning of the latter. Retracing this debate allows us to appreciate the role that a discursive conflict aimed at the production of world images and social representations played in the genesis of a collective subjectivity of labour.

"The men that made up this new caste only spoke of the people and for the people," we read in issue no. 4 of the *Écho de la fabrique*, published on the eve of the insurrection and featuring the opening editorial *L'aristocratie du comptoir*. Lyonnais silk merchants are described as a new kind of aristocracy seeking to exploit the popular revolution of 1830 to acquire the privileges of the old nobility, turning their backs on the masses, who had enabled the establishment of the new liberal regime. Within this scenario, the *canuts* claim that "the July sun has appeared for all" (ÉDF, II, 6 November 1831) and use the term *people* to portray themselves – and carve out a place for themselves – in public debate. This term allowed them to recall – and link their struggle to – the basic opposition between the people – the third estate claiming to be the entire nation – and the aristocracy: an opposition that engendered the 1789 break and which the Restoration regime only managed to mend for fifteen years. In 1830, the "three glorious days of July" suddenly and strikingly brought the term "people" back to the centre of public debate, paving the way for the development of that "romantic myth" of the people (Pessin, 1992; Jakobowicz, 2009) immortalised in the poem that Victor Hugo (1842, p. 18) composed to celebrate the revolution: "Hier vous n'étiez qu'un foule;/Vous êtes un peuple aujourd'hui." "After the victory, a hero was sought and a whole people was found," Jules Michelet (1831, p. 66) wrote, reflecting the effort to charge the body politic of the people with the salvific function of covering up the political-juridical ambiguities of the July regime – starting from the resounding contradiction of a monarchical regime established by means of an insurrection.[1] The full and close unity of the people-nation offered a kind of poetic, or romantic, solution, a rhetorical device bearing an evocative power that allowed it to conceal the contradictions underlying the revolutionary break of 1830 (Marbe, 1904; Pinkney, 1972, 1974; Merriman, 1975; Newman, 1975; Rosanvallon, 1994, 1998).

"These workers" – stresses issue no. 5 of the *Écho de la fabrique*, published during the uprising – "respect the dynasty which arose in July, and which they have contributed to establishing": by confirming their adherence to the Orléanist regime, the *canuts* claim the right to be reckoned as part of the collective body on which the new power rests. However, their very insurrection has brought out the polysemy of the notion of people – which encompasses and designates at the same time the whole nation and its lower social strata – and, with it, the very ambiguity of the July monarchy. Hence, republican journalists envisage the *révolte des canuts* as an opportunity to newly raise the question of the 1830 revolution's significance by launching a heated debate on the definition of its leading subject. To do so, they represent the latter as a "social people," a disadvantaged partiality to be integrated into the unitary political body of the people, envisaged as the holder of sovereignty:

> The Lyon events have just proven what had already emerged from our July days, namely that the *people* is now associated with all ideas of freedom . . . which the *middle class* has sought to affirm on its own against the Restoration regime.
>
> (*Le National*, 28 November 1831, emphasis added)

Thus wrote *Le National*'s editor-in-chief Armand Carrel to denounce the *volte-face* of those bourgeois elites who had "refused to recognise the popular side of the July revolution" (ibid.). His distinction between "the people" and "the middle class" reveals use of the term people as a subaltern *social part* of the political totality embodied by the people-nation. *Le National* then launched a campaign to grant amnesty to the rebellious weavers, stressing their upright conduct after they had taken the control of Lyon. In such a way, this newspaper established a parallel with the behaviour of the people who had risen up in Paris in July 1830, stressing the presence on the stage of the same political actor, which had expressed itself in the same terms:

> The more it is said that the two popular movements in no way resemble each other, that one was legitimate and the other is not, the more we appreciate the perfect conformity of mores displayed by the two populations. It seems to us that this people is far more advanced, far more capable of conducting itself, of governing itself, than what the champions of quasi-legitimacy and doctrinal corruption like to claim, they who for the past fifteen months have succeeded in turning the finest revolution of all into a lie.
>
> (*Le National*, 7 December 1831)

The liberal ideologists of Orléanism had sought to found the new regime on the presence of the unitary political body of the people on the public stage. But the *révolte des canuts* now brought onto the stage the "social side" of the notion of people, which embodied a subaltern partiality capable of threatening the power it had recently established. The insurrection of November 1831 revealed the people to be a two-faced Janus and a force more dangerous than the very ills it was intended to treat in the liberals' mind: for it recalled the fundamental contradiction of the Orléanist monarchy, namely its establishment by insurrectionist means. Indeed, Legitimist newspapers claimed that "the Lyon events are the natural outcome of the principles that prevailed in July" (*Gazette de France*, 28 November 1831, p. 2). The government circles sought to neutralise statements of this kind by juxtaposing the distinctly *political* character of the July days with the exclusively *social* and *unpolitical* one of the Lyon events (cf. § 6.6). The most authoritative mouthpiece of the Orléanist regime thus emphasised: "the lack of any political character in the workers' uprising," denouncing attempts to manipulate it to provide a misleading representation of the people: "what are the middle classes, if not a section of the people that work, industriousness, and enterprise have turned into a property-owner?" (*Journal des débats*, 1 December 1831 and 29 November 1831).

Le National reacted by harshly criticising this "revolt against the spirit and the character of the popular revolution of July, a revolution as *social* as it was *political*" (27 November 1831). The adjective "popular" (*populaire*) is used here to emphasise the central role of the people as popular classes in the July 1830 events, thus highlighting their social "spirit and character" and thereby associating them with November 1831. However, on the discursive level the possibility of affirming this representation ran up against the difference symbolised by the two different names – "people" and "workers" – that in public debate were used to describe the two events' leading subject. *People* is the noun stamped on the outcomes of the July revolution: a singular term, as it expresses unanimity and consensus, and a strictly political notion charged with lending legitimacy to the new regime. By contrast, *workers* is the name which the Lyon insurrection catapulted to the centre of the debate: an unpolitical, plural, and exclusively social notion, since – as we have seen – in this period it stood for little more than a generic description of the condition of being a manual labourer (cf. § 5.2).

Within the framework of republican discourse – and later the weavers' discourse – a solution to this antinomy between the political nature of the people and the social nature of workers would appear to have been sought in the use of the concept of *class*, which liberal historians such as Guizot had recently established as a key term in political debate (cf. §§ 1.3–1.4).[2] The "social side" of the concept of people made it possible to conceive of the latter also as a class, the *classe populaire*: "this class marked by toil, sacrifices, and tears which we call the people," as we once again read in *Le National* (13 April 1832). The term class here is used to designate the people as a subaltern partiality: the "popular class" is the class representing the lower stratum or disadvantaged part of the people-nation, that is, that stratum destined to be referred to as the "working class" in the political language of the following century. This representation was also highlighted by a bookbinder named Paillot in a letter addressed to the Saint-Simonian newspaper *Le Globe*: "in the days of July, when the ordinances appeared, there was much turmoil in the capital, and I believe that without this *class* of men we call *the people* there would have been much less" (cit. in Riot-Sarcey, 1998, pp. 182–183, emphasis added).

The concept of *classe* – employed by liberal historians in debates on the history of the French nation to justify the rise of bourgeois hegemony as a result of centuries-old conflict with the aristocracy – thus became a tool for representations designed to establish a point of contact between the political figure of the *peuple* – central to the republican discourse on popular sovereignty – and the subaltern social figures which the events of those months had placed at the centre of the political arena and which were chiefly designated through the term *ouvriers*. These three categories – class, people, and workers – thus came to function within a shared constellation of meaning that enabled the activation of dynamics of mutual signification and semantic transformation in the field of discourses justifying the insurrection. It was within this constellation that the concept of *working class* progressively began to be used to represent the world of the lower classes in the singular, paving the way for a unitary representation with which various different figures from the labour world and subaltern subjects could identify (Minler, 1983).

The notion of class also gained currency owing to its ability to overcome the intrinsic ambivalence in the concept of people, which was not entirely adequate to grasp and describe the complex social fabric resulting from the political and industrial revolutions. The idea of class could instead be used to encompass the social figure of the *ouvrier* – that is, the changing world of labour – and represent it as part of the unitary body of the people, thereby creating a point of conjunction between the political People of July and the social people of November. The juxtaposition between the *révolte des canuts* – the "workers" – and the July revolution – the "People" – thus triggered a process of mutual signification between the two terms whereby workers could be taken to embody the people, as the latter was also a class – the *classe populaire*, the class of the lower strata of the people. July 1830 must therefore be understood – as Carrel writes – as "the victory of the lower classes over the Restoration," a victory of that "working class" which in the society had "acquired . . . a hitherto unprecedented degree of esteem" (*Le National*, 27 and 28 November 1831).

6.2 The *Société des amis du peuple*: "professional" proletarians

The peculiar expression "social-republicans" already reveals the uncertain balance of this position. On the one hand, republican-social discourse is "social" because it draws upon the notion of class to emphasise the social side of the concept of people, understood as the subaltern part of the nation. On the other hand, it is still a "republican" doctrine because it is centred on the idea of popular sovereignty, and therefore remains based on the unitary political meaning of people, envisaged as the only legitimate foundation of power and of the constituent code of sovereignty. This discourse rests on a holistic and romantic conception of the people as a collective body with its own will, rationality, and ethics: "a people is a common principle made flesh, a living doctrine," *Revue républicaine* stated in 1834. This conception is strikingly embodied by the adage *Vox Populi Vox Dei*, used as an epigraph in the pamphlets by the *Société des Amis du Peuple* (see e.g. SAP, 1831), on which we can now focus to observe how the 19th-century emergence of the social question partly affected the republican discourse. This short-lived society (1830–32) is commonly credited by historians as having played a key role in the modern revival of the original Latin term "proletarians" (*proletarii*) and in its reception in modern political language, particularly through the trial involving fifteen of its leaders, which catalysed French public attention a few weeks after the *révolte des canuts*. At this trial, on 10 January 1832, Auguste Blanqui uttered his famous self-defence, which posed a unique semantic challenge to the judge:

- Your name?
- Louis-Auguste Blanqui.
- Your profession [*état*]?
- Proletarian.
- That is not a profession.
- What do you mean it's not a profession! It's the condition of 30 million Frenchmen who work for a living and are deprived of political rights.
- So be it, then. Clerk, write that the accused is a proletarian.[3]

The judge himself ultimately granted a kind of written juridical legitimation to the term "proletarians" and to its capacity to designate a collective condition. In those years, then, this neologism emerged alongside "pauperism" (cf. § 3.1) in an effort to designate a "new fact," as emphasised by the *Dictionnaire d'économie politique*: "contemporary to the proletariat, the latter [pauperism] in turn being an effect of the same causes" (Cherbuliez, 1873).[4] Based on this semantic proximity, the notion of proletariat would appear to have been employed to express in a subjective – that is, *political* – sense the condition which the term "pauperism" was designed to describe objectively. Indeed, in Blanqui's defence speech and in the SAP's republican discourse – inspired more by Babeuf's egalitarian perspective than by nascent socialism – the meaning of the term "proletarians" still appears to be modelled entirely after the ancient Roman one, making its political features predominant over any socio-economic ones (Rosemberg, 1939, p. 31).[5] "I, a proletarian, deprived of all rights by the *cité*," states Blanqui, thereby defining the meaning of the term primarily based on this condition of *political exclusion* – that is, of denial of political rights – rather than that of social subordination, labour conditions, and/or economic exploitation.

In republican-social discourse, the term proletarian thus emerged to indicate a condition of poverty that was primarily defined as a result of the bourgeois monopoly on the "manufacturing" of laws established by census-based representation. It exemplified a kind of deprivation determined by the political system, which is to say by exclusion from those decision-making mechanisms that regulate industry and trade, determining an "inextricable web of taxes, monopolies, prohibitions, customs rights, and concessions" that "affects the poor at every moment of the day" (Blanqui, 1971, pp. 60–62). Blanqui states that the protectionist legislation on grain was responsible for the high prices of bread, which made the poor go hungry; those on timber defended the expensive and poor-quality agricultural implements that farmers were forced to purchase against foreign competition. Overseas countries reacted with just as many tariffs, choking wine exports and thus crushing small landowners. Finally, taxes primarily imposed on consumer goods like salt and tobacco, combined with an inefficient credit system, accounted for the condition of the poor, who, being incapable of taking part in the decisions concerning such mechanisms, were therefore *proletarians*. Hence, Blanqui ascribes the latter's condition to a political order in which "the representative system . . . concentrates the three powers in the hands of a small number of privileged individuals sharing the same interests": these men are at once voters, jurors, and national guardsmen, and thus "manufacture," implement, and judge the laws – which are ultimately "designed for the same purposes of exploitation" (ibid.).

In the social and political context of the early 1830s, the emerging category of the proletariat displays a twofold disruptive capacity. On the one hand, it possesses a social depth that the concept of people lacks; on the other, it includes a political meaning that goes well beyond the mere designation of a social condition, to which both the term *ouvriers* and the notion of class are instead confined. Hence, the modern use of the term proletariat seems to emerge from the effort to lend republican discourse a social depth that its doctrine of popular sovereignty lacks. In the debates following the *révolte des canuts*, this neologism seems capable of covering the semantic field that opened up between the unitary political rhetoric about the people of July 1830 and the social partiality of the insurgent weavers of 1831. It is within this horizon of meaning that the republican discourse becomes charged with a new tendency to include and promote the figure of the "workers, these heroic proletarians" who have been the "brave and selfless soldiers of July" – we read in the pamphlet *Au peuple* of the SAP (1832, p. 43).

This "social bending" of SAP's republican discourse – that is, this effort to develop the latter by incorporating the growing relevance of the social sphere – also takes the form of actual social initiatives. Under the leadership of Raspail –

who was elected president of the SAP in May 1831 following the young doctor Ulysse Trélat's arrest on a conspiracy charge – the SAP promotes the provision of legal protection to "poor families" and the "creation of a primary education school for adults" (ibid., p. 49) in every Paris *arrondissement* to teach grammar, mathematics, science, hygiene, history, and singing. Right from its founding *Manifesto*, the SAP states that "compared to other patriotic associations," it also sets itself "the aim of defending" the "interests of the lower classes of society" and of "improving their physical and moral condition" – expressions that vividly reveal the influence of Saint-Simonian language (cf. § 6.4). The theme of the social classes, and of their interests and needs, thus becomes grafted onto the republican mystique of the people, orienting the SAP's discourse "not only towards the lower classes, but also towards the manufacturing classes" and "citizens from all industrious classes" (SAP, 1830, pp. 15–26).

The SAP's adoption of the ancient term "proletariat" crystallises the conjunction between the traditional theme of popular sovereignty and the emergent one of the material needs of the lower social classes – brought into the limelight by the Lyon events. By describing a social class and at the same time interpreting it politically, the term *prolétaires* thus proves to have the potential to narrow the gap between the political nature of the concept of people and the social feature of that of class. In other words, in republican-social discourse, the figure of the proletarian seems to serve as a bridge between the unitary political figure of the *citoyen* – the rights-bearing citizen as the fundamental unit of the people-nation – that was at the centre of traditional republicanism and the social figure of the *ouvrier* – the individual member of the working class whose needs and interests were to become the centre of the nascent socialist discourse. Hence, in the SAP's publication concerning the *canuts'* insurrection we read:

> Those who have made their arms accustomed to working and their brain to reason, the proletarians of today, wish to live free and through work: their well-being – but at the same time their dignity! The profit from labour must return to the worker. . . . It is necessary for the laws to tend towards this end.
> (SAP, 1831, p. 4)

This pamphlet – especially the article "La guerre civile" on the Lyon events – has been identified as the republicans' first significant display of active support for the workers (Dolléans, 1936, Vol. II, p. 78). Then, the last pamphlet published by the SAP – entitled *Discours sur la misère du peuple* and presented by Guillame Desjardins (1833) at the Court of Assize during the SAP's trial – defined the law of the future as the "progressive advent [*avènement*] of the proletariat," on both the level of social conditions ("interests") and that of political rights ("capacities"). According to Rosanvallon (1992, p. 260), the Société des Amis du Peuple exemplifies those "republican and popular societies that will become the matrix of the labour movement and of French socialism." Indeed, as is widely known, Auguste Blanqui was to play a prominent role in the development of the French labour movement in the 19th century – from the 1848 revolution to the Paris Commune of 1871.

6.3 The *Écho de la fabrique* and the language of association

With the *révolte des canuts* a new subjectivity burst onto the stage that escaped the traditional coordinates of the notion of people. Blanqui, therefore, chose to describe this subjectivity by drawing upon an ancient word, proletarians, which he primarily used to designate a condition of political exclusion. The political philosopher Jacques Rancière has repeatedly explored the significance of Blanqui's gesture in court by framing it as "a statement of belonging to the community that takes account precisely of those who do not count," a "class which does not exist if not in the declaration by which these people count themselves as those who are not counted": the name "proletarian" would thus subjectivise "this part of those *with no part*." Hence, this author suggests that we frame the processes of working-class subjectivation in France in the years 1830–48 as a "heterology" corresponding to an "identification with the one who is designated as excluded." This process of identification primarily occurs through "the invention of names" that are used to lay claim to acts that come into play in the relationship between the level of discourse and the level of social conditions, "promoting within shared space unprecedented subjects and new forms of legitimacy" (Rancière 1992, 2007, 1981).[6] The "novelty" determined by the turn which followed the 1830 revolution would therefore coincide with this "unique effort made by a class to define itself" in a climate marked by the irruption of a conflict that revolves around the "right to qualify workers," and hence of a "struggle for the appropriation of words" whereby the latter are in each case rejected or asserted, challenged or redefined (Rancière, 2007, pp. 9–17, 1985, p. 37).

This perspective seems particularly in tune with the way in which the Lyonnais weavers' weekly newspaper draws upon the neologism *prolétaires*, activating a critical hermeneutics that eventually leads them to appropriate the term by including it within a new language of the emerging working class – that is the language of "association," which the *Écho de la fabrique* was developing to promote the *canuts*' mutualism in the political discourse of its time (cf. § 5.4). In this newspaper, the neologism proletarians, first of all, appear as someone else's word, as the prerogative of those who view the "worker" as "an inferior being" and "believe they have defeated him and knocked him down by telling him that he is a *proletarian*" (ÉDF, IX, 25 December 1831, p. 1). In other words, this category is at first *rejected*, so much so that the *Écho de la fabrique* calls for "the word proletarian, an insulting term that has become odious, to disappear" (XIII, 22 January 1832, p. 2). However, alongside this rejection, what also emerges is a gradual process of challenge, *detournement*, reception, and appropriation of this term. This happened through a resemanticisation which, in this case as well, makes the idea of proletariat a point of conjunction between the term "workers" – by which the *canuts* defined themselves and were defined – and the (revolutionary, political, and legitimate) figure of the "people." Hence, a few weeks after the insurrection, we read in the *Écho de la fabrique*: "the worker today senses his own dignity, and knows his own strength. Little does it matter whether he is called a proletarian; he knows he is necessary for the organisation of society" (ÉDF, IX, 25 December 1831, p. 1). This declaration of indifference subsequently turned into a possibility for identification: "qui est-tu? je suis homme du peuple . . . c'est-à-dire prolétaire" (ÉDF, XXVIII, 6 May 1832, p. 3, cf. also *supra* note 14 in Ch. 5). This semantic-political development – which in the first months of 1832 led the *canuts* to appropriate the word proletarians – is vividly represented in an important editorial aimed at retracing the history and purposes of the weavers' newspaper four months after the insurrection:

> It is *peoples* that carry out revolutions; some for the interests of big men . . ., other to achieve liberty; and the well-being of the *lower classes* has always sprung from the latter . . .; and one of the greatest benefits that these revolutions have brought peoples is no doubt freedom of the press.
>
> Nevertheless, an omission unworthy of our century had been committed: a sizeable *class*, interesting on account of the services it renders to the State and to society, had no organs to defend its rights; this sizeable, boundless class is that of the *proletarians*. . . . It is for this eminently *popular* [populaire] aim that the *Écho de la Fabrique* has been created. . . .
>
> Some generous men, sprung from the *popular class* [classe populaire], have come together for this bold task and . . . also think that *industrialists, proletarians across all crafts*, across all professions, will join them . . . because their paper is not at all an exclusive one, and the manufacturer, whatever his status, will always find protection within it. The *Écho de la Fabrique will ultimately be the proletarians' newspaper.*
>
> (ÉDF, XXIII, 1 April 1832, p. 1, emphasis added)

Here we find the whole range of categories and meanings considered so far: the "people" as the revolutionary actor par excellence; the "class" as a partiality that acts within the people – as a social part of it – and which has the potential to encompass it through the figure of the "popular class"; and, finally, the notion of the "proletariat" as a semantic space to achieve a possible synthesis in this dialectic between social and political signifiers.[7] This editorial, then, shows how the reception and resemantisation of the term *prolétaires* in the labour field ultimately plays a crucial twofold role. On the one hand, it helps to associate the working-class condition of the *canuts* – the social partiality of the *ouvriers* as a class – with the revolutionary figure of the *people*. On the other hand, it also serves as a springboard for a new space of collective recognition, within which the weavers are able to question the traditional boundaries between professions, transcending the guild structure and legacy of their struggles. In denying the "exclusive" character of their newspaper and inviting "proletarians across all crafts, across all professions" to join it, the Lyonnais weavers made a disruptive gesture, which expressed the emergence of new forms of cross-category solidarity among workers. This gave rise to the idea of *association* which served as the generative principle of the French labour movement (Sewell, 1980, 1981).[8] Indeed, the latter's crucial discontinuity with respect to the guild tradition lay in its overcoming of the exclusively sectorial and professional character of workers' organisations: the discourse developed by the ÉDF's editorial bears witness precisely to this shift and to its linguistic dimension. Workers' reception of the neologism *prolétaires* – which had first emerged in the republican milieu as a means to assign social depth to the doctrine of popular sovereignty – expresses this emerging identity of the labour world that goes beyond the distinction between different professions and sectors. It embodies the rise of a new collective representation of the workers that paves the way for the establishment of the collective singular "working class" and, with it, the space for a unitary movement of French workers.

6.4 The Saint-Simonian movement and the "poorest and most numerous class"

"The industrialists [*industriels*], proletarians across all crafts, across all professions": this passage from the above-quoted editorial of the *Écho de la Fabrique* (XXIII, 1 April 1832, p. 1) reflects the gradual seeping of Saint-Simonian doctrine into Lyonnais mutualism, whose language and discourse it contributed to changing – as is witnessed by the increasing use of the term "industrialists" in the *canuts*' newspaper. "The Saint-Simonians only suggest senseless solutions, but at least they are addressing the question," writes Rémusat with regard to the 1831 insurrection,[9] expressing a view also shared by Villermé (1989, p. 368) in his *Tableau*: "Saint-Simonianism has unwittingly partly paved the way for the regrettable events in Lyon." "An unfortunate event soon revealed in what sense and with what effects their influence was unfolding," writes Guizot (1959, p. 167), evoking the *révolte des canuts* as a symptom of the "worsening of the anarchic perturbation" produced by the penetration of Saint-Simon's and Fourier's ideas into the "popular masses." These worlds reveal the elite's concern about the intertwining of workers' struggles with the first socialist movements, between the "utopian" activists and the workers involved in the emerging forms of mutualism and association. This is a particularly relevant conjunction because the French labour movement first emerged under the theoretical aegis of so-called "utopian" socialism. Equally significant are the tensions, impacts, and shifts which the first labour struggles produced within the nascent socialist discourse of "utopian" movements.

This impact becomes quite evident when we look at the effects of the Lyon insurrection on the politics of the Saint-Simonians, whose pacifist and reformist principles initially led them to distance themselves from the event. "Your place could be neither among the bourgeoisie's ranks nor among the workers' ones; it was in between the two" (Chevalier, 1831, p. 10), the Parisian "fathers" wrote to the Lyonnais "apostles," stressing how their doctrine ruled out any hostile stance vis-à-vis the *fabriquants* insofar as they too were *industriels* like the *canuts*.[10] Hence, the industrialist doctrine of the movement initially resulted in an equidistant position aiming to express "the voice of the upper classes among the poor, and the voice of the lower classes among the rich" (ibid.). And yet, precisely the *canuts*' revolt would appear to have brought about a significant shift within Saint-Simonian discourse: a growing focus on workers' conditions, even at the expense of other issues that until then were been central to the movement's politics.

We have already noted the leading role that this movement came to play in French political debate, particularly through the acquisition of the *Globe* in 1831 and the circulation of Saint-Simonian ideas ensured by this newspaper (cf. § 1.5). These ideas were summarised by the two catchphrases "improvement of the condition of the poorest and most numerous class" and "to each according to his ability, to each ability according to its works." Hence, the movement developed a reformist programme, suitable for the climate of its day and revolving around two fundamental proposals. First, the Saint-Simonians' critique of the property led them to call for the abolition of the juridical institute of heredity. This was presented as the logical outcome of both the processes that in 1789 had led to the abolishment of aristocratic privileges and the principle that private property must be safeguarded only insofar as it derives from work and is socially useful, because it stimulates the development of abilities. Second, the Saint-Simonians' new religious morals translated into a critique of the bourgeois family centred on the question of female emancipation and of the "absolute social equality" between the sexes:

> With respect to morals, we perform something akin to what the revolutionaries of the past three centuries have done with respect to politics and religion . . . because no one before us has been as pervaded by faith in the social equality of man and woman. . . . We will give every woman the strength to speak, that she may now challenge not only her shackles but also her judges.
>
> (Transon, 1832, pp. 5 and 9)

The relative suspicion with which the Saint-Simonians initially viewed the Lyon insurrection is therefore quite understandable. The issues at the heart of the insurrection were not directly related to the movement's core programme and its violence seemed foreign to Saint-Simonian doctrine, as did the antagonism within the industrialists' ranks (i.e. between *canuts* and *fabriquants*). However, it was precisely this event that first led to the growing intertwining of Saint-Simonian discourse with that of the first workers' struggles. From November 1831 onwards, the movement's propaganda in Lyon intensified: in February 1832 it issued a "Call to Lyonnaises of all Classes" – manufacturers, merchants, workers, artists, and women – while in the same months, *L'Écho de la fabrique* started publishing excerpts from the *Globe* with increasing frequency. To grasp this growing intertwining, it is sufficient to consider one of the last Saint-Simonian publications: the pamphlet *À Lyon! 23 novembre 1832*, which was circulated on the first anniversary of the revolt. This announced the first volunteers' departure to Lyon to establish there the "peaceful army of the workers" and fraternise with the weavers, in view of the dawning of a new social order:

> *Theoretical* politics is over for us; *practical* political life has begun. We shall practice it in Lyon, because down there new things are blossoming. . . . *We have become proletarians*: salary day, baptism day, has come . . . we will go and look for the air that is breathed and the wind that blows in the greatest manufacturing and economic centre that the European continent boasts. . . . It is to this mighty

worker that we will go to ask for the baptism of salary. . . . We will go to him with the proletarians of Paris as comrades.

(Chevalier, 1832, pp. 2–8)

We have already noted the crucial importance of the Saint-Simonian language of association's reception in the field of labour: equally relevant is this affirmation in the Saint-Simonian field of the category of "proletarians," which testifies to the emergence of an unprecedented centrality of the workers' conditions with respect to the master's doctrine and the original programme developed by his disciples. As early as 3 February 1831, the *Globe* had hosted the *Pétition d'un prolétaire à la Chambre des députés* (*Petition by a Proletarian to the Chamber of Deputies*), written by the *ouvrier horloger* Charles Béranger – a pioneering example of the adoption of this term in the labour context.[11] Then in April 1832, the Saint-Simonian Reynaud (1832) published an important article on the "representation of the proletarians" in the *Revue encyclopédique*. This growing focus on labour conditions also emerged from the workers' mounting participation in the Saint-Simonians' activities and from the way in which the Menilmontant Saint-Simonian community was affected by, and in turn affected, the lives of the young workers involved in the first workers' struggles in Paris: in other words, by the many encounters between intellectuals acting as the apostles of a new religion of humanity and proletarians searching for a way out of their painful condition as labourers. This was the "history of the complex relations between emancipated workers and the leaders of utopian schools," writes Jacques Rancière, who devoted remarkable studies to such encounters, aiming to reconstruct the tensions, short-circuits, and changes that proletarian involvement brought about with respect to the forms of Saint-Simonian apostleship and its doctrine, but also – conversely – the influence of Saint-Simonianism on the development of the nascent labour movement and its overcoming of the guild tradition through the new language of association (Rancière, 2003, p. 59, 1981). This author speaks of "an organic workers' utopia" to describe the spread in the labour world of the issue of the abolition of wage labour as the outcome of cross-fertilisation between workers' movements and Saint-Simonian, Fourierist, and Icarian-Cabetist projects (Rancière, 1975, p. 88).

6.5 The work of utopia

The interweaving of utopian socialism and the first workers' struggles that we have just considered is part of the process that brought the condition of wage labour at the centre of the projects for the emancipation of the subaltern classes that had emerged in the first half of the 19th century. But what I wish to emphasise here is how this process also coincides with the progressive removal from this field of a whole range of issues that were later to be presented as *utopian*, such as for instance the Saint-Simonian criticism of the family and of morality in the name of female emancipation. Johann Wallach Scott (1988) has rigorously reconstructed certain aspects of this "gender politics of class formation" by investigating the way in which claims and movements centred on the condition of the workman as the head of the family became predominant, stigmatising all references to the gender issue defining other movements, which were accused of immoral, fanciful, or "womanly" views.[12] This position is also shared by Michèle Riot-Sarcey (1998), who has further emphasised the way in which the adjective "utopians" itself was used in a pejorative sense to marginalise perspectives such as the Saint-Simonian one and to "banish them from the political field." Rancière (1975, pp. 96–98) has stressed the "ideological price" paid by the labour movement through its progressive detachment from the "utopian criticism of the civilised order," which in his view led to outcomes such as the acceptance of the "status quo in the domestic sphere" and the "defence of the marital order and of female subordination."

The process of the subjectivation of work we are retracing here also unfolded through the erasing from the horizon of emancipation projects of other issues that had originally been defining elements of "utopian" socialism. The affirmation of the centrality of wage labour coincides with the obliteration not just of the woman question, but of any positions promoting a break with the paradigms of rationality characterising bourgeois civilisation, that is, any discourse on sensualism, esoterism, and the criticism of labour, pedagogy, technology, consumption, the family, punishment, and the penal system (Rancière, 1985; Abensour, 2013; Tomasello, 2017). Such discourses were to be marginalised by confining them to the field of "utopias" – and hence of the non-political. In the case of Saint-Simonianism, what contributed to this marginalisation was initiatives such as the publication of *Appel à la Femme libre* in 1831, the eccentric forms which the movement took under Enfantin's leadership, and the effort to develop a criticism of morality through the creation of a new kind of family in the Menilmontant community. Furthermore, in January 1832 the Rue Taitbout amphitheatre, the Saint-Simonians' preaching venue, was searched and sealed off, while the movement's leading representatives were charged with the crimes of unlawful association and contempt of public morals. The subsequent arrest of Prosper Enfantin, Michel Chevalier, and Charles Duveyrier eventually led to the dissolution of the movement.[13]

For all these reasons, the Saint-Simonians also became an object of mockery, which obscured the cogency and depth of their proposals for reform. We have seen how the questions they raised were actually quite consistent with the political and theoretical climate of an age of palingenesis such as in the 1830s in France. This was a period generally marked by the search for new strategies for governing and ordering the new society of individuals forged by the revolutionary breaks, as well as for laying radical new foundations for the social body, in such a way as to draw together the threads of the long post-revolutionary transition and heal its wounds (cf. §§ 1.3 and 1.5). The Saint-Simonians are prominent representatives of this climate fraught with uncertainty and marked by a deep eagerness to find rational means of governing modern liberties, discover the laws that bind together those individuals who makeup society, invent catchwords and concepts to establish a new shared sensibility, and develop emancipatory projects which were up to the challenges of the 19th century. This complex range of problems is masterfully captured by the way in which Victor Hugo evokes the climate of 1832 in *Les Misérables*:

> In the meantime, at home, pauperism, beggary, wages, education, the penal code, prostitution, the fall of woman, wealth, misery, production, consumption, assessment, exchange, money, credit, the rights of capital, the rights of labor – all these questions were multiplied above society; a terrible precipice . . . Thinking men meditated, while the soil, that is to say the people, traversed by the revolutionary currents, trembled beneath them.
>
> (Hugo, 1893, pp. 42–43)

It was from this vast and diverse field of subjects and problems, and its intertwining with the fast-paced events of the early 1830s, that a *socialist discourse* emerged. From the wide range of phenomena and ways of life initially encompassed by expressions such as "pauperism" and "social question," this discourse eventually came to focus on more specific pragmatics of the "labouring classes," and progressively came to express this notion through the singular "working class." This collective singular also served to reduce the complex range of problems recalled here through Hugo's words by processing it and establishing a somewhat unitary representation revolving around the strong figure of the wage worker. The very meaning of the concept of class was thus anchored in the question of wage labour, and the Saint-Simonian theme of "the poorest and most numerous class" thus became that of the working class. This resulted in a powerful politicisation of labour that had also the effect of consequently marginalising other social claims and subjects, which were to be confined to the sphere of the "unpolitical." The spread of the expression "working class" within political language would therefore appear to express a movement of resignification of the needs and interests of the subaltern classes that represent, unifies, and politicises them through the centrality of work and the condition of wage labour.

What I aim to highlight here is the contingent nature of this development which, far from realising a kind of necessity immanent in the transformation of industrial society – or in the very ontology of the modern subject – stems from a complex, sticky, and heterogeneous subjectivation process that is historically determined by the intertwining of the course of events with the transformations of political discourse. On the other hand, this subjectivation process revolving around the figure of the wage workers only becomes fully intelligible if we also consider its points of conjunction with the social representations produced by the processes of "objectivation" of the workers' condition as a sphere of investigation and governance that were the focus of this book's first part.

6.6 The labour movement and the borders of politics

Through this reading of the 1831 insurrection, I have sought to intertwine its historical singularity as an event with its long-term effects in terms of political ideas, concepts, and languages. I have therefore stressed its capacity to stir republican and utopian movements into action by stimulating the genesis of a socialist discourse, and to impact the public debate developed over the course of the long post-revolutionary transition by challenging established representations and leading to new interpretations of shared truths and world images. These effects also clearly emerge from the discursive strategies deployed by the ruling elites to affirm their interpretation of the Lyon events in public debate. These discourses chiefly aim to establish the *non-political* nature of the insurrection and its "otherness" with respect to politics – to the field of political facts and discourses. In the government's report to the Chamber, Prime Minister Périer states:

> We are glad to confirm one of the first observations made concerning these deplorable events, namely that their causes, as much as their consequences, would appear to be generally alien to any kind of political thought . . . and this constitutes a point of strength for our authorities.
>
> (Périer, 1831, p. 7)

The very issue of the political – or unpolitical – character of the insurrection also lies at the centre of the polemic between the republicans of the *National* and the liberal Orléanists of the *Journal des débats*. The latter constantly stressed the "lack of any political character in the Lyonnais workers' uprising," and hence the radical difference "between the Lyonnais social movement and the Parisian political movement" of July 1830 (cf. § 6.1).[14] Hence, the metaphor of the 'new barbarians' – presented in Girardin's famous editorial of 8 December 1831 (cf. § 2.1) – crystallised this representation of the insurrection's alterity with respect to the political sphere. "It was then fully established [*bien établi*] that there was nothing political about the Lyon riots," recalls Rémusat (1959, p. 538), bearing witness to the active effort to validate this interpretation while bemoaning the fact that, in parliamentary debate, little attention had been paid to the "dangers of a new sort" that "could be hazily glimpsed in the insurrection."

In contrast to these representations, the theme of labour and workers' condition was destined to acquire increasingly disruptive political meanings within public debate. In the first relevant historical reconstruction of the *révolte des canuts*, liberal physician Jean-Baptiste Monfalcon accurately grasps this point by writing that "one of the most momentous consequences" of the event was that it turned "the Lyonnais workers into a political class."

> This large and powerful weavers' association . . . had established itself as an authority vis-à-vis the lawful authorities, turned the interests of 80,000 individuals into a single interest and their wills into a single will, and gave their vast class the unity of thought and action of a single man. . . . Practically the whole weavers' class had established itself as a deliberating and acting society . . . operating, in the face of the lawful authorities, as a new authority – the most obeyed one of all.
>
> (Monfalcon, 1834, pp. 99, 2, 149, 151)[15]

By drawing upon the notion of the general will – by which the French Revolution had translated the social contract principles into political institutions – to describe the actions undertaken by the weavers and their transformation into a "political class," this author presciently seems to grasp the rise of the constituent power of labour. The emergence of the category *working class* would appear to express this fact and the process of producing a political subjectivity that somehow established itself alongside the sovereign one of the State. Just as the latter's sovereignty – according to the modern tradition of Western thought from Hobbes to Rousseau and Hegel – unified the multitude of individuals into the singular political body of the people, so the figure of the "working class," by progressively expressing the world of the subaltern classes in the singular – and offering an image of integration far more solid than the category of the proletariat – embodied the rise of a powerful new actor. The latter emerged within – and sometimes against – the sphere of the political State, even leading to a significant redefinition of the State's aims and functions, and along with them, of the forms and boundaries of the political sphere. Ultimately, over the course of the 20th century, this actor – the working class organised as the labour movement – succeeded in establishing the protection of the interests, needs, and rights of "labour" as one of the normative horizons of the democratic state, while at the same time creating an unbreakable link between the condition of wage workers and the very meaning of labour (cf. Conclusion).

After overcoming their initial reluctance, the *canuts* too came to affirm the political significance of their insurrection, against the government's arguments:

> Yesterday, even yesterday, bullets were ringing in our ears, and blood was running on both sides, misery was there, hideous, flagrant . . . . ; a social problem of immense scope was posed before our legislators; that of harmonising the demands of hunger with those of competition . . . . ; this petition was presented to the Chambers, blackened by the smoke of battle, still warm with French blood . . . What mockery! . . . Capitalists . . . . Workers . . . Your representatives and rulers have not focused on the remedies to be adopted, but on the causes of your ills, and it will be a great consolation to you to know that there was nothing political about this movement! Nothing political – that's what they think! Ah! Is *our own politics* not the well-being of our women and children?
>
> (ÉDF, XIII, 22 January 1832, emphasis added)

The expression *notre politique à nous* reveals the conflict which the insurrection had given rise to concerning the meaning of the word "politics." We must "show those politicians who insist on isolating politics from all other questions that they are heading in an opposite direction compared to the aim of politics," writes Pierre Leroux (1832, p. 281), who was one of the founders of the *Globe* leading it towards Saint-Simonianism, a theoriser of the union between utopian socialism and the democratic question, and the "inventor" of the term "socialism" (Abensour, 2013; Tomasello, 2017). Similar perceptions that the *canuts*' uprising was ultimately engendering a redefinition of the political field also emerge from the readers' corner in the *Globe*, which gave voice to many workers' opinions: "The Lyon events have changed the meaning of the word *politics*; they have broadened it. Labour interests have entered the sphere of *politics* for good and are increasingly extending within it" (Chevalier, 1832, p. 16).

While future historians were to regard the Lyon insurrection as marking the birth of the labour movement, these sources from the period primarily associated the event with the semantic transformation and broadening of the word "politics" determined by the emergence of the political meaning of labour. As far as this book's aim is concerned, the historic-political significance of the Lyon insurrection lies precisely in its capacity to bring out and call into question the *borders of politics*, the borders of the political sphere. In other words, it lies in the challenging and transforming of the boundaries of the notion of politics that define the conditions which statements and events must meet to be acknowledged as part of the "political" realm. For most of the 19th century, these shifting boundaries were the object of conflicts designed to redefine the forms and aims of politics, until these became crystallised in an idea of citizenship founded on labour which made its first, extemporaneous appearance with the 1848 events and was subsequently epitomised by the emergence of modern social rights and welfare principles.

Discussing these events from his exile, François Guizot – whose theory of capacity-based representation envisaged the condition of paid manual labour as the general threshold for exclusion from political rights (cf. § 1.4) – denounced precisely this process of mutual "resignification" that had emerged between the notion of politics and that of labour:

> By what chance has the word labour, so glorious for modern civilisation, become a war cry and source of disaster among us today? Because this word conceals a great and deplorable lie. It is not at all labour, its interests, and its needs that are at stake in the turmoil caused in its name. . . . Look at the meaning that the word labour usually carries in the language of this antisocial war. . . . it is material labour alone that people are concerned about, that is constantly being presented as labour par excellence and which overshadows all other kinds of work. Words are being uttered that are bound to foster and sustain a feeling in the spirit of manual labourers that theirs is the only kind of labour worthy of this name and carrying the rights associated with work. . . . All rights are being assigned to the abstract quality of being a labourer, regardless of individual merits.
>
> (Guizot, 1849, pp. 86–89)

In the face of the powerful workers' mobilisations that marked the 1848 events in France, Guizot thus stressed the transformation of the "meaning of the word labour," which had come to revolve around the condition of workers as "manual labourers," to the point of establishing a direct connection between it and "all [citizens'] rights." It is possible to detect in this a first crystallisation of the whole range of processes examined throughout this book, coinciding with the affirmation of the *political character of labour* and the connection between the concept of labour, the workers' condition, and the political sphere of citizenship rights. Hence the possibility of interpreting the process of the French labour movement's formation as a heterogeneous sum of events, claims, and linguistic acts that gradually came to revolve around a set of common principles, thereby contributing to the emergence of the kind of unitary representation of popular needs and interests that came to be called the working class. Within the broader field of subjects and problems related to the social question, pauperism, and subalternity, this representation affirmed the centrality of wage labour. This enabled workers to emerge as a "social class" that was to become politically entitled to claim a new set of citizenship rights linked to its specific collective condition – that is, the rights resulting from the principles of modern labour-based welfare. In this regard, the emergence of the labour movement may be understood as a subjectivation process unfolding on the political-discursive level and as a "discursive formation and practice" designed to affirm the political significance of labour.[16] This necessarily implied a redefinition of the very meaning of the word politics and of the boundaries of the political sphere through the inclusion of hitherto foreign subjects and problems.

Notes

1 On the contradiction represented by the revolutionary foundations of the Orléanist monarchy, see Morabito (2008), Rosanvallon (1985, 1994, 1998), and cf. *supra* § 1.2.

2 With regard to the use of the term class I am proposing here, see J-C. Minler (1983). On the discursive strategies adopted by republicans with respect to the November events in Lyon, see Rude (2007, pp. 235–238) and Riot-Sarcey (1998, pp. 179–188).

3 Société des Amis du Peuple (1832, pp. xxix and 2–3). All 28 publications issued by the SAP in the two years of its existence are collected in the volume *La Société des amis du peuple 1830–32*, which is the second of the twelve-volume series *Les révolutions du XIXe siècle*, published by EDHIS in 1974. The most substantial of such publications is entitled *Procès des quinze* and brings together the banned pamphlets and the addresses of the defendents (who had been charged with press offences). The trial "was huge," recalls François-Vincent Raspail (1984, pp. 192–199): "from early morning the court building's corridors were teeming with members of the public, police, and soldiers." On the SAP's history see also Caron (1980).

4 The historical dictionary of the French language traces the modern "establishment" of the term *prolétariat* back to 1832 (Rey, 1992, vol. III, p. 112). The term indeed appears in the 1832 edition of F. Raymond's *Dictionnaire général de la langue française* (Paris, André, p. 304: "among the moderns, it is said of those who are propertyless") and in the 1835 edition of the *Dictionnaire de l'Académie française* (vol. II, pp. 514–515): "by extensions, in modern states it is said of those who have neither wealth nor an adequately lucrative profession." In April 1832 the *Revue encyclopédique* published the important article *De la necessité d'une réprésentation spéciale pour les prolétaires*, in which Jean Reynaud (1832) compared modern proletarians to the Spartan 'helots', serfs owned by the State and lacking any rights.

5 Starting with the reorganisation of the army carried out by Servius Tullius in the 6th cent. BC, the *proletarii* were defined as those individuals who lacked the income required to be registered as members of one of the five classes into which the *populus* was divided; they were therefore exempted from taxes and military service (they only served the State through their offspring). While being socially part of the Roman population, they

were therefore excluded from the *populus* and from participation in State life on account of their condition of indigence.

6 It is on the basis of this interpretation of the process of proletarian subjectivation in France in the years 1830–48 that – from the early 1970s – this author moved away from Althusserian Marxism and embarked on an investigation of political philosophy's theoretical status that eventually led to the theses expressed in *La Mésentete* (1995). Furthermore, by contrast to the kind of interpretations focusing on popular and artisan cultures that are typical of the "new social history" school (cf. § 5.3), Rancière primarily interprets working-class sources – proletarian writing and the voicing of proletarian views – as a "work of disidentification," as a break with the established relations between the level of discourse and that of social conditions, with an imposed identity that assigns the worker specific modes of expression that correspond to a specific social position.

7 See also Guilhaumou (2008), who analyses the "forms of lexicalisation" of the signifiers *travailleurs*, *industriels*, and *ouvriers* in relation to the notions of *peuple* and *prolétaire*, highlighting the way in which the workers overturned the meaning assigned to the latter notion by the bourgeois press.

8 It is worth noting that the powerful impact of the idea of association also involved the republican field of the SAP, whose pamphlet on the 1832 trial states: "Association. This word encapsulates our thought as a whole. We associate to be stronger and to give those thoughts we feel to be good and fruitful the kind of authority which can ensure their dominance. . . . We are proud to act by means of association" (SAP, 1832).

9 Rémusat's letter of 13 December 1831, cit. Barante (1894, p. 400).

10 All the Saint-Simonian movement's publications are filed under Michel Chevalier's name, as he was the movement's treasurer and the editor-in-chief of *Le Globe*.

11 The text was also published separately as Béranger (1831).

12 See Scott (1988): cf. esp. the chapters "Women Workers in the Discourse of French Political Economy, 1840–60" – noting the construction of a gender-based division of labour in the studies by French political economists, and the reception of this perspective within the nascent labour movement – and "Work Identities for Men and Women: The Politics of Work and Family in the Parisian Garment Trades in 1848" – which analyses the different claims advanced by Parisian seamstresses and tailors, emphasising how gender oppositions structured different programmes and claims among workers. Hence, this author highlights the gendered character of a category such as "working class," which emerged as a new universal category by confining women to a condition of invisibility or "exception."

13 The trial was then held in August 1832 and attracted broad public interest, also owing to the conduct of the defendants, who would only speak when authorised by Prosper Enfantin. Concerning the "utopian-political" history of Saint-Simonianism see Tomasello (2015).

14 *Journal des débats*, 6 and 7 December 1831, p. 1: "once politics has been removed from the Lyon uprising, what does it amount to? A deplorable attack on the rule of law, a painful crisis, but of the sort that is ultimately found in the history of all nations and trade cities."

15 Chateaubriand (1831, p. 4) stresses a similar aspect when he writes "These workers who negotiated, by despatching envoys, engaged with the July monarchy on an equal footing."

16 I am employing the notion of "discursive formation" – or simply "discourse" – in the sense described by Michel Foucault (1969, 1971), i.e. as a set of *enoncés* (utterances) originating within different spheres which, nonetheless, obey to a single logic, arise from the same system of formation, develop through common principles of articulation, and deploy their truth effects through the production of forms of knowledge, practices, and strategies.

References

Abensour M. (2013), *Utopiques I. Le procès des Maîtres rêveurs (2000)*, Sens & Tonka, Paris.

Barante P.B. de. (1894), *Souvenirs du Baron de Barante de l'Académie française*, vol. IV, Calman-Levy, Paris.

Béranger C. (1831), *Pétition d'un prolétaire à la Chambre des deputes*, au Bureau de l'organisateur, Paris.

Blanqui, L-A. (1971), *Textes Choisis*, Éditions Sociales, Paris.

Caron J-C. (1980), La Société des Amis du Peuple. *Romantisme*, 28–29: 169–179.

Chateaubriand F.R. de. (1831), A Mm. les redacteurs de la Revue Européenne. *La Revue Européenne*, 2(4): 1–10.

Cherbuliez A. (1873), Pauperisme, in *Dictionnaire d'économie politique*, Cocquelin-Guillaumin, Paris, p. 574.

Chevalier M., dir. (1831), *Événements de Lyon*, Éverat, Paris.

Chevalier M., dir. (1832), *A Lyon! 23 novembre 1832*, Duverger, Paris.

Desjardins G. (1833), *Discours du citoyen G. Desjardins sur la misère du peuple, prononcé à l'audience de la Cour d'assises du 22 février, dans l'affaire de la Société des amis du peuple*, impr. de A. Mie, Paris.

Dictionnaire de l'Académie française, Firmin-Didot, Paris 1835.

Dolléans É. (1936), *Histoire du mouvement ouvrier*, vol. I, Collin, Paris.

Écho de la Fabrique. (1831–1834), Lyon. Retrieved from: http://echo-fabrique.ens-lyon.fr/index.php

Foucault M. (1969), *L'archéologie du savoir*, Gallimard, Paris.

Foucault M. (1971), *L'ordre du discours*, Gallimard, Paris.

Gazette de France. (1797–1848), Paris. Bibliothèque nationale de France, département Philosophie, histoire, sciences de l'homme, 4-LC2–1, Identifier: ark:/12148/cb41265446t/

Guilhaumou J. (2008), De *peuple* à *prolétaire(s)*: Antoine Vidal, porte-parole des ouvriers dans *L'Écho de la Fabrique* en 1831–1832. *Semen*, 25: 101–115.

Guizot F. (1849), *De la démocratie en France*, Plon-Masson, Paris.

Guizot F. (1959), *Mémoires pour servir à l'histoire de mon temps (1859)*, Laffont, Paris.

Hugo V. (1842), Dicté après juillet 1830, in Id (ed.), *Les chants du crépuscule (1835)*, Cans&Cie, Bruxelles.

Hugo V. (1893), *Les Miserables*, vol. IV, book 1, trans. M. Edouard Jolivet, George Barrie & Son, Philadelphia (or. ed. *Les misérables*, Paris 1862).

Jakobowicz N. (2009), *1830 Le Peuple de Paris. Révolution et représentations sociales*, PUR, Rennes.

Journal des Débats. (1814–1944), Paris. Retrieved from: https://gallica.bnf.fr/ark:/12148/cb39294634r/date&rk=42918;4

Koselleck R. (1975), Geschichte, Historie, in Otto Brunner, Werner Conze, Reinhart Koselleck (eds.), *Geschichtliche Grundbegriffe: lexikon zur politisch-sozialen Sprache in Deutschland*, vol. 2, Klett-Cotta, Stuttgart, pp. 647–717.

Koselleck R. (1979), *Vergangene Zukunft: Zur Semantik geschichtlicher Zeiten*, Suhrkamp Verlag, Franfurt am Main (Eng. trans. *Futures Past: On the Semantics of Historical Time*, Columbia University Press, New York 2004).

Le Globe. (1824–1832), Paris. Retrieved from: https://gallica.bnf.fr/ark:/12148/cb327828335/date&rk=21459;2

Le National. (1830–1851), Paris. Retrieved from: https://gallica.bnf.fr/ark:/12148/cb32822285p/date

Leroux P. (1832), De la Philosophie et du Christianisme. *Revue Encyclopédique*, LV: 281–340.

Marbe M. (1904), *Ètude historique des idées sur la souveraineté de 1815 à 1848*, LGDJ, Paris.

Merriman J.M. (ed.) (1975), *1830 in France*, New View Point, New York.

Michelet J. (1831), *Introduction à l'histoire universelle*, Hachette, Paris.

Minler J-C. (dir.) (1983), *Les noms indistincts*, Ch. 11: *Les classes paradoxales*, Seuil, Paris.

Monfalcon J-B. (1834), *Histoire des insurrections de Lyon en 1831 et en 1834*, Perrin, Lyon.

Morabito M. (2008), *Histoire constitutionelle de la France (1789–1958)*, Montchrestien, Paris.

Newman E. (1975), *What the Crowd Wanted in the French Revolution of 1830*, in J.M. Merriman (ed.), *1830 in France*, New View Point, New York, pp. 17–41.

Périer C. (1831), *Communication faite au nom du gouvernement à la chambre des députés sur les troubles de Lyon par M. le président du conseil*, Imp. Royale, Paris.

Pessin A. (1992), *Le mythe du peuple et la société française de XIXe siècle*, PUF, Paris.

Pinkney D.H. (1972), *The French Revolution of 1830*, Princeton University Press, Princeton.

Pinkney D.H. (1974), The Crowd in the French Revolution of 1830. *American Historical Review*, 70: 1–17.

Rancière J. (1975), Utopistes, bourgeois et prolétaires. *L'homme et la société*, 37/38: 87–98.

Rancière J. (1981), *La nuit des prolétaires. Archives du rêve ouvrier*, Fayard, Paris (Eng. transl. *The Nights of Labor: The Workers' Dream in Nineteenth-Century France*, Temple University Press, Philadelphia 1989).

Rancière J. (1985), Savoirs hérétique et émancipation du pauvre, in *AA.VV. Les sauvages dans la cité. Auto-émancipation du peuple et instruction des prolétaires au XIXe siècle*, Seyssel, Champ Vallon, pp. 34–53.

Rancière J. (1992), *Les mots de l'histoire. Essai de poétique du savoir*, Seuil, Paris.

Rancière J. (1995), *La Mésentente. Politique et philosophie*, Editions Galilée, Paris (Eng. transl. *Disagreement: Politics And Philosophy*, University of Minnesota Press, Minneapolis 1999).

Rancière J. (2003), La scène révolutionnaire et l'ouvier émancipé (1830–1848) (1st ed. 1988). *Tumultes*, 20(1): 49–72.

Rancière J. (2007), Introduction, in J. Rancière, A. Faure (eds.), *La parole ouvrière* (1976), La fabrique, Paris, pp. 9–17.

Raspail F-V. (1984), *Les Avenues de la République. Souvenirs de F-V. Raspail sur sa vie et sur son siècle 1794–1878*, a cura di Y. Lemoine e P. Lenoel, Hachette, Paris.

Raymond F. (1832), *Dictionnaire général de la langue française*, André, Paris.

Rémusat C. de. (1959), *Mémoires de ma vie, volume 2: La Restauration ultra-royaliste. La Révolution de Juillet (1820–1832)*, Plon, Paris.

Rey A. (dir.) (1992), *Dictionnaire historique de la langue française*, vol. II, Le Robert, Paris.

Reynaud J. (1832), De la necessité d'une réprésentation spéciale pour les prolétaires. *Revue encyclopédique*, April: 1–20.

Riot-Sarcey M. (1998), *Le réel de l'utopie. Essai sur le politique au XIXe siècle*, Alvin Michel, Paris.

Rosanvallon P. (1985), *Le moment Guizot*, Gallimard, Paris.

Rosanvallon P. (1992), *Le sacre du citoyen. Histoire du suffrage universel en France*, Gallimard, Paris.

ROSANVALLON P. (1994), *La monarchie impossible. Les Chartes de 1814 et 1830*, Fayard, Paris.

ROSANVALLON P. (1998), *Le Peuple introuvable. Histoire de la représentation démocratique en France*, Gallimard, Paris.

ROSEMBERG A. (1939), *Democracy and Socialism: A Contribution to the Political History of the Past 150 Years*, Knopf, London (or. ed. *Demokratie und Sozialismus, Zur politischen Geschichte der letzen 150 Jahre*, De Lange, Amsterdam 1938).

RUDE F. (2007), *Les révoltes des canuts 1831–1834*, La Decouverte, Paris (or. ed. 1982).

SAP-SOCIÉTÉ DES AMIS DU PEUPLE. (1830), *Manifeste de la Sap*, Auguste Mie, Paris.

SAP-SOCIÉTÉ DES AMIS DU PEOPLE. (1831), *La voix du people: brochure publiée par la Société des amis du people* (Décembre 1831), David, Paris.

SAP-SOCIÉTÉ DES AMIS DU PEUPLE. (1832), *Procès des quinze*, Auguste Mie, Paris.

SCOTT J.W. (1988), *Gender and the Politics of History*, Columbia University Press, New York.

SEWELL W.H. (1980), *Work and Revolution in France: The Language of Labor from the Old Regime to 1848*, CUP, Cambridge.

SEWELL W.H. (1981), La confraternité des prolétaires: conscience de classe sous la monarchie de Juillet. *Annales. Économies, Sociétés, Civilisations*, 36(4): 650–671.

TOMASELLO F. (2015), Utopia e politica del movimento sansimoniano (1825–1835). *MORUS. Utopia e Renascimento, 10*: 55–75.

TOMASELLO F. (2017), L'utopia come politica dell'emancipazione. Miguel Abensour, Jacques Rancière e le eredità del socialismo utopico. *Scienza & Politica*, 28(56): 57–86.

TRANSON A. (1832), *Religion saint-simonienne. Affranchissement des femmes, prédication du 1er janvier 1832*, Bureau du Globe, Paris.

VILLERMÉ L-R. (1989), *Tableau de l'état physique et moral des ouvriers employés dans les manifactures de coton, de laine et de soie*, Études et documentations internationales, Paris.

Conclusion

The present investigation has led us to approach the 1848 events, which are generally regarded as a major turning point in 19th-century European history, insofar as they led to the affirmation of a different hierarchy of subjects and problems, marked by the growing role of the working class and the rise of socialist discourse. On 21 February, the first edition of Marx and Engels' *Manifesto* was published in London. Two days later, in Paris, the revolution drove out the king and the Guizot government, ushering in the French Second Republic. The events that followed this revolutionary break represent the first crystallisation of the processes we have been considering so far. Work and its organisation became an entirely political issue at the centre of the claims concerning social conditions that were now being advanced in addition to the kind of petitions for political rights which had triggered the Parisian upheaval. The core of the political arena came to be occupied by the growing claim for the "right to work," the creation of the Luxembourg Commission to debate the labour question, the establishment of *ateliers nationaux* (national workshops) to ensure government-funded jobs, and the political struggle culminating in the dramatic workers' insurrection that took place between 22 and 26 June 1848. As Alexis de Tocqueville stressed, people, pundits, and thinkers at the time struggled to make sense of these debates and events through traditional political categories:

> It was not, strictly speaking, a political struggle, in the sense which until then we had given to the world, but a combat of class against class, a sort of Servile War. . . . What distinguished [this revolution] also, among all the events of this kind which have succeeded one another in France for sixty years, is that it did not aim at changing the form of government, but at altering the order of society.
>
> (Tocqueville, 1995, p. 136)

According to Tocqueville's words, what appeared to have been called into question and reshaped by the events following the revolution of February 1848 was the very "sense" of the "word" politics – as it had been understood until that moment. This was the result of the new claims that were being raised in relation to the social

DOI: 10.4324/9781003303497-10

sphere and, more specifically, of the new role and political significance that labour was acquiring in the public sphere.

Within the revolutionary process, the popular masses primarily represented themselves as "working classes," and laid claim to rights that were inherent to this social condition. They pressured the new authorities into passing the decree of 25 February 1848, which stated: "the provisional government of the French Republic undertakes to ensure workers' subsistence through work. It undertakes to guarantee work for every citizen" (Lamartine, 1849; Marx, 1850, 1852; Garnier-Pagès, 1866; Blanc, 1870). The following day the *ateliers nationaux* were established (Thomas, 1848). By marking a substantial break with respect to the political conflicts of the past and to the field of problems that had shaped the whole post-revolutionary transition, the people of Paris now struggled for the "right to work" (Scotto, 2021). In such a way, it claimed labour and its organisation to become a new specific field of mediation of the relationship between the State and its citizens. It was precisely this struggle that determined the subsequent course of the revolution, as in June 1848 the Parisian working classes rose up against the plan to close the *ateliers nationax*, thus deploying that emerging form of contentious politics that was destined to take the name of "class-struggle" and to mark the rest of the century.

> The June revolution – wrote Friedrich Engels (1977, p. 130) – offers the spectacle of an embittered battle such as . . . the world in general have never seen before. . . . The workers of June 23 are fighting for their existence and the fatherland has lost all meaning for them. . . . The *Marseillaise* and all memories of the great Revolution have disappeared. The people as well as the bourgeoisie sense that the revolution which they are experiencing will be more significant than that of 1789 or 1793.

Viewed from the perspective of the present enquiry, the profound break marked by the 1848 events was due to in the fact that a political demand was advanced to generalise the condition of wage labour as the new horizon of a society in which each *citoyen* had the right and duty to be a *travailleur*. This was a struggle to affirm a new idea of the State and of its functions, now charged with the mission of promoting the advent of a "civilisation of work."[1]

* * *

Quashed in 1848, this demand nonetheless expressed a principle destined to permeate European political culture as a whole, starting from the socialist and social democratic fields but then largely transcending their boundaries. Indeed, several post-WWII constitutions in Europe define work as a major right and duty of all citizens, to be promoted by the State to achieve a substantive democracy. "Each person has the right to work and the right to find employment," reads the Preamble to the French Constitution of 1946. The first chapter of the Italian one of 1948 states that "Italy is a democratic Republic founded on labour," while Chapter 4 grants "all citizens the right to work" and commits the State to promote "conditions that render this right effective." A similar "workist" framework marks the Spanish constitution (1978) – which affirms "the duty to work and the right to work" (art. 35) – and the Greek one, which describes work as "a right" that enjoys "the protection of the State, which shall care for the creation of conditions of employment for all citizens" (art. 22). Hence, this horizon of "full employment" has been actively pursued by governments to fulfil the right and duty to work for all citizens as the pillar of substantive democratic citizenship. It has offered one of the most cogent expressions of the idea that the State is called to realise the full identity between the figure of the citizen and that of the worker. This points to the affirmation of the dyadic figure of the *citizen-worker* as the quintessential subject of rights, the figure which defines the political anthropology of citizenship throughout the European 20th century.

This political anthropology emerges from the image of societies in which it is through work that an individual becomes a full citizen and expresses himself as such; the very idea of social security primarily designates employment security; participation in the public life of the political community is tied to participation in the labour market; and work "ethic" and "discipline" are considered to crucially underpin the social order. In this framework, the figure of the "good citizen" tends to reflect that of the earnest worker who contributes to national welfare through his daily hard labour. This conception also reveals an understanding of work as a moral obligation, social duty, and public value regardless of the harsh and petty material forms it has often taken – e.g. in the assembly lines of big factories. In this sense, we can regard the mature industrial societies of democratic post-WWII Europe as being based on an implicit social contract, which exchanged social security and a certain standard of living for subjection to the discipline of the repetitive – and sometimes alienating – work producing the nation's wealth. Welfare regulations and social citizenship rights embodied the legal technology making such an exchange possible through redistribution policies that supported the growth of a secure working class able to enjoy full inclusion in citizenship guarantees and to act as confident consumers within a mass-production economy. In this scenario, labour and citizenship became overlapping institutional spheres and the nexus between the two shaped the whole architecture of social citizenship down to the present day.

However, the "citizen-worker" that embodies the political anthropology of this model of citizenship does not encompass or refer to the world of labour as a whole. Rather, this figure crystallises the hegemony of a specific historical idea of work: male adult-paid (formal) employment. This is a representation of work primarily based on a distinction – underpinned by a gender hierarchy – between paid productive labour and unpaid reproductive labour. Such a division has played a crucial role in designing social protections in mature industrial societies and a structure of welfare regulations ultimately based – albeit to different degrees – on employment. Most social rights have been conceived of as insurance for workers who are unable to participate in the formal labour market: social insurance for sickness, injuries, and disabilities, pensions as a social right upon retirement, insurance for unemployment, active labour market policies, family benefits, etc. Although formally universalistic, social rights ultimately reveal an implicitly conditional character, insofar as they are closely connected to employment conditions: the elderly, the unemployed, and the poor living on welfare are regarded as a workforce that has been – either permanently or temporarily – excluded from the job market owing to objective circumstances.[2] We can therefore describe European systems of social citizenship as based on an implicit anthropology identifying labour with paid employment and the figure of the citizen with that of the worker as the quintessential subject of rights.

This edifice has come to be regarded as the defining feature of a "European model" of citizenship, in which social insecurity has been largely reduced through the provision of universalistic and constitutionally recognised welfare services. Over the last four decades, however, such a model has entered into an enduring crisis owing to several factors, including a deep transformation of the role and meaning of work. New social cleavages – often related to generational differences – have emerged and grown between "citizen-workers" who are still fully included in welfare regulations and the emerging figures of a contingent and precarious workforce, reproductive and unpaid labourers, self-employed and gig workers, and underemployed citizens who are – partly and to different degrees – excluded from such regulations. This rift indicates an emerging point of crisis with regard to the political anthropology of citizenship that has emerged from 1848 and developed throughout the 20th century. In many European countries, social security systems still seem to be largely modelled on a work standard that has ceased to be typical. While employment is still considered a major citizen right, duty or even virtue, and still represents the main means of inclusion into the institutions of social citizenship and our systems of social recognition, rights claims on the grounds of lifelong full-time paid employment can no longer be considered the norm. Digital automation is increasing the number of jobs performed by thinking machines, while the horizon of full employment seems to have turned into an illusory goal in several European countries. Moreover, the so-called "great resignation" that we have witnessed in recent years bears witness to the fact that the social and existential meaning associated with labour is changing (Tessema et al., 2022; Serenk, 2022). As I have argued elsewhere (Tomasello, 2022), the magnitude of these phenomena is vast enough to call into question the very social contract underlying our labour-based societies and systems of welfare. Major phenomena of our times such as globalisation, technological transformation, demographic change, neoliberal economic governance, and post-industrial transition have profoundly challenged the very nature and meaning of labour, to the point that even the simple dichotomy between employed and unemployed is losing its heuristic value.

This range of processes is profoundly eroding the nexus between labour and citizenship that has emerged since 1848, and the enduring crisis of European welfare states is also the result of this political fracture. The latter ultimately corresponds to a potential crisis of civilisation stemming from the condition in which societies find themselves once they become incapable of providing the kind of support that they themselves have established as the fundamental means for social and political inclusion. In my view, this fracture brings out the need for a new political anthropology of citizenship and of the modern subject capable of overcoming the dyadic figure of the citizen-worker as the quintessential bearer of rights. This means rethinking the social contract underlying our labour-based societies, the very meaning of the idea of work beyond its identification with paid employment, and the role that the latter should play in the systems of citizenship and social recognition of a democratic society.

* * *

By examining the context of post-revolutionary France in the first half of the 19th century, the present book has retraced some of the processes by which the conditions for the profound entanglement between labour and citizenship emerged. Compared to more established interpretations centred on the rise of the labour movement and of the democratic and socialist perspective, I have sought to stress other factors as well, such as epidemic crises, the unfolding of liberal strategies for dealing with the social question, and the role played by the rise of the modern social sciences. I have thus sought to reconstruct the spurious and multifaceted character of those processes which led to the establishment of labour at the centre of an emerging architecture of citizenship rights. In doing so, I have sought to present this centrality of labour for the world images that define contemporary subjectivity not as a timeless truth that realises a necessity immanent in the development of our civilisations, but as a historically defined configuration which, as such, is structurally destined to change. My aim has been to provide a contribution in view of interpretations of our times capable of newly firing the imagination, understood as a critical capacity for innovation, so as to outline perspectives and ways out of the present crisis that goes beyond the mere reformulation of trajectories already undertaken in the past.

Notes

1 The position assigned to labour in the constitution of the French Second Republic already reveals a first crystallisation – within the sphere of public law – of the processes this book has been considering. Even though the debate on the "right to work" eventually led to the compromise formula of the "right to assistance" – which established the Republic's duty to secure work for citizens "within the limits of its resources" – the constitution passed by the National Assembly on 4 November 1848 assigned unprecedented relevance to labour in the legal-political sphere (cf. Garnier, 1848; Donzelot, 1984; De Boni, 2002; Scotto, 2021). Art. 4 of the Preamble presents labour as the "basis" of the Republic, along with the family, property, and public order, while art. 12 of the second *Chapitre* reads: "society favours and encourages the development of labour" through education, civil equality between employers and employees, credit and social security institutes, and public work for the unemployed.

2 See e.g. Beveridge (1942), which is usually regarded as a crucial milestone in the establishment of universalistic social rights.

References

Beveridge W. (1942), *Social Insurance and Allied Services*, MacMillan, London.

Blanc L. (1870), *Histoire de la révolution de 1848*, vol. I, Lacroix, Verboeckhoven et Cie, Paris.

De Boni C. (2002), *Il diritto al lavoro nel 1848. Antologia di scritti e discorsi*, Mimesis, Milano.

Donzelot J. (1984), *L'invention du social. Essai sur le déclin des passions politiques*, Fayard, Paris.

Engels F. (1977), The 23rd of June, in *Marx-Engels Collected Works*, vol. 7, Lawrence & Wishart Ltd., pp. 130–133 (or. ed. Der 23. Juni, *Neue Rheinische Zeitung*, No. 28, June 28, 1848).

Garnier J. (ed.) (1848), *Le droit au travail à l'Assemblée nationale, recueil complet de tous les discours prononcés dans cette mémorable discussion*, Guillaumin et Cie, París.

Garnier-Pagès L-A. (1866), *Histoire de la Révolution de 1848. Tome III: gouvernement provisoire*, Pagnerre, Paris.

Lamartine A. de. (1849), *Histoire de la Révolution de 1848*, F. Michel, Bruxelles.

Marx K. (1850), Die Klassenkämpfe in Frankreich 1848–1850. *Neue Rheinische Zeitung. Politisch-okonomische Revue*, February–November (now in Marx-Engels, *Werke*, Band 7, Dietz Verlag, Berlin 1990, pp. 9–107; Eng. trans. *The Class Struggles in France, 1848 to 1850*. In Karl Marx and Frederick Engels, *Collected Works*, vol. 10: 1849–51, Lawrence & Wishart Ltd. 2010, pp. 45–146).

Marx K. (1852), Der Achtzehnte Brumaire des Louis Bonaparte. *Die Revolution*, May–July (now in Marx-Engels, *Werke*, Band 8, Dietz Verlag, Berlin 2009, pp. 111–207; Eng. trans. *The Eighteenth Brumaire of Louis Bonaparte*. In Karl Marx and Frederick Engels, *Collected Works*, vol. 11: 1851–53, Lawrence & Wishart Ltd. 2010, pp. 99–196).

Scotto P.B. (2021), *Los orígenes del derecho al trabajo en Francia (1789–1848)*, Centro de Estudios Politicos y Constitucionales, Madrid.

Serenko A. (2022), The Great Resignation: The Great Knowledge Exodus or the Onset of the Great Knowledge Revolution? *Journal of Knowledge Management*. doi: 10.1108/JKM-12-2021-0920

Tessema M., Tesfom G., Faircloth M., Tesfagiorgis M., Teckle P. (2022), The "Great Resignation": Causes, Consequences, and Creative HR Management Strategies. *Journal of Human Resource and Sustainability Studies*, 10: 161–178. doi: 10.4236/jhrss.2022.101011

Thomas É. (1848), *Ateliers nationaux*, Impr. de A. Appert, Paris.

Tocqueville A. de. (1995), *Recollections: The French Revolution of 1848*, trans. George Lawrence, Transaction, New Brunswick, NJ (or. ed. *Souvenirs de Alexis de Tocqueville*, C. Lévy, Paris 1893).

Tomasello F. (2022), From Industrial to Digital Citizenship: Rethinking Social Rights in Cyberspace. *Theory and Society*. https://doi.org/10.1007/s11186-022-09480-6

Index

For Product Safety Concerns and Information please contact our EU representative GPSR@taylorandfrancis.com
Taylor & Francis Verlag GmbH, Kaufingerstraße 24, 80331 München, Germany

www.ingramcontent.com/pod-product-compliance
Lightning Source LLC
Chambersburg PA
CBHW070533051126
54393CB00004B/477
* 9 7 8 1 0 3 2 3 0 1 1 4 3 *